CIS £19.91

MW00353125

Organizational Ethnography

Daniel Neyland

WITHDRAWN

THE UNIVERSITY OF BOLTON
THE LIBRARY   CAMPUS

Accession No. 361681

Classification No. 302·35072 NEY

SAGE Publications
Los Angeles ▪ London ▪ New Delhi ▪ Singapore

THE UNIVERSITY OF BOLTON

361681

LCN=10193217

© Daniel Neyland 2008

First published 2008

Apart from any fair dealing for the purposes of research or private study, or criticism or review, as permitted under the Copyright, Designs and Patents Act, 1988, this publication may be reproduced, stored or transmitted in any form, or by any means, only with the prior permission in writing of the publishers, or in the case of reprographic reproduction, in accordance with the terms of licences issued by the Copyright Licensing Agency. Enquiries concerning reproduction outside those terms should be sent to the publishers.

 SAGE Publications Ltd
1 Oliver's Yard
55 City Road
London EC1Y 1SP

SAGE Publications Inc.
2455 Teller Road
Thousand Oaks, California 91320

SAGE Publications India Pvt Ltd
B 1/I 1 Mohan Cooperative Industrial Area
Mathura Road, New Delhi 110 044
India

SAGE Publications Asia-Pacific Pte Ltd
33 Pekin Street #02-01
Far East Square
Singapore 048763

Library of Congress Control Number 2007924967

British Library Cataloguing in Publication data

A catalogue record for this book is available from the British Library

ISBN 978-1-4129-2342-2
ISBN 978-1-4129-2343-9 (pbk)

Typeset by C&M Digitals (P) Ltd, Chennai, India
Printed on paper from sustainable resources
Printed in Great Britain by The Cromwell Press Ltd, Trowbridge, Wiltshire

Contents

Introduction

How this book works

This book is a guide to becoming an organizational ethnographer. No single set of instructions can hope to cover the multitude of experiences, settings, issues and dilemmas each ethnographer will face in particular organizational settings. In place of a single set of instructions, this book will begin by providing a background to the development of ethnography (through anthropology, sociology and management research). This background will highlight the practical and methodological issues ethnography has historically involved. I will then introduce ten sensibilities with which organizational ethnographers can engage. Each of these sensibilities will in turn form the focus for subsequent discussions. Esteemed, illuminative and notorious ethnographic studies will be used to provide further insights into these sensibilities. These ethnographic exemplars will be presented in a different typeface for ease of navigation. Each sensibility will conclude with three recommended resources for readers to pursue.

Ethnography

What is ethnography?

Ethnography is a research methodology developed originally in the field of anthropology which is now utilized in a range of work (in, for example, anthropology, sociology, management theory, organization studies and cultural studies). It involves the observation of, and participation in, particular groupings (such as local indigenous groups, management consultants, medical students and so on). This observation and participation aims to engage with questions of how a particular group operates, what it means to be a member of a particular group and how changes can affect that group. The origins of ethnography in anthropology were closely tied into western European colonial endeavours, where the anthropologist to some extent sought to bring the 'exotic' back 'home' (for an example, see Evans Pritchard's study of the Nuer, 1940). However, as the next section will underline, such endeavours were also focused on colonial management.

Throughout the twentieth century these ethnographic origins were taken in many directions through anthropology (for an augmentation of the 'exotic' through thick description, see Geertz, 1973), sociology (from the study of slums, see Whyte, 1955; through to youth culture, see Cohen, 1972), science and technology studies (see, for example, Latour and Woolgar, 1979) and the development of new avenues of exploration such as visual anthropology (see, for example, *Visual Anthropology*, 2005). In the twenty-first century, discussion of ethnography has found focus in considerations of the understanding and use of technology (see Miller and Slater on Trinidadians' use of the internet, 2000) and in questions of ethnography's ability to engage with messy, complex and chaotic organizational forms (Law, 2004).

Claimed strengths of ethnographic data are that: a detailed, in-depth picture of a group, organization and its members can be developed; the social, cultural and political issues which other methods find intangible can form the focus for analysis; and ethnography can be strongly participative, allowing for members of groups to comment on the data and data gathering as it occurs. With more practical ethnography (see, for example, Neyland and Surridge, 2003), these strengths can be augmented by a translation of this in-depth data into practical recommendations. It is claimed these recommendations are particularly robust as they are developed in tandem with local members (rendering them inclusive), pay attention to the detail of members' interests (and so are informed) and allow for research to be an iterative and participative process (rather than an enforced set of top-down management or researcher-led decisions).

In recent years these claimed strengths have seen an expansion in the area of organizational ethnography. This has involved ethnography forming a growing presence in business schools, in practical research methods courses and in organizational activities such as marketing and technology development. Ethnographic observation of, and participation in, particular organizations, locations and social activities is now frequently noted for its utility in providing in-depth insights into what people and organizations do on a day-to-day basis. This picture of day-to-day activity has been used to inform a broad array of actions from the augmentation of strategy processes to the design of mobile phones.

However, readers should proceed with caution. Many of the strengths of ethnography have the status of 'claims' because ethnography is not a straightforward methodology. Ethnographies require a great deal of access to the field being studied, a participative role for researchers, a great deal of time spent in the field and a great deal of researcher involvement in gathering, organizing and analysing observations. Such issues can lead to critical questions for ethnographic studies regarding the possibility of objectivity, excessive researcher involvement, research participants influencing outcomes and so on. Rather than take such issues as demonstrative of ethnography's fallibility, these issues have been incorporated into ethnographic analyses. The following sections on the history of ethnography will introduce the variety of ways in which ethnographers have engaged with these issues.

The anthropological tradition

It should not be assumed that the recent increase in interest in organizational ethnography is posing practical questions of the methodology for the first time. Indeed, the very beginnings of ethnography in anthropology were closely involved in western colonial activities. The early pioneering work of Malinowski (1929) and Radcliffe-Brown (1922) has been identified by many (see, for example, Burgess, 1984) as providing the basis for the development of ethnographic fieldwork. Prior to these studies, many ethnographers had simply collected second-hand accounts of exotic lands from travellers returning to, for example, Britain (Urry, 1984) or had been involved in the development of questionnaire-type approaches to map out practices of colonial groups (Ellen, 1984). Malinowski advocated direct participation in the groups being studied and using such participation as the central focus for developing an understanding of the group. The ethnographic principles of getting close to the group and spending a great deal of time in the group emerged at this time.

Baba (2005) suggests that the popular view that this colonial entanglement provides something of a blot on the history of ethnography is a relatively recent reading of events and that early anthropology involved both practical and scholarly pursuits. She argues: 'In the past, relationships between pragmatic and scholarly interests were fuzzier and more entangled than the received version would have us believe' (2005: 206). Drawing on the work of Kuper (1983), she points out that forms of applied anthropology date from at least 1881, 'when British anthropologists used it to advocate the potential utility of their emerging profession which did not yet have a firm constituency' (Baba, 2005: 206). Early ethnography combined practical and scholarly pursuits, but not in seamless ways. Often practical work (depending on funding and availability) was handed over to junior colleagues (often women), beginning a separation between (more esteemed) theory and (lower status) practice. This representation of research funding, involving a combination of work required to meet the funders' prerequisites and (more interesting) theoretical work which can be done under the auspices of the same project, still characterizes much current research activity (see, for example, Coopmans, Neyland and Woolgar, 2004).

Histories of ethnography (such as Baba, 2005) suggest that the funding for such theoretical-practical work continued through the Second World War in line with endeavours to engage with colonial groups. Post-independence and the end of empire, such interest dwindled. Schwartzman (1993) argues that simultaneous to the decline in colonial, practical studies, anthropology moved into new and distinct settings, raising new practical questions for ethnography. The Hawthorne studies of the 1920s and 1930s involved ethnography moving in to the workplace. Schwartzman (1993: 9) highlights how Lloyd Warner suggested 'work groups could be studied as a type of small society'. Although these studies were subsequently criticized for apparently representing the workers as less logical than their superiors, this research began to indicate that anthropological techniques, spending time in the setting, producing a detailed picture of the mundane and the ordinary, could have potential for studies 'at home' as much as in 'exotic' locations abroad. The practical approach taken by these ethnographers was emphasized by Lloyd Warner who went on to found a consulting firm, Social Research, Inc.

It should be noted, however, that such practical endeavours have by no means dominated the history of anthropological ethnography. Although it could be argued that practical questions of ethnographic utility were formative of the field, these questions have not retained their presence in significant amounts of anthropological fieldwork. Instead, questions of the role of the ethnographer in the field, of the appropriate means to represent the field studied, and of the best means to give research participants a voice in the study, form just a few of the issues to which a great deal of anthropological writing has been committed (see following sensibilities).

In recent years there has been something of a reinvigoration of questions of ethnographic utility. The Xerox Palo-Alto Research Centre (PARC) employment of ethnographers has shifted attention (at least partially) from scholarly ethnographic research to the scholarly in combination with practical and pragmatic considerations. A question for Suchman (2000) regarding these ethnographic endeavours is the extent to which anthropology has now become a brand. While anthropological ethnography has always been resistant to setting a single and definitive methodological set of rules by which ethnography should be done, does organizational interest in the method risk restricting ethnography to a particular kind of practice, adhering to a particular set of rules? In conversation with hi-tech corporations, employers have tried to convince me of the importance of rapid and routinized ethnographic training for observers to be carried out in ethnographic boot-camps. This suggests a form of packaged ethnographic method developed without regard for the particular problems, questions, issues, barriers, practices and customs of the setting to be studied. Such a suggestion would be anathema to most anthropologists.

However, as Suchman (2000) points out, brands are not single things (but often groups of things, people, logos, lifestyles, and so on). Furthermore, Wakeford (2003) highlights the multiple possibilities offered by corporate–scholarly ethnographic collaborations. Wakeford provides a recent history of developments in the field of corporate ethnographic collaborations from PARC, through E-lab, Sapient and her own INCITE (Incubator for Critical Inquiry into Technology and Ethnography). Drawing on these examples, such developments in organizational ethnography and corporate interest in anthropology need not be problematic for the field, but instead provide a new or revisited set of questions (these will be taken up in the section 'Ethnography in organizations' below).

The sociological tradition

Anthropology has not had an exclusive hold on the use of ethnography for social science research. While anthropology began through ethnographic engagements with 'exotic' tribes in far-flung places, sociological ethnography began with subject matter closer to home.[1] These sociological beginnings also drew together ethnography as a scholarly pursuit with practical and pragmatic (in this case, political) questions. The Chicago School (for a discussion, see Fielding, 2001) used ethnography for the practical political purpose of enhancing knowledge of particular groups within inner-city slums, who, they claimed, were poorly represented by statistical analyses which offered little information on who people were, what they did, how they organized their lives, what problems they faced, and so on. Ethnography was deployed here in order to get close to those who dwelt in the poorer areas of cities in order to make insights into their lives which might create some political leverage. The explicit political aim of the likes of Whyte (1955) and his study of the street corner life of Boston slums was one of adequate representation.

Although it would be incorrect to argue that such pragmatic and political questions have dominated sociological ethnography, there have been many studies over the years which have retained this aim to provide an adequate representation of groups who have been somewhat marginalized. Willis's (1977) study of working-class school children in the UK drew attention to the logics and rationales these kids employed in coming to terms with their education and their future (possible lack of) employment prospects. This study attempted to illustrate, in a similar manner to Whyte (1955), that faceless and nameless statistical figures for crime, unemployment and educational failure only provided one version of 'what was going on' in these people's lives. The sociology of deviance has engaged with similar ethnographic rationales, engaging with the mundane and everyday activities of particular groups. These studies were not designed to make available the obvious, or 'things we all know about' the particular group under study. Instead, these studies made available detailed, insightful and often counter-intuitive pictures of, among other things, the complex organization of marijuana users (Becker, 1973) and fighting between rival gangs (Cohen, 1972). This counter-intuitive aspect of ethnographic research has been important in making available detailed analysis of the activities of particular

---

1 Once anthropologists also began deploying ethnography 'at home' this distinction became less obvious. Readers should keep in mind that the separation employed here is to some extent for purposes of clarity.

groups which had been absent from media and legislative discourse. Thus Becker demonstrated that becoming a marijuana user was as much about a process of becoming a member of a particular group, taking part in particular activities and adopting particular attitudes, as it was about smoking.

In recent years questions of practical and pragmatic ethnography have been brought to the fore in research in the field of Science and Technology Studies. For example, research in the Public Understanding of Science has tackled, among other things, issues of the environment and pollution (Rayner and Malone, 1998), genetically modified (GM) foods (Oreszczyn, 2005) and forms of risk and trust (Wynne, 1996). These studies have again involved making available detailed pictures of the everyday and unexpected. They have also, on occasions, involved specific policy orientations. Such policy work raises a range of questions regarding the ways in which ethnographic research can be translated into useful and useable practical advice (see Neyland and Surridge, 2003; also see sensibility eight and Conclusion).

Management research

This brief history of the anthropological and sociological tradition of ethnography has begun to highlight some of the salient features of practical ethnographic research. However, the distinction between a sociological and anthropological tradition is difficult to maintain. There is much research at the margins which would appear to fit both traditions. A third and more recent focus for ethnographic development has been the field of management research. Sporadic calls have been made for the relevance of ethnography for addressing quite traditional concerns within organizational and management research. In, for example, organizational behaviour (Bergman, 2003), strategy (Whittington, 2004) and accounting research (Dey, 2002), forms of ethnographic research have been utilized in order to address questions of 'culture', 'strategic practice' and 'change'. Each of these areas is incredibly complex and has involved both ethnographic advocates and backlashes against attempts to 'capture' culture or waste time in its pursuit (for a discussion, see Bate, 1997). Several ethnographers sit at the juncture between anthropological and management research through the use of ethnography (see, for example, Darrah, 1996; Rosen, 2000).

Baba (1986) suggests that the origins of organizational behaviour lie in anthropological research such as the Hawthorne studies. It was in these studies that the grounds for in-depth, up-close studies of the everyday, routinized, informal activities of the workplace were established. Czarniawska-Joerges (1992) traces the historical shifts which saw the fields of anthropology and management research move apart over time. She suggests that organizational-management research developed rapidly in the 1950s and 1960s, moving away from anthropological ideas towards supposedly scientific notions being developed in much sociological research at the time (for example, sociological researchers were pushing the development of survey sampling techniques, statistical formulas, experimental designs and data processing). However, Bate (1997) argues that it may be time for reconciliation. Bate identifies moves being made in the UK and more prominently in the USA to bring together anthropological and organizational behaviour concerns, highlighting the importance of getting close to subjects under study, making available routine aspects of organizational activity for analysis and studying 'history' and 'context'. The latter need not be considered as abstract or background features of organizational activity but can be studied by the ethnographer for the ways they are made relevant by members of the organization in the organizational present. Thus the way employees relate stories of 'how things have always been done' can tell the ethnographer much about the regular, routinized and everyday character of organizational activity. Furthermore, although management and anthropological research has been separated in the past by anthropologists' study of the exotic and management researchers' focus on organizations 'at home' (Burack, 2002), this is no longer such a clear distinction, with many anthropologists also studying the exotic at home.

Bate (1997) suggests that ethnography has an important part to play in demonstrating counter-intuitive aspects of this organizational activity. Bate draws on examples such as Latour and Woolgar's (1979) study of laboratory scientists, which suggested that objective, factual scientific method is far more complex and far less clear-cut than may be taken for granted. It is such counter-intuitive results, Bates argues, that offers ethnographic researchers the possibility of producing revelatory findings. Getting close to the organizational action is not just about telling the audience what they already know, but also involves a refusal to take anything for granted. In the same way that anthropologists encountered exotic locations, tribes and customs, the organizational ethnographer can shift the everyday into the exotic, by carrying out detailed and close examination of their subject matter. In the same way that Chicago School sociologists made available rich and textured detail of life in the ghetto, which (counter to media reporting at the time) demonstrated the level of organization of street corner life, organizational ethnographers have the opportunity to scrutinize even the most apparently banal features of organizational activity to analyse what they suggest about the characteristics of the organization under study. For example, Weeks (2004) provides a detailed ethnographic analysis of organizational complaining, at once both an ignored and frequent feature of workplace settings. Through a thoroughly sceptical treatment of each aspect of organizational activity, the ethnographer can get close to those everyday features of activity which hold the organization together. Van Maanen (1979: 540) argues that the purpose of organizational ethnography is 'to uncover and explicate the ways in which people in particular work settings come to understand, account for, take action, and otherwise manage their day-to-day situation'.

It should not be assumed that management research engages with ethnographic analyses without encountering problematic issues. For example, management research often operates with particular expectations regarding the number of publications to be produced. Ethnographic analyses generally operate at a far slower pace than alternative management research methodologies. In business schools, the utility of ethnography thus requires some demonstrative effort on the part of the ethnographer in convincing colleagues, heads of department and so on of some specific form of value. Organizations may also be reluctant to allow researchers prolonged or unfettered access to all areas of an organization. Ethnographers may have to work hard to convince organizations of the utility of their study. Questions could also be asked of ethnographers' attempts to render the everyday exotic, to lift the banal or the mundane to the status of a legitimate focus for research. This requires effort on the part of the ethnographer and may run counter to some management research expectations that research should involve more straightforward data collection and less researcher involvement (these issues will be dealt with in more detail in the subsequent section on sensibilities).

One final question to ask in this section on management research is: what should count as an organization for organizational ethnography? The exemplars throughout the following discussions are drawn from each of the different approaches to ethnography. This may suggest that the 'organization' in organizational ethnography is vague. If anthropologists' study of Balinese village life can be considered alongside management researchers' study of globally franchised fast-food firms, what does this tell us about organizations? My argument will be that although this text is designed as a guide to becoming an organizational ethnographer in what might be termed 'conventional' organizational settings for management research, each of the exemplars can help us to think through the issues faced by ethnographers and can provide us with imaginative ways of engaging with the concept of organization. Thus when Geertz (1973) talks of the unstable and temporary organizational features of Balinese cockfighting (exemplar five), this can help us to think about the ways in which features of organizational activity come together, hold together momentarily and dissipate through changes in the interaction between members of the organization. When Leidner (1993) talks of the routinization of McDonald's employees (exemplar nine) this can help us to think of the ways in which certain features of organizational activity hold together and endure over time. Although this book is designed as a guide to becoming an organizational ethnographer, where organization might be taken to relate to those settings usually studied by management research, the exemplars drawn on will situate these studies within a broader range of organized, sometimes routinized, sometimes chaotic and messy ethnographic studies.

Ethnography in organizations

The brief history of ethnography provided by this introduction has suggested that ethnography in both the anthropological and sociological tradition has from its very beginnings involved a practical and pragmatic element. This might raise the question, why write this book now? The timeliness of this guide lies in the recent growth of ethnographic studies in forms of management research, on courses being taught in business schools and in the co-option of ethnography (as a term at least and partly as a method) by organizations.

Hi-tech corporations such as Intel, Kodak, Microsoft and IBM are employing ethnographers to address a range of questions regarding the ways in which technologies are used. Often this involves questions of attempting to access arenas not conventionally available for corporate insight. For example, the way technology gets used in homes (information on which is not conventionally easily accessible to corporations, Mainwaring and Woodruff, 2005), in far-flung places (which may have increasing markets, but about which corporations may not know a great deal, Bell, 2003) and slightly unusual environments (such as virtual gaming, Ducheneaut and Moore, 2005) have formed a focus for ethnographic analysis. Corporate ethnographic interest has also focused on particular types of user, identified as possibly market relevant, whose everyday activities remain less than clear (for example, teenage girls, March and Fleuriot, 2005). Beyond hi-tech corporations employing ethnographers, there are increasing numbers of ethnographic consultancies in operation. These offer potential client organizations ethnographic insights for hire. Such developments have generated an amount of media interest with a variety of articles investigating the activities and utility of ethnographers (see *Sunday Times*, 2003; and for a discussion, see Suchman, 2000).

This raises an important distinction here between ethnography *of* and ethnography *for* organizations. The former relates to scholarly studies of an organization, the latter refers to research carried out for (or on behalf of) an organization. Hammersley (1992) suggests that the two are incompatible, that forms of practical and academic ethnographic research should not be drawn together. However, the distinctions between scholarly pursuit and more practical and pragmatic ends have always been unclear throughout the history of ethnography. It is not certain that the recent rise in ethnography *for* organizations signals a definitive change in practical and scholarly ethnography. Indeed, the work of Wakeford (2003) highlights a number of innovative and interesting directions that a hybrid of scholarly and corporate ethnographic research could take. Often, in negotiating access to a corporate setting, the ethnographer can discuss what might be of use to the organization being studied and what use the ethnographer might make of the organization for their own purposes.

However, questions have been raised regarding whether or not business interest in ethnography threatens some of the traditional values associated with ethnographic research. Bate (1997: 1150) suggests that '[o]rganization anthropologists rarely take a toothbrush with them these days', alluding to the rushed, short-term, non-immersive strategies frequently employed in these forms of ethnographic research (similar points are made by Blythin, Rouncefield and Hughes, 1997). Such studies may miss out on the strengths of ethnographic research – that it can provide a detailed, in-depth, up-close examination of a particular group and the way that group operates. This is not a direct threat to ethnographic research as such, as there is no reason for all ethnographers to buy into this rushed mode of study. However, if ethnography were to become associated with such forms of rapid research and such research were notably to fail to produce the insights promised by ethnographers, this could become problematic for organizational ethnography further down the line. If access to an organization depends on convincing the organization of the utility of the research, and ethnography becomes known as a less than useful approach, then access may be more difficult to gain. It may be more appropriate for ethnographers to spend time negotiating the values of ethnography with particular organizations, emphasizing the benefits of long-term, deeper immersion in the field being studied.

Ten sensibilities for organizational ethnographers

What is a sensibility?

Many research methods texts begin by establishing the impossibility of producing a set of instructions (Atkinson, 1990) or a recipe (Brewer, 2000) for the particular method in focus. This avowal usually takes the form that researchers (particularly ethnographers) need to go out and do the research and develop their method in association with the field being studied. Instructions or recipes for methodical success are inappropriate as the researcher is required to tailor any research method to the environment in which they are studying. However, it is the job of methods texts to provide readers with sufficient insight into the method to enable them to approximate, develop and engage with a version of the method under discussion. This is sometimes achieved through discussing common problems associated with the method, through providing multiple examples of the method in practice or through providing a series of tasks for readers to consider in engaging with the method.

Alongside these questions of method are questions of methodology. If method can be thought of as the tools and techniques which researchers need to engage with and develop in doing research, methodology can be thought of as the theoretical underpinning for such research activity. Methodological questions involve issues of the approach to knowledge the researcher will take, such as, does the world exist out there independent of the research waiting to be collected and analysed, or is the researcher and research heavily involved in the collection, construction and attribution of meaning to the setting (in which case, how will the researcher take this into account)?

This provides for two closely intertwined issues. First, if we accept the impossibility of providing a single set of rules appropriate for all forms of organizational ethnography, a methods text needs to provide guidance of use for a broad range of possible ethnographic experiences. This issue is referred to by N. Lee (1999) in relation to legislation as the problem of the general and the particular: how to make, for example, broad legislative (or in this case, methodological) principles relevant in each particular occasion on which some aspect of the general principle is deemed relevant. Second, the complexity for ethnographers of considering the possible methodological underpinnings of each research project (in which the method has been made appropriate for its particular setting) lies in attempts to figure out the specifics of their approach to engaging with the world. This initiates questions such as, what kinds of approach to knowledge has the researcher carried into and engaged with during the ethnography, how heavily has the researcher been involved in the production of the data for the research, would another ethnographer report the same experiences and would these experiences be made available to subsequent ethnographic entrants into the field?

Organizational ethnographers can address these two issues – of method and methodology – through consideration of ethnographic sensibilities. Sensibilities do not have the same status as recipes or instructions, but neither do they leave issues of method and methodology vague or incoherent. Instead, this guide on becoming an organizational ethnographer will provide ten sensibilities which can be engaged by ethnographers in working their way through ethnographic research. The sensibilities will provide information, background, questions and a range of alternative answers, and tricks (Becker, 1998) available for ethnographic consideration. The sensibilities will provide ethnographers with possibilities for orienting their ethnographic study. The text will further illuminate these sensibilities through a range of exemplars from ethnographic fieldwork. These exemplars are drawn from anthropological, sociological and management research ethnographies and provide particularly useful, relevant or notable (sometimes notorious) insights into the practicalities of ethnography. The sensibilities and exemplars will enable organizational ethnographers to navigate between the general and the particular.

The following sections provide an introduction to each of the sensibilities.

▷▷▷▷▷Sensibility One: Ethnographic Strategy

Ethnographic research takes time, requires a great deal of access to the field and involves close engagement with members of the group being studied.

This generates ethnographic complexity, resulting in the ethnographer managing multiple features of the research while engaged in the very completion of the research. The kinds of questions an ethnography addresses can range from fairly open questions, which can develop over the course of doing the ethnography, to very precise questions to be answered through the study of very particular groups. This complexity is best managed through the development of an ethnographic strategy. Like all the best strategies (Neyland, 2006a), an ethnographic strategy should not be considered as written in stone, unchanging and non-negotiable. Instead, ethnographers need to develop an approximate strategy which should then orient the study and be available for constant consideration, challenge and adaptation as the study progresses. Such a fluid (Law, 2004) strategy is the best means for an ethnographer to retain coherence in the research while also dealing with contingency, interesting new possibilities and directions that arise during the research and new problems that show as research continues.

The ethnographic strategy does not need to be complete prior to entry into the field. The ethnographer can begin their strategy in a variety of ways. The ethnographer can aim to engage with a particular group or type of organization (for example, fast food restaurants, Leidner, 1993) which the ethnographer feels has not been studied a great deal or is available to provide new insights. Alternatively, the ethnographer may be interested in a particular material thing (for example, mobile phones or the use of computers to access particular internet sites, Cooper et al., 2002) and may seek out particular places where that material thing is made prominent and made available for study. Or the ethnographer may have a particular question they wish to answer (such as how do mobile workers understand their membership of the organization for which they work when they are seldom 'in' that organization, Whittle, 2001).

These different beginnings – choosing a type of group or activity, a place, material object or a very specific question – form the initial stage of producing a strategy. Once the ethnographer has made these kinds of choices, the following sensibilities require consideration in fulfilling an initial version of the strategy. The ethnographer needs to begin thinking about the terms on which they will engage with the focus of study (see sensibility two), how they can access the area, group or thing to be studied (see sensibility three) and how they will go about completing the practical aspects of the study – how they will observe, record, represent and exit the field (see subsequent sensibilities).

The ethnographic strategy needs to be developed in tandem with the situation being studied and needs to be constantly made relevant for that situation. Ethnographers need to consider the possibility of rewriting the strategy if necessary, stubbornly sticking to the strategy at times and/or using a version of the strategy as a negotiating point with the group or organization being studied. Under sensibility one, more detail will be offered on the tactics to employ in ensuring organizations meet any obligations they have signed up to in the research and the times and grounds during which an ethnographer should consider radical alterations to an ethnographic strategy.

▷▷▷▷▷Sensibility Two: Questions of Knowledge

Tied in closely with considerations of a research strategy are methodological issues of knowledge. Briefly stated, there are three principle approaches to knowledge in ethnographic research.

Realist ethnography

Early anthropological ethnography could be said to fit the realist approach to knowledge. The work of, for example, Radcliffe-Brown (1922), straightforwardly assumed that the activities being observed existed independently of the study and could be gathered together as a more or less definitive representation of the group being studied. This approach to ethnography is still characteristic of some more recent research, most commonly in management research. Realist approaches to knowledge are in many ways the most straightforward for questions of observation and representation. What is seen is taken (more or less) as a definitive version of what is going on. Questions then need to be asked regarding whether or not there is anything else going on that should be taken into account, whether the observations gathered are likely to reflect common practices among the group being studied (that is, is this what the group normally does?) and whether there are any further locations which require study. For realist ethnographers, time spent in the field and close access to informants is important for answering these questions of representation.

Narrative ethnography

Realist ethnography has been criticized for paying insufficient attention to ethnographers' own roles in completing the research and to the possibility that an ethnographic version of events is only one of several possible versions. Narrative ethnographies (for example, Whyte, 1955) pay closer attention to these questions. Often they are based around a notable informant whose views of 'what is going on' are taken as a valuable (but not the only possible) version of events. These narrative accounts of the field are often utilized to get close to a group who may not be easily accessed. In management research, if the focus of research was on the CEOs of major international corporations, then a narrative ethnography providing a detailed account of the activities of one particular person, embedded within their accounts of the broader organization, might prove useful. It could be seen as one of several possible accounts of the organization. (For a discussion of alternative ethnographic styles, see Van Maanen, 1988.)

Reflexive ethnography

Narrative and realist ethnographies are criticized by more radical reflexive ethnographers who suggest that the ethnographic 'reality' being studied is not independent of the ethnographers' work to produce an ethnographic text. Reflexive ethnography makes no claims for objectivity then, but rather seeks to emphasize its validity through reflexive subjectivity. That is, the involvement of research participants in the collection, organization and analysis of data, their opportunities to reflect on these processes and reflection on the researcher's own involvement in these processes all form a part of the data collection, organization and analysis. Such ethnography seeks validity by not making claims to objectivity and instead through carrying out analysis of its subjectivity, its involvement in the production and continuation of the field. Ethnographers in this view are one feature of the membership making up the organization being studied.

▷▷▷▷▷Sensibility Three: Locations and Access

Having produced an initial strategy for the kind of ethnographic question to be addressed and the appropriate form of engagement to be entered into, ethnographers need to consider where their study will take place and how that place (or places) can be accessed. The traditions of ethnographic anthropology involved travelling to far-flung places, posing difficulties with travel, language, and with getting close to and producing an understanding of the group being studied. For some anthropologists, such difficulties remain a sign of high-quality ethnography and a prerequisite for gaining a job in particular university anthropology departments.

Organizational ethnography tends to happen closer to home, but this does not mean that access and location issues are any more straightforward. Access can involve prolonged negotiations with the organization, offers from the ethnographer of benefits for the organization from the study (remembering the issue of ethnography *of* and *for* the organization), and discussions relating to exactly what the ethnographer might do, where they might sit, who they might talk to and what they might do with the results. Some of these issues will be discussed further (in sensibility nine on ethics), however, it can be important for the ethnographer to be reasonably up front and establish precisely the grounds for the research and what the organization will allow. Gaining a firm commitment from the organization can then form one means to avoid access problems later in the research.

At the beginning or during the course of the research it may become apparent that the primary site is not the only site where interesting things are going on or where potential answers to ethnographic questions may be found. Ethnographers then need to choose between sticking with the primary location and producing an up-close and detailed study of that particular location or incorporating further sites into the study. Simply because further sites exist does not mean that the ethnographer necessarily has to study them. It may be that secondary ethnographic sites are talked about by members of the primary site and can be analysed on this basis. It may be that secondary sites have an important role to play in the study simply through the way they are talked about by the members already incorporated into the study (for example, studying fans of a football team may reveal interesting insights about the way those fans talk about fans of opposing teams, but this would not necessarily mean the ethnographer should pursue and study the fans of those other teams).

Having introduced this caveat that not all secondary sites are worth pursuing, in certain studies further ethnographic field sites can prove illuminating. For example, Hirsch's (1992; exemplar six) study of families' use of technology involved moving with the family through the various locations in which they used technology, revealing the variety of ways in which technologies could be used for different purposes in different settings and the ways in which the family could understand something of their own identity in relation to the location and use they were making of the technology. This is often referred to as multi-site ethnography. Multi-site ethnography involves the ethnographer moving between field-sites, exploring boundaries and connections, and investigating the multiple locations of the subject matter under consideration. Ethnographers should keep in mind that multiple sites can involve multiple access negotiations, even more time spent in the field and even more complex research strategies. Such questions require careful consideration.

▷▷▷▷▷ Sensibility Four: Field Relations

Ethnographers spend a great deal of their time in the field focused on establishing relations with those they study. This close relationship is important for gaining in-depth, up-close views on what it is like to be a member of a particular group or organization. By participant observing, the ethnographer becomes an effective member of the group. This membership can be illuminating for ethnographic research, providing insights into what status membership confers, how individuals shift from being non-members to members and what it means to cease membership (see sensibility ten on exits).

Close involvement

Close involvement with members of the ethnographic group under study is important, but can take several distinct shapes. First, ethnographers can establish rapport with one or a few key informants who provide much of the observational data for the research (Whyte, 1955; exemplar three). These key informants often provide illuminating tales of the group under study and know every member of the group. Second, ethnographers often

15

establish relations with gatekeepers – members of the group who are particularly useful in providing access to the group being studied, who introduce the ethnographer and aid the ethnographer's move from location to location (Geertz, 1973; exemplar five). This can sometimes be the same member who is also a key informant. Third, close involvement can be more pervasive, with ethnographers simply trying to establish themselves as members of a particular group. Being a convincing member can be central to the ethnographic study (for example, in studying football fans, not being a convincing member of the group can leave the ethnographer very much on the outside, Armstrong, 1998).

Establishing trust

A particularly complex feature of field relations is establishing trust. There are a variety of different social science approaches to trust. However, for the purposes of this succinct introduction, trust can be thought of as those close relations established between ethnographer and research subjects which lead to the mutual exchange of relevant information. Trust relations can involve work on the part of the ethnographer to establish that the research being carried out is rigorous, relevant and/or has some utility. This can be aided by presentations to those being studied. Alternatively, trust can be a given at the start of the research, perhaps through introduction by a gatekeeper. In this case the ethnographer needs to work on maintaining trust. For both the building and maintenance of trust ethnographers can utilize particular tactics, such as asking questions in a naïve rather than challenging way, beginning conversations with 'safe' topics before moving on to more challenging issues and attempting to contribute something positive and constructive to the group (Hine, 2001).

Too close?

Getting close to research participants is not without problems. The ethnographer constantly needs to shift between insider and outsider status to maintain ethnographic strangeness and avoid taking what the tribe say for granted (see, for example, Cooper, 2001). The extent of close contact between ethnographer and group studied needs to be negotiated; some ethnographers get closer than others (see, for example, Coffey, 1999, on sexual relations in the field).

▷▷▷▷▷ Sensibility Five: Ethnographic Time

Ethnographic time operates on a different time scale than most methods in management research. Bate (1997) suggests that much ethnographic work in management research and in ethnographies for organizations is now more focused on quick description than thick description. This move to quick description threatens some of the principles of ethnographic research – that the researcher gets close to the members of the organization being studied, that time spent in the field enables the researcher to produce a detailed and in-depth picture of what is going on in the organization and that the time spent in the field allows the ethnographer to move back and forth, going over previous observations and assessing their merit in relation to constantly emerging new observational materials. This latter point is often referred to as being both an ethnographic insider and outsider (or emic and etic perspective, see Fetterman, 1989; Hammersley and Atkinson, 1995). The ethnographer shifts between being 'in' the organization (actively participating in what is going on) and being 'out' of the organization (writing and reviewing observations and taking these into account when observing further aspects of organizational activity). This insider/outsider position is managed by the ethnographer through time spent in the field. Neither are absolute positions – as the research develops, at times the ethnographer will be more 'inside' and at other moments more 'outside' the organization.

Thick description

Geertz (1973) developed the term 'thick description' for his ethnographic fieldwork in various locations, notably Bali (see exemplar five). Thick description has been perceived as a literary style of ethnography, with rich story-telling of incidents in the field providing the backdrop for a developing understanding of what is going on. Such a style of writing may not be appropriate for all forms of organizational ethnography. However, the principles of thick description may prove valuable to the organizational ethnographer. Ethnographic time for Geertz was about years, not minutes, spent in the field. Adequate representation was developed through living with the groups being studied for prolonged periods. Geertz provides incredible detail on the moment-to-moment ways in which features of the field under study were made and remade by participants in the setting (for example, information on Balinese betting is incredibly detailed in this account, but such detail is intended to convey the complex and sometimes temporary forms of organization which characterize Balinese life).

Quick description

This is the term Bate (1997) uses as a criticism of some management research on ethnography and is also characteristic of much ethnography completed for organizations. An employee of a corporate organization suggested to me that his ethnographic studies were a little like drive-thru McDonald's. He did not intend to stay around too long and was happy to move through the setting collecting what he assumed were the important ingredients he required for his ethnographic research. Such an approach to ethnography puts at risk many of the advantages of doing ethnography. Key features of the setting may be missed or may be misunderstood (not understood in the same way as members of the setting understand them) and then those missing details may form a problematic absence from representations of the setting studied. It has been suggested that quick ethnography is not ethnography at all (Smith, 2001) but a conventional organizational snapshot of a particular setting which utilizes the term 'ethnography' to enhance its status.

▷▷▷▷▷Sensibility Six: Observing and Participating

A central feature of ethnographic research is developing observational skills. Ethnographers need to develop these skills while participating in particular fields of study. There are few universally helpful points that will aid ethnographic observations in all situations. However, the following are issues with which ethnographers can engage to orient ethnographic research.

What to observe?
The principle I employ in ethnographic research is a form of scepticism. This has a long ethnographic tradition dating back to early anthropological fieldwork. Ethnographers entered field settings in remote places and were confronted by a range of unusual, uncomfortable and occasionally unsettling activities. Everything for early ethnographers was treated as strange. To some extent this treatment of colonial outposts as strange has been criticized (see Burgess, 1984, for a discussion) for its western-dominated viewpoint on what should count as normal. However, this treatment of ethnographic strangeness has utility for organizational ethnography. When asked the question – what to observe? – the answer for ethnographers should always be everything. That is, nothing should be taken for granted and nothing should be assumed to be uninteresting. The organization should receive the traditional ethnographic treatment of strangeness. Lifting everything up for potential analysis can result in revealing something of the organization which others (even others in the organization) are unaware of or have not considered in detail. This treatment of strangeness is difficult to maintain. The longer the ethnographer remains in the group the more things, activities and people begin to seem familiar. Initial stages of ethnographic fieldwork are thus most likely to reveal most about the organization and provide the moments where ethnographers find it most straightforward to treat the setting as strange.

Writing field notes

Writing field notes enters the ethnographer into a further series of complex problems. It is not always possible to record observations as things happen. In meetings where writing is part of the routine activity of the setting, ethnographers may find the time and space to write down observational notes at will. In the middle of a conversation with an organization's employee, stopping to write down something the person has said may be the quickest way of ending that conversation. Ethnographers employ a range of tactics for overcoming these problems. Some ethnographers scribble down as much as they can in a rapid shorthand and later write those notes up into something more coherent. Other ethnographers use a technological means to record the field (see sensibility seven). Other ethnographers rely on their memory to effectively retain all the relevant detail until such time that they are free to write detailed field notes. Whichever technique is employed, the ethnographer should develop keen sensibilities in the field to initially record everything and treat it as strange, to try to keep in mind other things that have been observed during previous visits, to gauge the importance of pursuing particular events, and attempt to develop relations with other members of the organization to develop further understanding of particular features of the organization. During the course of what might be a prolonged stay in the field of research, ethnographers should keep all fieldnotes reasonably well organized in a diary or some other format which enables them to order, recall and later analyse particular events (also see sensibility eight).

▷▷▷▷▷Sensibility Seven: Supplementing

In much the same way that organizational ethnographers should constantly keep in mind their ethnographic strategy and the possible need to review the strategy, the possibility of supplementing the research in a variety of ways should be a frequent consideration. Alongside observations, researchers may want to consider the possibility of carrying out field interviews, using video and still cameras, engaging with the vast amount of organizational activity that occurs through computers and employing a variety of other technologies to record and/or enable others to access the research as it progresses.

Field interviews

Although the principle feature of ethnographic research is observation of the setting being studied, ethnographers also employ interview techniques to elicit further information. Organizational ethnographers need to decide what they are managing to accumulate in observational material and what (if any) further areas of the organization require study. It may be appropriate to consider organizational documents or interviews when or if there are particular members of the organization whose activity is less than observable, who are keen to talk about a select feature of the organization, or if the ethnographer wishes to capture members' stories about the organization, its past, its competitors and so on. Field interviews can be more or less structured, ranging from specific conversations to be recorded in the setting to semi-structured discussions oriented around a set of topics selected as relevant by the ethnographer (around which interviewees can hold expansive discussions).

Cameras and visual ethnography

An alternative means to engage with the field is to take photos or video of particular activities or locations. Such an approach forms part of the growing disciplines of visual anthropology and visual ethnography (see *Visual Anthropology*, 2005). The value of visual material needs consideration by the ethnographer. Organizations and their employees may find it uncomfortable to have their activities under surveillance or may find the camera a useful way of having things recorded they think are important features of the organization. Ethnographers also need to take into account the purpose to which they will put visual material. It can be used to supplement observational field notes, to illustrate particular aspects of the organization, to catalogue particular types of incident or primarily to show aspects of the organization to its members.

Computers and virtual ethnography

A great deal of organizational activity takes place through computers. In order to consider this activity, ethnographers can engage with the newly emerging discipline of virtual ethnography. Many of the same questions should be asked as per visual material. Why does the ethnographer want to engage with this aspect of activity? What will it add to the study? How should it be used by the ethnographer? Will it make organizational members feel uncomfortable? Sensibility seven provides more details on this and the range of other forms of technology that ethnographers can utilize in engaging with the field, from using MP3 recorders to setting up blogs on the research for members to reflect on and contribute to during the ongoing development of the research.

▷▷▷▷▷Sensibility Eight: Writing

There are two principle forms of writing in which organizational ethnographers can expect to engage. The first of these is utilizing observational material in scholarly pursuit. The second involves translating something of the ethnography for an organizational audience. Each of these can involve different challenges and can be designed for different purposes. However, in general, the starting point for each writing activity is the same: making sense of ethnographic material. Although ethnographies are often noted as taking time due to long periods spent in the field, ethnographic output does not necessarily accelerate outside the field. Average times between the initiation of an ethnographic project and its publication have been put at eight years (Smith, 2001). Why so slow? Important insights derived from ethnographic writing involve detailed and thorough analysis of observational material. Ethnographers should spend a great deal of time with their data, going through the data again and again and then again. Some ethnographers recommend sleeping with the data in case the ethnographer has an idea in the middle of the night. This time spent with the data should involve reading through the observational materials many times, developing possible ways of ordering, categorizing or producing themes for the data. These can help the ethnographer to think of questions the data answers, ways of producing a version of what goes on in the organization and even highlight further areas that the ethnographer has not covered in sufficient detail.

Scholarly pursuit

Translating this more or less ordered data into a scholarly representation often involves addressing a specific question (for example, what happens when a doomsday cult reaches doomsday and nothing happens? See Festinger, Riecken and Schachter, 1956). Such questions are occasionally carried into research, sometimes develop during research and often become more focused as research develops. Addressing a question can help to give an ethnographic write-up a distinct structure. The ethnographer can include other pieces of research which might shed light on the question, give a background to why this question is relevant; provide a background to the study and why it forms a useful way to address the question, and/or attempt to provide some answers to the question. Often, ethnographers will also conclude with possible further questions, organizations or areas of the organization that other ethnographers could pursue. This modesty can be an important feature of establishing the ways in which a scholarly research write-up should be read (as provocative, or as opening up a new field, as posing questions, or challenging previous research).

Writing for the organization

Translating more or less organized field notes into a representation for the organization can pose some different questions. Ethnographers should think carefully about what they want to get from presenting research to the organization studied. The aim can be to fulfil a promise made during access negotiations (for example, a detailed picture of a particular area of organizational activity, carefully avoiding exposing research participants to any untoward criticism from other members of the organization), presenting research to the organization in order to get feedback on what the organization makes of the research (to provide useful further insights for the study), or, alternatively, presenting research in the middle of the study in order to establish trust between members of the organization and the researcher (see sensibility four).

▷▷▷▷▷Sensibility Nine: Ethics

Ethics are a complex area for organizational ethnographers to navigate. From an academic perspective, ethnographers should establish what the ethical requirements are in relation to their own academic institution. There are three principle forms of ethics. First, there are *ethics as rules,* which attempt to define in a relatively rigid manner the ethical direction of the research. Second, there are *ethics as guidelines,* which attempt to provide general principles which researchers should make relevant for each piece of research. Third, there are *ethics as accomplishments.* Due to the complexity and diversity of research settings, this third area depends on researchers producing ethical outlines tailored to the setting for corroboration by academic peers, ethics committees and so on. Ethical clearance from an academic institution is one thing, clearing ethical hurdles in relation to an organization can be quite another. Access negotiations in relation to an organization can involve discussions of ethics. This may require the ethnographer to demonstrate knowledge of another organization's ethical guidance, such as an accepted, professional body's ethical research guidelines. Alternatively, the organization may wish to enter into a pre-research agreement on ethics.

These ethical discussions should feature the following: which areas of the organization the ethnographer will study (to assess the sensitivity of the organization to particular activities); whom the ethnographer will incorporate into the research; how subjects will be incorporated (through signed or verbal agreement, through the agreement of senior management and so on); what the ethnographer will do with the observational data (how will it be written up, where might it be published, will it be anonymous or not); and whether or not the organization will have access to the observations or write-ups of the observations (and at which stage, all the way through the research, or prior to publication). Although these might appear complex negotiations to enter into, particularly at an early stage of the research when the ethnographer may still be trying to figure out exactly what they want to study, these discussions can prove useful for grasping initial impressions of the organization. For example, if an organization wants to take out insurance against market damage being inflicted by the researcher, this may say something interesting about the ways in which the organization assesses its own worth.

In the past, one means through which ethnography steered clear of these negotiations was through covert ethnography. Covert ethnography involves becoming a participant in the setting without informing members of the setting that they are part of an ethnography. Notable ethnographies have been completed in the past (for example, homosexual activities in public toilets, Humphreys, 1975). These have since been criticized for exploiting research participants who knew little or nothing of the research. For academic ethnography it is increasingly difficult to gain ethical clearance for covert ethnography. Covert research is generally identified as contravening important ethical principles of informed consent. Covert research also reduces many of the avenues open for ethnographers to pursue, such as gaining feedback from the organization on their view of the research, asking members how they feel about participating in research, and using this kind of feedback to further the ethnography. Ethnography for organizations is generally constrained by the same set of principles.

▷▷▷▷▷Sensibility Ten: Exits

Although this forms the tenth sensibility, exits should not be left until the end of the ethnographic study. Exits are an important consideration from an early stage of the research. There are five kinds of exit from ethnographic research (and some are more recommended than others).

Studying a phenomenon

Organizational ethnography often focuses upon study of a time-specific organizational phenomenon. This may involve a particular change process occurring in an organization, such as a merger, the introduction of a major new technological system or a change in management. This may involve time in the setting prior to the change, a study of the change and then some time gaining reflection from organization members after the change. Such an approach to a particular organizational phenomenon can usefully bracket the time allocated to the study (taking into account the vagaries of organizational activity and the possibility of delays) and this can then inform the ethnographer's research strategy.

Studying a time frame

An alternative way to establish a particular time frame for a study is to enter into a deliberate fixed entry and exit to the field. This could be presented to the organization in negotiating access and in research write-ups as, for example, a year in company x, six months in the company of CEO, 23 and so on. This approach may be useful for establishing some boundaries to a study that may otherwise seem endless to both the ethnographer and the organization.

Negotiating with an organization

The demands of the organization and its members may dictate the time spent in the organization by the ethnographer. If the time allowed for the ethnography appears short, the ethnographer is faced with three options. First, the ethnographer could decide that another organization might be more appropriate and decline to study the initial organization. Second, the ethnographer could agree to access and then carefully plan and structure the time and access they do have prior to making their exit. Such limitations should then form part of the ethnographic write-up and could be taken into consideration when analysing the way the organization operates. Third, the ethnographer could accept the short-term access offered and move into the field in the hope that once they are in, the organization may be willing to let them stay longer (see sensibility four on establishing field relations).

Ethnographer constraints

There may be particular time constraints on the ethnographer due to other expectations, such as deadlines, course schedules, and so on. Ethnographers should design research appropriately (for example, by asking a very specific question) and report on such limitations (by suggesting questions for further research).

Unexpected events

It is always possible that unexpected events may arise which question the ethnographer's continued stay in the field. Although such emergency exits are unwelcome, they are an occasional necessity.

Recommended reading

Bate, S. (1997) 'Whatever happened to organizational anthropology? A review of the field of organizational ethnography and anthropological studies,' *Human Relations* 50(9): 1147–76

Hammersley, M. and Atkinson, P. (1995) *Ethnography: Principles in Practice* (2nd edition, Routledge, London)

Schwartzman, H. (1993) *Ethnography in Organizations* (Sage, London)

1

▷▷▷▷▷Sensibility One
Ethnographic Strategy

Introduction

This first sensibility sets out some of the basics that ethnographers frequently take into account prior to entering the field. Like each of the sensibilities in this book, it does not set out a single set of instructions to follow in doing ethnography (as each ethnographic setting and each experience of doing ethnography is different). Instead, I will set out some questions to address, ideas to consider and possible paths to take in entering into ethnographic research, and ground these in the experiences of other ethnographers. First, I will address what is meant by an ethnographic strategy and why a strategic vocabulary is useful for organizational ethnography. Second, I will look at ways ethnographers have conceived strategies for entering into and staying in research settings. Third, some alternative takes on ethnographic strategic content will be presented. Finally, the discussion will close with a look at ethnographic strategies in action, including questions of adapting, scrapping and stubbornly sticking to an ethnographic strategy.

Prior to this analysis of ethnographic strategy, I should point out that I will not deal in detail in this discussion with the question of whether or not to complete a study ethnographically. I am assuming to some extent that readers choosing a book entitled *Organizational Ethnography* have already demonstrated some interest in ethnography. Briefly stated, there is no simple, single formula for calculating if ethnography is the most appropriate methodology for addressing a particular research question or whether ethnography is any better or worse than another method for addressing particular research objectives. However, readers contemplating ethnography for the first time should be able to decide by the end of this discussion if ethnography is for them.

What is an ethnographic strategy and why should I have one?

In the Introduction to this book I suggested that ethnographies can be exploratory in nature and can involve long periods of immersion in the field of study. This can involve the development of numerous relations with those who ordinarily go about their business in the field of study. It can also involve the ethnographer in a constant move between being at times more of a participant in the field and at other times being more of an observer. This can generate an amount of ethnographic complexity, centred around the ethnographer themselves, who must manage a set of relationships, a research project, observations, being a participant member, trying to figure out what they want to find out as an ethnographer, while also not limiting the exploratory scope of ethnography, sticking to a budget, a deadline and producing something (hopefully insightful, interesting and/or useful) at the end of the ethnography. This sounds like hard work – and it is. However, the complexity of completing an ethnography can be managed through the development of an initial ethnographic strategy.

Prior to entering into a detailed analysis of the likely contents of an ethnographic strategy, it is important to note the kind of strategy I am recommending. The aim of developing an ethnographic strategy is not to build a step-by-step plan to be followed slavishly in subsequent research. The aim is also not to build a hypothesis to be tested in the field (see sensibility two). Instead, an ethnographic strategy involves collating an initial set of ideas that the ethnographer can carry into the field, use to negotiate access, adapt as the research progresses, scrap if necessary or stubbornly stick to at times when it appears the ethnography might be under threat (see 'Ethnographic strategy in action', below). An ethnographic strategy can be developed in line with recent management research on questions of strategy.

Much of the management literature on strategy tends to search for a prescriptive means of establishing the ideal method for carrying out strategy. For example, Goodman and Lawless (1994: 288) look at ways in which to build 'defensible competitive advantage' and Thompson (1995: 199) suggests 'successful change needs planning, champions and persistence'. Corrall (1994: 3) argues in the academic arena that 'Planning helps us to prepare for a better future; it is good management practice and an organisational requirement'. This kind of prescriptive plan of action remains unavailable for ethnographers. Ethnographic research needs to develop in the field, in connection with the experiences the ethnographer has in the setting they are studying. Also, most ethnography tends to have at least an exploratory aspect which would be undermined by a rigidly prescriptive strategy developed prior to entering into the research (see next section).

However, recent developments in management research on strategy can provide us with some more compelling ways to think about doing ethnography. First, recent research treats strategy as an ongoing, inclusive process. In much of this work, prescriptive approaches to strategy are replaced through considerations of strategy as providing opportunities to draw people together around particular focal points for discussion (see, for example, the work of Ackoff, 1981; Pettigrew, 1987; Morton, 1988; Reponen, 1993; A. Smits et al., 1997; Lee, 1999; Orna, 1999; Fjelstad and Haanaes, 2001). Hence Ackoff (1981: 70) argues that strategic processes should involve 'continuous monitoring, evaluation and modification', and Reponen (1993: 102) suggests that 'strategy development is seen more and more as an interactive organisational process'. According to Reponen (1993: 103), the 'strategy generation process is thus a kind of research project where multiple participants are involved and multiple methods are used'.

Second, the possible futures that strategy might involve are engaged with as problematic possibilities, rather than things which can be definitively planned. Problematizing the future is treated as a way of thinking about strategy (see, for example, Ackoff, 1981; Arfield, 1995; Smits, van der Poel and Ribbers, 1997; Earl, 1999). Earl (1999: 162) suggests that: 'The future has to be brought back into strategy-making.'

Exemplar One

R. Harper (1998) *Inside the IMF: An Ethnography of Documents, Technology and Action* (Academic Press, London)

Harper's ethnography stems from a tradition of research known as Computer Supported Collaborative (or Co-operative) Work (CSCW). This tradition is technology focused and uses a form of ethnography to shed light on interactions between people and technologies. Harper's ethnography looks at the International Monetary Fund (IMF) and analyses the features which make and maintain the IMF as an organization. Harper particularly concentrates on the life of documents in the organization and the ways in which documents move between particular groups of people within the IMF to help us to understand something of the way those groups operate. Harper suggests that the documents are used and understood differently by different sections of the IMF and this tells us something of the practices of each aspect of the organization. Harper draws on broader ethnographic experience within other organizational settings (such as air-traffic control centres) to help illuminate the particular organizational issues that arose in his study of the IMF.

This ethnography is not solely a study *of* the organization. To some degree it is also a study *for* the organization. Harper suggests, however, that making what might be termed practical recommendations based on ethnography raises a range of questions regarding precisely how an ethnography will be carried out, how it will be written up, how an analysis based on the ethnography will be produced and what kinds of recommendations could be made from the analysis. This summary of Harper's ethnography will begin by looking at how the ethnographer went about designing a research strategy and the questions involved in producing practical recommendations. It will then go on to investigate what organizational ethnographers can find of use in Harper's study.

Designing an ethnographic strategy

Harper is clear on the principle behind his ethnographic work: 'My concern in this book is to report on how ethnographic findings can be used to improve the design of organisational work practice and supporting technologies' (1998: ix). Initially, however, Harper points to the problems of defining what ethnography might mean and to whom. For some within the IMF ethnography was described as the 'E word': a mythical method by which (what appeared to be) just looking at what people did was transformed into 'a marvellous new technique that will revolutionise computer systems' (1998: 49).

For Harper, the key to navigating the ethnography of the organization and translating its findings into something useful for the organization lay in establishing a 'field work programme' (1998: 50). Such a programme would involve 'the vexing and obdurate problem of how to make ethnography robust enough as a method to prise open the kinds of issues made salient by design type concerns' (1998: 9).

Harper suggests that what makes a good ethnography stand out are the ways in which the ethnographer manages to evoke the particular situation that has formed the focus of study and intertwine this evocation with insights from other ethnographies, making available a variety of forms of argumentation and analysis. Although this might appear somewhat unspecific, it is designed as a counter to ethnographic textbooks which sometimes suggest 'recipe book' type approaches to ethnography (as if the methodology were entirely unproblematic and easily mobilized from one setting to another). There is a problem of ethnography being indefinable on the one hand and too rigidly defined on the other. In order to avoid such difficulties Harper develops a programme (or what I term a 'strategy') which establishes that not just anything gets to count as ethnography. Harper's programme/strategy has three principle elements.

First, he sets out to follow 'the career of information' (1998: 68) through an organization. He focuses on a particular form of information to study and tracks this information through its various moves within an organization, and the various interpretations and uses made of the information. This provides a set of ethnographic material from which to build arguments.

Second, Harper focuses as an ethnographer on going through ritual inductions within the organization. A ritual induction is an ethnographic moment through which the ethnographer is made aware of some features of the organization that are taken as important by members of the organization. Although this varies widely between organizations, a ritual induction is an event noted by members of the organization as a necessary thing to go through to understand something of the organization. The first part of the programme provides material for judging the second part of the programme.

Third, Harper suggests that ethnographers should develop, analyse and further develop reasons for doing observations and interviews in the field. 'Reasons' here are taken fairly broadly to cover such matters as what kinds of thing the ethnographer might want to find out about an organization (for example, the ethnographer might develop an interest in how a seemingly diverse organization manages to hold together as a coherent unit). These 'reasons' may develop as the research progresses and through consideration of the first two parts of the programme.

What does Harper's programme tell us about organizational ethnographic strategies? First, it confirms the notion that an ethnographic strategy should not be fixed and rigid. Despite using the title 'programme', it is by no means a straightforward ethnographic recipe to apply to all settings. Instead, Harper's approach provides a fluid way of thinking about the organization, of thinking through what might count as an adequate ethnography and, in Harper's case, of considering what might count as useful.

Second, the programme provides three areas that ethnographers could take into account in thinking about engaging with an organization. These areas offer a starting point which each ethnographer can consider in terms of its relevance for their own ethnographic research. Considering (1) the career of organizational information, (2) ritual inductions and (3) what the ethnographer wants to find out could all be useful points to orient an ethnographic study. Thus, Harper's programme provides for three ethnographic starting points which can be utilized and moulded for a particular research project.

Third, Harper's programme gives us an opportunity to begin thinking about ethnography for, and not just of, an organization. What are the advantages of being able to set out an ethnographic programme or strategy? How might this help us negotiate access to an organization? Would an organization look more favourably on research which appears to have a clear programme of work, a clear rationale, and a reasonably clear set of questions? On the other hand, would this risk limiting the exploratory scope of the research? These are questions which cannot be answered in general, but need consideration in relation to specific research experiences (they will be taken further under sensibilities three and four).

Aside from this focus on ethnographic strategy, Harper's work provides several stimulating insights for organizational ethnographers to take into consideration.

Why has ethnography risen to prominence in organizational IT settings?

Harper identifies three trends which can help account for the recent rise in interest in ethnographic research in organizational IT settings. The first of these trends has been the development of research into social issues involved with computing from sociology and anthropology, and from those involved with computers themselves. This melding of social science and IT, Harper suggests, has led to an increasing number of researchers and research outputs on social and organizational aspects of computing. The second trend, developing from the first, has involved the production of a 'set of seminal publications that were a kind of clarion call for a new interpretive, loosely sociological/anthropological approach to requirements capture' (1998: 52). In place of more rigid requirements capture, which might not look far beyond narrowly construed technical issues, these newly emerging publications opened up the question of requirements more broadly. The third trend involved organizations themselves taking a greater interest in ways of getting more from technology or in ways of losing less between the marketed promise of technologies and their introduction into the organization. Harper suggests that the willingness of the IMF to support his own research is further evidence of this attitudinal shift.

Ethnography doesn't just have to be about people

Although this may seem an obvious point, given the previous discussion in this exemplar about organizational documents, it is worth drawing out. Ethnographic research can be all too easily restricted by assumptions that it is focused on culture or cultural variables or social issues which can often be taken to mean people not things or technology. Of course an ethnographic study cannot draw such stark boundaries. From the traditions of anthropology we find tribes studied as people, but also through their material artefacts and the ceremonial significance of things. In the same way, most modern organizations would make little sense if they were studied without the range of things, technologies, processes, documents and so on upon which the organization's day-to-day operation is focused. What Harper's study does, which is particularly useful for organizational ethnographers, is to centre on the things (in this case, documents) rather than people. It is through the movement and work done to make sense of the documents that we find out something about the people. This shifting of focus opens up a range of options for organizational ethnographers, who could consider centring their ethnographic strategy around, for example, technology, documents or processes; they need not limit their central focus to people.

Treating strategy as an ongoing process is a useful way of thinking about ethnography as a method of drawing together multiple participants and views and co-ordinating those people and views. Problematizing the future avoids tying the ethnography into a prescriptive process which might carry with it assumptions that the ideas established at the start of research are the ideas which should define the research. Holding on to the possibility that the future is not always clear, that research develops in the field and that outcomes for research cannot be determined prior to doing the research, means the direction of the research is always available for further consideration.

Although I have presented here two aspects of thinking about ethnographic strategy (strategy as an ongoing process and treating the future as problematic), it should not be assumed that these two areas are straightforward. The ongoing process of ethnographic strategy is (I think) most usefully conceptualized as connecting multiple opportunities to dispute, redirect and reconstitute the direction of study. The 'process' of ethnographic strategy is not a smooth, linear progress towards a fixed goal, but is the (sometimes multiply sited) location for ongoing disputation, the purpose of which is to allow for multiple reconstructions of the research to exist in a reasonably coherent, connected form (for more on improvisation and ethnography, see Humphreys, Brown and Hatch, 2003).

I have called the ethnographic strategy a sensibility because it provides a basis for ethnographers to think about what it is they are doing while they are doing research, to reflect on the principles they carry into the research and because it gives a basis for ethnographers to move back and forth between the everyday practicalities of their research and the general direction in which they would like the research to move. Such movement also involves constant consideration of the appropriateness of the direction in which the research is going and constant questions regarding the possibility of taking an ethnographic study in a new direction. Just as ethnographers can be thoroughly sceptical about the field of study (holding everything up for ethnographic inspection and attempting to take nothing for granted, see sensibility two), ethnographers can apply that scepticism equally to the development of their own research. If strategy can be usefully thought of as a fluid and interpretable set of principles for drawing people together, then what kinds of principles should an ethnographic strategy incorporate?

Conceiving an ethnographic strategy

A research question

Although I have recommended treating an ethnographic strategy as an ongoing process, a focal point to bring people together, and have suggested thinking about futures as problematic possibilities (rather than a single target to aim towards), in this section I will begin looking at ways to build initial content for an ethnographic strategy. This content is not designed as a step-by-step ethnographic programme, but instead provides a series of areas that ethnographers can consider in building a strategy to be subsequently worked on in doing the research. The first of these areas involves the development of a research question. Such questions can be broadly or narrowly conceived and the subject of particular constraints (time, funding, colleagues' expectations) which might set some of the scope for the kind of question to be addressed.

The development of an initial outline research question can form the starting point for developing an ethnographic strategy. If an ethnographer wants to study conflict among corporate executives (see exemplar thirteen), the difficulties of unionisation in Japanese automobile transplants (exemplar seven) or the social organization of marijuana users (exemplar twelve), this can form the starting point for considerations of where the study might take place, who might be included in the study, how the study might be initially shaped and so on. However, these initial research questions can be more or less broadly defined prior to doing the research. Hence entering into research in order to analyse the use of documents in the IMF (exemplar one) provides a narrower definition of the scope of the research than exploring the possibilities of ethnographically studying the internet (exemplar ten). A narrower question might well set some more strict parameters for developing an ethnographic strategy. This can be advantageous in that the field-site for doing the research appears to follow on from the question and the participants to be included in the research can be more or less clearly defined ahead of doing the research because of the site chosen. Thus choosing to study documents in the IMF (exemplar one) establishes a setting (the IMF), narrows the participants to be studied (according to the documents to be selected) and establishes a series of practical questions regarding access and time allowed in the field. However, narrowly prescribed research questions also limit the exploratory scope of ethnography. Alternatively, choosing a broader question, such as researching the possibility of studying the internet ethnographically (exemplar ten), does not dictate a particular research field-site or particular set of research participants (however, as exemplar ten demonstrates, this exploration of methodological possibilities did involve the gradual development of a very specific study).

Types of ethnographic question

I have found in doing ethnographic research that one way to develop a research question is to think about the type of question to be addressed. Although the following typology is reasonably detailed, it is important to note that often an ethnography will cover more than one of these areas, that ethnographies sometimes shift between areas (as an exploratory strategy should allow) and ethnographers may always find new areas to work in or new types of question to ask (as ethnographers often seek to innovate).

A narrowly prescribed research question The work of Morrill (1995; exemplar thirteen) ethnographically engages with questions of conflict among corporate executives. This provides one way of thinking about an ethnographic research question. In Morrill's case the research question to be addressed prescribes some features of the ethnographic strategy. The question establishes that Morrill's interest is in top-level executives. In terms of thinking about where to study, what to study and who to study, Morrill's research question sets some parameters. It is not such a narrowly prescribed question, however, that a particular type of executive should be studied, or that executives from a particular region or nation should be studied. Even a narrowly prescribed research question then entails further work relating to location and access (see sensibility three), relations to be established in the field (sensibility four) and time to be spent in the field (sensibility five). A narrowly prescribed research question thus carries some restrictions, without entirely defining the research. Even in ethnographic studies which focus on a particular research question, experiences in the field can shape the direction of the study. Ethnographers should think carefully about developing narrowly prescribed questions prior to entry into the field and the commitments which follow from such narrow questions.

Utilizing a focal area Whyte's (1955) work (exemplar three) does not utilize a narrowly prescribed research question. Instead, Whyte establishes that the purpose of his ethnography is to provide an account of what goes on in the day-to-day activities of those living in a poor part of the USA. Whyte does not delimit his study to conflict (as Morrill does) or any other specific feature of life in the area to be studied. Instead, Whyte's approach is relatively exploratory (although see next section on Malinowski). Whyte is keen to understand and offer a portrayal of everyday life in a slum and is focused on organizing his ethnography in relation to what he finds happening in the field. Using a focal area as the basis for doing ethnographic research does not free the ethnographer from all constraints. Having selected a type of area (slum), a geographical region (Italian neighbourhoods of Boston), a specific location (the street corners of a particular Italian neighbourhood), there follows a series of further commitments. The participants to be included in the research are those people living around the street corner selected. This introduces some very specific access questions (how to become a member of this particular group) and sets some challenges for the ethnographer (particularly how to become a convincing member of an Italian neighbourhood street corner). Although Whyte's (1955) work appears to begin with a less narrowly prescribed research question, the development of an ethnographic strategy involves the successive building of commitments. Each of these commitments (such as access, field relations, time to be spent in the field) needs to be considered in relation to the developing ethnographic strategy. For Morrill, commitments had to be managed in relation to attempts to keep the research focused on conflict. For Whyte, these commitments (gaining access and time spent in the field) formed achievements in getting to know more about the community he was trying to study. The choice to base an ethnographic strategy around a region can be a useful way of developing an ethnographic focus without having to produce the kinds of commitments prior to doing the research that a narrow research question can entail.

A commitment to exploration It should not be assumed that Whyte's (1955) work is purely exploratory. Whyte had a specific political purpose in attempting to provide a picture of street corner life, counter to the mostly negative media stories available at the time of his study of street corner crime and poverty. The anthropological tradition of ethnography, such as the work of Malinowski (1922/2002; see exemplar two) has perhaps a more explicit exploratory aim. Malinowski presents his ethnographic experiences as an engaged exploration of a culture entirely foreign to his own. The study is exploratory in that Malinowski's aim is to uncover the organization of the society he is studying (this has problematic epistemological commitments, see sensibility two). This 'purely' exploratory approach to ethnography should not be overplayed, as many of these early anthropological studies also involved issues of European colonial management and at the very least involved introductions to the native culture by missionaries or colonial administrators (thus introducing the researcher on management terms). A commitment to 'pure' exploration is not then an achievable, practical research aim. Any ethnographic research is predicated upon particular needs (such as a need to get the research done in a particular time, fulfil a particular obligation in a course one is studying, meet the expectations of research funders, and so on). However, Malinowski's and Whyte's work demonstrate that in place of a narrowly prescribed research question developed prior to research, there are other ways of providing a focus for developing an ethnographic strategy (which can be as open as seeking to ask 'what is going on in this particular area?' or 'what are the organizational features of this local culture?').

The pursuit of things   There are a variety of other ways of thinking about the development of a focal point for an ethnographic strategy. One of these is provided by the work of Harper (1998; see exemplar one). Harper's strategy is to follow, first, the career of information in a particular organization, second, organizational rituals which demonstrate particular features of the way the organization works and, third, constantly attempt to develop further observational opportunities in the field in line with experiences that develop during the research. Harper's study of organizational documentation thus combines carrying into the research a reasonably narrow research question with attempts to strike a balance between strategic commitments (such as following documents) and exploration (seeking further opportunities for observation in line with field experiences). Other similar focal points can be found in the work of Suchman (1987; exemplar eight), who looks at the development and testing of particular technologies in workplace settings. In Suchman's work the pursuit of documentation is replaced by the pursuit of photocopier testing.

Methodological development   Hine's (2000) work on virtual ethnography takes methodological development as its focus (see exemplar ten). In place of a narrowly prescribed research question, a commitment to exploration of a particular area or the pursuit of a specific aspect of organizational activity (such as documentation), comes a study of the possibility of using ethnography to study the internet. This methodological focus involves the development of particular research commitments as the study develops. Hine selects a particular event (or series of events) surrounding a particular legal case as it develops both in traditional media and on the internet. Hine uses this event to pursue the questions that arise in attempting to produce a virtual ethnography. Such methodological development provides a focus for the production of an ethnographic strategy free of many commitments prior to doing the research. In Hine's case, the internet is available for study and she is in a position to set the parameters of the research. In line with previous ethnographic focal points, as the research develops, Hine builds a series of commitments in attempting to develop an ethnographic means of studying the internet.

Theoretical development   An alternative focus from exploring possible methodological developments in ethnography is provided by the work of

Latour and Woolgar (1979; exemplar four), who seek to develop some specific theoretical insights. They argue that the study of science and scientists can be devised ethnographically and that such ethnographic study can offer a picture of the day-to-day activities of what goes on in a laboratory. For Latour and Woolgar, this study of the day-to-day accomplishment of science offers a distinct alternative to what were contemporary philosophical analyses of the nature of, for example, scientific discovery. Latour and Woolgar use their study of the practices of scientists to argue for the development of alternative ways of conceptualizing science, scientists and the production of order through laboratories (this study is also noted for its methodological originality, see exemplar four). Pursuing this kind of theoretical aim (that there might be an alternative way of conceptualizing what goes on in the organized world of the laboratory), also carries with it particular kinds of commitments: to find a laboratory to study; to uncover ways of engaging with scientists in action; and figuring out ways of understanding and reproducing accounts of scientists and science. For management researchers, a theoretical focus could involve pursuing ethnographic research to question, challenge or contribute towards any number of traditional management research areas (accountability, strategy, outsourcing, and so on).

Practical questions A final potential focal point around which to develop an ethnographic strategy is the possibility of addressing a practical question. With the move of ethnographic research into organizational settings, practical questions are becoming an increasingly common feature of ethnographic work. Exemplar fourteen, based on some of my own work, looks at the kinds of issues raised in trying to enter into an organizational setting not just to produce an account of that setting, but also to produce an account which has some practical resonance for the members of that setting. In exemplar fourteen I present some of the ethnographic work I have been doing in university settings. This draws together both ethnography *of* and ethnography *for* the particular setting under study. Practical ethnography (see Conclusion) often involves a protracted period of negotiation, prior to entering the field, which establishes some of the questions to be addressed during the research. I have always found it useful to carry my own ethnographic strategy into such negotiations in order to manage my way around questions I will not answer (either because they are beyond the scope of the research or the scope of my interest) and establish at least the direction of the early stages of the research project (which areas of the organization will be studied, why they are of practical import, what kinds of things it might be possible to say about those areas). These negotiations also involve frequent reiterations (by me) of the importance of the exploratory aspects of ethnography and of the need to frequently revisit the ethnographic strategy with members of the organization to see what we are doing and where we might go next. Using practical questions as a focal point for the development of an ethnographic strategy involves a clear emphasis on using the strategy as a process for bringing people together (see the section on 'What is an ethnographic strategy?' above).

Building a strategy

How to turn a question into a strategy

In outlining some of the differing broad types of question an ethnographer might seek to ask it should be clear that different types of question come with different forms of commitment. We can see that a narrowly conceived research question carries with it particular demands in relation to the location that will be studied, the participants required for the study, perhaps even the length of time the ethnography will require. We can also see that more exploratory research questions carry far fewer or at least less rigid commitments. With more exploratory questions, commitments to a particular location, to a particular set of participants and to a length of time to be spent in the field are developed as research progresses. However, I have suggested that even narrowly prescribed research questions should also retain the possibility for further exploration as the ethnographer gains more experience in the field and can make more informed decisions regarding the appropriateness of the research question.

Once an ethnographer has established an initial type of question to be asked and the broad area which will form the subject of ethnographic investigation, a more detailed initial strategy can be developed. I have always found the following areas to be frequent features of my ethnographic strategies (however, given the variety of forms of ethnographic research entered into, some readers may find other areas more or less relevant). Each of these areas will provide the basis for subsequent discussions, but it is worth briefly stating how each can be utilized in building a strategy. First, I pay close attention to the possible locations to be ethnographically studied. This can involve drawing up a long or fairly short list of possible organizational settings. I analyse these potential field-sites in terms of their suitability for the research I want to pursue and in relation to a range of practical questions (such as how easy will it be to get to each location). I have always found it necessary to have more than one potential field-site in which to do the research. Second, closely tied into issues of location, I make some initial considerations of access. Looking at my list of potential field-sites, I assess my likelihood of being able to gain access to the site, to spend an amount of time in the site and to spend time talking with the members of the particular site (similar discussion can be found in the work of Morrill, 1995; exemplar thirteen). Assessing access then leads into more detailed assessment of time (how long do I want to spend in the field?; how long do I estimate the study will take?), observation (how will I go about doing the observation?; how will I collect observational material?; how easy will it be to collect such material?; how sensitive will such material be?), ethics (particularly incorporating into the strategy that the work will adhere to a professional code) and exit (how long do I want to stay in the organization?; do I want to predetermine the exit point?; am I going to make any promises to the organization regarding my exit, such as providing feedback?). For me, such considerations are brief prior to entering the field. As the study develops I will enter into much more detailed analysis of these areas.

Building each of these areas into an initial strategy can prove helpful for three purposes here. First, the strategy can be used in negotiating access to the organization. Having something to present and having some confidence in what I am asking for has proved useful for me in gaining access to organizational settings. However, I have also always found that an important feature of negotiating access to an organization has been to emphasize the exploratory scope of ethnography, that the strategy is there for all parties to revisit and that we should schedule some discussion during the research regarding the progress (and any changes in direction required) of the research. These negotiations also form ethnographic moments which can reveal a great deal about the way the organization operates (see sensibility three).

Second, the strategy can be useful once research is under way. A particular problem with doing ethnography (see sensibility four) is that the ethnographer works hard in building relationships in the field but can lose any sense of ethnographic distance. That is, relations in the field become the focus for development and the research itself slips into the background. Having a strategy (even one that requires constant development and reassessment) offers the ethnographer something to prise them away from the field, to remind them of their research project and to enable them to re-introduce some ethnographic distance to their actions.

Third, an ethnographic strategy can document the expectations that the researcher carried into the field. This can be useful for providing an analysis of the role of the researcher in carrying out the research. Briefly stated, such analysis can form an important part of ethnographic research in making available a methodological account of an ethnographic study which subsequent readers can use to assess the study (for more detail on this, see sensibility two). Retaining a version of the assumptions the ethnographer carried into the field can help the ethnographer reflect on the journey they have been on, in doing any particular piece of research.

Ethnographic strategy in action

It may appear that having considered a focal point for the ethnography, a type of question to be asked, the commitments that question entails and some possible details of the proposed study (such as location and time), ethnographers would have completed an amount of strategic work.

LIBRARY
The University of Bolton
Eagle Campus

However, I should emphasize here that an ethnographic strategy is only preparatory work for entering the field. The ways in which ethnographic strategies are reworked, dumped, retained or otherwise adapted needs some attention.

Although reading ethnographic research often provides us with a sense that the ethnographer knew what they were doing, it is not always the case that an ethnographer sets out a narrowly prescribed research question early in the research and then adheres to that single question. Often, ethnographic write-ups feature an analysis of the ways in which the question developed, how this led the ethnographer to engage in a series of practical questions and how these led to a further series of practical and theoretical insights regarding ethnography and what can be done. There are many differing degrees of messiness in this development of research questions and ethnographic strategies. I will present three very brief experiences from my own ethnographic work to illustrate this point.

Developing a strategy

In a recent ethnographic study of traffic regulation (particularly speed limits) in the UK, I constructed an initial strategy highlighting the importance of speed cameras (as prevalent across UK traffic management discussions, as controversial in media reporting, as a development drivers have been keen to express views on). Despite developing a strategy which focused on speed cameras, it was not clear where the action was taking place. Indeed, it was only after talking with various local authorities and some management consultants (who had previously been involved in setting up the first national programme of speed cameras in the UK) that I gained some sense of where and whom I could study ethnographically. It turned out that there were bodies called 'local safety camera partnerships', which had responsibility for installing, maintaining and publicizing cameras. Although studying traffic regulation in the UK, particularly relating to speed cameras, might appear to form the basis for a narrowly prescribed ethnographic strategy, this strategy was still subject to a great deal of developmental work in the early stages of the research. The strategy had to retain an exploratory aspect to incorporate these developments.

Stubbornly sticking to a strategy

Prior to the ethnography of traffic management I had been studying the introduction of new technologies to university settings (see exemplar fourteen). For this study I had developed a detailed ethnographic strategy in collaboration with the participants in the study. This strategy set out the technology projects I would study, the members of the university to be incorporated into the research and a commitment to present findings from the research. The strategy left open the kinds of findings that the research would produce. As the study progressed it became increasingly apparent that several of the areas of university activity, which had formed the basis for proposed research under the strategy, were raising difficulties in allowing me ethnographic access. In this case, rather than develop the strategy, I felt it was appropriate to stubbornly stick to the strategy and hold meetings with those who had agreed the terms of the original research. In this case the strategy proved to have utility in ensuring access promises were met.

Abandoning a strategy

My first ethnographic experience involved an over-ambitious study of English football fans travelling abroad. Counter to the media attention at the time directed towards supposed hooligans, I hoped to demonstrate that English football fans travelling abroad were actually organized, albeit boisterous, social groups. Needless to say, towards the end of my first match travelling abroad with the fans (during which the English team were losing 1–0), there was trouble. The stadium stewards locked the doors preventing fans from leaving the stadium (to prevent clashes with local rival fans). The English fans proceeded to break down the doors and exit the stadium *en masse* only to be met by riot police with shields and batons. During the ensuing fight I decided that my ethnographic strategy had been somewhat misdirected and my research project as a whole misconceived. There was little in the way of an ethnographic get-out here (claiming to 'merely' be an ethnographer at this point did not seem a viable way of avoiding trouble). After half an hour or so of batons and shields, stones and bottles of urine being thrown, we were taken as a group to the airport and flown back to England where several fans were arrested. Abandoning an ethnographic strategy in this way emphasizes the importance of always being open to radical changes in research according to circumstance. An ethnographic strategy always needs to be made locally appropriate.

Summary

An ethnographic strategy is not a step-by-step guide to be slavishly followed in the course of an ethnography. Instead, developing an ethnographic strategy involves drawing together a range of ideas, principles, initial questions and assumptions that the researcher has prior to starting the ethnography. An ethnographic strategy can be important for negotiations at the point of entering the field and for establishing the early development of an ethnography. However, the strategy should be treated in a fluid manner, constantly available for redirection and should be treated as sceptically by the ethnographer as the field-site itself. An ethnographic strategy can form an initial attempt to scope out the kinds of things the researcher might do – it is only in doing the ethnography that further successive commitments (in terms of access and locations, field relations and time spent in the field) will be made, as the following sensibilities will highlight.

Recommended reading

Burgess, R. (1984) *In the Field: An Introduction to Field Research* (Routledge, London)

Spradley, J. (1980) *Participant Observation* (Holt, Rinehart and Winston, New York)

Wakeford, N. (2003) 'Research note: working with new media's cultural intermediaries', *Information, Communication and Society* 6(2): 229–45

2

▷▷▷▷▷Sensibility Two
Questions of Knowledge

Introduction

This sensibility introduces the tricky question of knowledge in ethnography. The discussion is designed to build on the previous strategic sensibility. I will, first, establish some initial definitions for the concepts to be used in the subsequent discussion. Second, I will look at three distinct approaches to knowledge in ethnography – the realist, narrative and reflexive approach. I will suggest in this section that each of these approaches is complex and can sometimes overlap, and that all are subject to many arguments regarding, for example, the most appropriate way to approach realism or reflexivity. Third, I will consider some traditional questions of research methodology and knowledge (questions of validity, usefulness and rigour) which are appropriate to forms of organizational ethnography.

Questions of epistemology and ethnography

Definitions

Under the last sensibility I suggested that ethnographers can begin building an ethnographic strategy prior to entering the field and can use such a strategy to orient their activities in the field. The strategy can be useful for negotiating access, for figuring out appropriate first steps in the field and for prising the ethnographer away from full immersion in the field setting. However, I stressed under the last sensibility that an initial strategy should not be treated as a step-by-step guide to be slavishly followed in completing ethnographic research. Instead, the strategy should be constantly worked upon and kept at the forefront of considerations of what to do next. One important aspect for building an ethnographic strategy is entering into questions of knowledge: what kind of claims to knowledge can ethnography make? On what basis can ethnography demonstrate the validity, usefulness or rigour of its claims? Do assessments of ethnographic claims to knowledge represent further opportunities for ethnographic investigation?

Such questions of knowledge are intertwined with forms of ontology and epistemology. Prior to entering into an analysis of different claims to knowledge made through ethnography, I will propose some outline definitions of these areas. First, *ontology* relates to questions of the status of the world, including questions of how the world is made up and how aspects of the world hold together. Second, *epistemology* relates to the kinds of claims to knowledge we can make about the world. An epistemology establishes the basis for what can be known and how that knowledge can be assessed. As we shall see in the next section, forms of ontology and epistemology shift between different approaches to ethnography. That is, the kinds of approach to the world (what the world is made up from) and the kinds of claims to knowledge about the world (what it is we can say about the world) vary between ethnographic approaches.

Third, we should note that different forms of ontology and epistemology are frequently positioned in social science research in terms of oppositions. There are oppositions composed between *essentialism* (that things in the world, for example technologies, have certain properties) and *relativism* (that the properties of things are not fixed and need to be understood in their varied ways), between *positivism* (that the world exists to be analysed and that predictive, scientific laws can be developed) and *interpretivism* (that the world is open to multiple claims as to what is going on), and between *realism* (that the world exists to be explained, although not necessarily through predictive laws) and *constructivism* (that any version of a local aspect of the world is a local accomplishment, including ethnography itself). Such oppositions can be shifted around so that, for example, essentialism is understood as opposed to constructivism. These oppositions are also mapped on to distinctions made between *objective* (the world provides the material from which research extracts) and *subjective* (the research is the inevitable product of the researchers' engagement in the world) forms of research and between *inductive* (research which draws general conclusions from specific research) and *deductive* (research which involves the production of a hypothesis to be tested) approaches to research. While I only offer a very brief introduction to some possible ways of thinking about these topics here, the following section will provide more ethnographic detail on the ways and means through which these areas are made to make ethnographic sense.

The following section collates different ethnographic approaches under three headings. I have done this in order to provide a reasonably succinct and coherent description of the principal ontological and epistemological considerations entered into by ethnographers. However, readers should note that these three headings also incorporate a variety of subtle (and not so subtle) ontological and epistemological distinctions which I shall begin to discuss here and will pick up on under subsequent sensibilities.

Ontology, epistemology and ethnography

Realist ethnography

In exemplar two, the work of Malinowski is used to establish one version of a science of ethnography. The claim to science invoked in this exemplar is that there exists a rigorous and coherent means of engaging with an ethnographic field-site. Malinowski aimed to establish ethnography as an academic discipline. Hence his appeal to rigour, to standards and to regular ways of doing ethnography need to be understood in this light. For our purposes, Malinowski's scientific approach to ethnography introduces a particular set of ontological and epistemological issues. Malinowski enters into the ethnography claiming that the world is there to be understood and that a rigorous, robust and routinized (ethnographic) way of engaging with the world can be developed. The ontological underpinnings of this approach are realist: the world is available for engagement by the ethnographer. The epistemological approach here is also realist: the data collected can be assessed for the extent to which it accurately reflects the field-site from which it has been collected. Although 'science' is proclaimed as the standard to be achieved, Malinowski's work need not be thought of as positivistic, at least in the sense that he is not seeking to establish universal laws that govern both Trobriand islanders and those living in other parts of the world, and he makes no attempt at predictive modelling. Realism and positivism do not necessarily need to be understood as one and the same (for more on this, see Blaikie, 1993).

Exemplar Two

B. Malinowski (1922/2002) *Argonauts of the Western Pacific* (Routledge, London)

The purpose of this exemplar is to provide three principle insights for those interested in organizational ethnography. First, this summary will offer an introduction to the work of Malinowski, and provide detail on how his work formed an important contribution to the historical development of ethnography. Second, Malinowski's approach to realist, objectivist, scientific ethnography will be introduced, providing insights into the epistemological underpinnings of his work. Third, ideas of exchange and the ways in which apparently economic relationships are heavily implicated in issues of magic, myth and religious belief in Malinowski's work will provide a starting point for considering the usefulness of early anthropology for studying the modern corporation.

Malinowski and the history of ethnography

Malinowski's *Argonauts of the Western Pacific* is based on a two-year ethnographic study of Trobriand society in New Guinea. Malinowski's work was an important contribution to early anthropology, resisting the convention for dependence upon second-hand accounts of particular settings in favour of getting close to the action. This 'getting close', however, involved Malinowski living with the tribes being studied, actively participating in their rites and rituals, learning their language and ways of life. This was something of a departure from most anthropology of the time, which involved 'getting close' by living with missionaries or colonial dignitaries who were, to an extent, 'outsiders' to the local setting. For Malinowski, although such relations with missionaries or colonialists were an important starting point for a study, it was far more valuable to shed off the shadow of the colonial administrator in favour of attempting to get as close to the action as possible. However, this was not a straightforward methodological development. Malinowski opens his book by expressing concern that ethnographic research:

> …is in the sadly ludicrous, not to say tragic, position, that at the very moment when it begins to put its workshop in order, to forge its proper tools, to start ready for work on its appointed task, the material of its study melts away with hopeless rapidity. Just now, when the methods and aims of scientific field ethnology have taken shape, when men fully trained for the work have begun to travel into savage countries and study their inhabitants – these die away under our very eyes. (2002/1922: xv)

Malinowski suggests that ethnography in the early part of the twentieth century occupied a tense position between the need to establish its methodological rigour (see next section) and the constant loss of suitable sites for study. The colonial domination and (what might be termed) 'civilization' (in the sense of transforming a tribe to live along the principles of western European moral, religious and cultural principles) of tribal cultures resulted in fewer locations to study. This was to be followed by the dissolution of colonial territories and the concomitant decline in the number of opportunities to study tribal settings through the auspices of colonial management. For Malinowski, however, this decline in field-sites was particularly painful as he felt the field of anthropology was only just setting about the business of establishing its methodological principles. To emphasize, the importance of Malinowski's work lay in his attempts to establish rigorous anthropological principles, through living in the setting under study.

> I therefore had constantly the daily life of the natives before my eyes, while accidental, dramatic occurrences, deaths, quarrels, village brawls, public and ceremonial events, could not escape my notice. (2002/1922: xvii)

This theme of ethnographic immersion in the field might appear similar to modern ethnographic concerns. However, two points require careful consideration. First, Malinowski was working hard to render this principle of immersion in the field as the proper approach to ethnography. It was by no means settled that this was the 'proper' way to go about ethnographic research. Second, he wanted to tie this immersion in to the development of ethnography as a scientific method of enquiry.

Realist, scientific ethnography

Malinowski's work can be seen as part of an attempt to establish and secure a future for ethnographic research through paying particular attention to (Malinowski's own version of) methodological rigour. In this book he clearly sets out the principles by which he argues research should be done.

> One of the first conditions of acceptable ethnographic work certainly is that it should deal with the totality of all social, cultural and psychological aspects of the community, for they are so interwoven that not one can be understood without taking into consideration all the others. (2002/1922: xvi)

For Malinowski, forms of exchange needed to be considered in relation to social relationships, myth, magic and rituals. However, this was part of a scientific, realist and objectivist study. Thus economic exchange alongside myth and magic were opened up for ethnographic analysis. Each of these areas was now accessible for ethnographic investigation and, furthermore, the methods and techniques of collection were to form an important aspect of writing.

> The results of scientific research in any branch of learning ought to be presented in a manner absolutely candid and above board. (2002/1922: 2)

> I consider that only such ethnographic sources are of unquestionable scientific value, in which we can clearly draw the line between, on the one hand, the results of direct observation and of native statements and interpretations, and on the other, the inferences of the author, based on his common sense and psychological insight. (2002/1922: 3)

Malinowski did not restrict his thoughts on the science of ethnography to declarations regarding the ways in which ethnographic writings should be presented. He argued that there were three principles which needed to be followed in completing a scientific ethnographic enquiry. First, the organization of the tribe and an anatomy of its culture needed to be recorded clearly. The ethnographer should provide a 'concrete, statistical, documentation' of the tribe (2002/1922: 24). Second, this documentation should provide the basics of an ethnography which could then be fleshed out through the provision of detail on what Malinowski termed 'the imponderabelia of actual life,' (2002/1922: 24). Third, these ethnographic details needed to be recorded alongside documentation of the 'native mentality' (2002/1922: 24). This mentality should be sought through statements from natives, characteristic narratives of the natives' concerns and items of folklore and magic. He argued that the final goal of such scientific ethnography should be to 'grasp the natives' point of view … his vision of his world' (2002/1922: 25).

This talk of a scientific, objectivist, realist approach to ethnography appears to situate Malinowski's approach to ethnography within a different set of epistemological concerns from the narrative and reflexivist approaches. However, the need to get close to the action, to immerse oneself in the setting, and to attempt to take into consideration multiple 'things' which might be going on (the economic, social and religious, not just exchange relationships) each appear as relevant now as they did in the early part of the twentieth century. It is difficult to comprehensively assess from a contemporary perspective the need to establish ethnography as a field of research (given that anthropology and sociological forms of ethnography are now well established) and the necessity of invoking science as the basis for methodological rigour. It could be argued that this attempt to establish anthropological ethnography as useful and rigorous finds a close match in contemporary attempts to establish the usefulness of ethnography in organizational settings (see sensibilities one, four and the Conclusion).

Exchange and the value of early anthropology

Beyond this comparison between establishing ethnography in colonial and organizational settings, Malinowski's work provides a variety of further insights for organizational ethnographers to consider. First, his approach to exchange relationships among Trobriand islanders offers insights into the way exchange forms a focal point for social organization of the islanders. 'Kula' is the local term for a form of ceremonial exchange which maintains reciprocal relations between islanders. To give establishes and maintains the reciprocal obligation to receive something of similar status. However, Malinowski argues that the equality of such exchange is not held together by any particular law or sanction. Instead, the expectation and social order is subtle and held together by a variety of status, symbolic, mythic and ritualistic relations. These ideas might aid the organizational ethnographer in throwing into relief (thinking about things from a different perspective) the informal, non-sanctionable relations which pervade the modern workplace and are crucial for the maintenance of the workplace. The ways in which employees interact might be held together by similar complex social and psychological relationships as the Trobriand islanders.

Second, Malinowski's analysis of exchange focuses on the material artefacts involved in social organization. The canoe forms a focus for holding together these social exchange relations. The building of a canoe, in a similar vein to the introduction of a new technology in the workplace, is a site for superstition, suspicion and ritual. Treating objects as the centre for social interaction and observing the complex social relationships in which an identity for the object is made and maintained can be an important means through which to develop an ethnographic understanding of the local organization.

Third, Malinowski's approach to ceremony among those he studied reminds organizational ethnographers of the importance of staged interactions among corporate employees. Ensuring ceremonies are carried out in the correct manner, with members taking appropriate roles, responding in conventional ways, doing things at the right time, ensures the continuation of the tribe, its rituals and its members' identities. Corporate presentations, product launches, press conferences and boardroom meetings, among other organizational events, could be approached in much the same way, revealing something of the organization and its members.

This form of realist ontology and epistemology has led to debates in ethnography about the quality, accuracy and reliability of some ethnographers' findings. For example, Margaret Mead's (1928) work claimed that teenage girls in Samoa experienced a less troublesome transition from teenagehood to adulthood than, for example, American teenage girls. Yet other ethnographers visiting the same islands argued that Mead's findings were flawed (Freeman, 1983). Critics such as Freeman argued that Mead did not know the language, had not immersed herself fully in the field (by staying with non-natives), had been duped by locals who were playing a joke on her and had misunderstood key aspects of Samoan life. These criticisms were established on further realist grounds: Freeman was closer to the action, lived with the islanders more closely, was more closely incorporated into their ways of life, learnt the language and was not so easily misled by locals' stories. In this criticism, the ontology remains the same: that there is a world out there from which observational data can be extracted. The criticism is also predicated on the same epistemology: that the version of the world presented is available for testing in terms of how accurately it represents the world out there.

However, responses to this criticism have shifted the ontological and epistemological grounds for debate. Critics have suggested that work such as that of Freeman failed to apply the same standards of criticism to their own work. Rather than finishing the argument here, Shore (1983) goes on to suggest that perhaps Mead and Freeman experienced different aspects of Samoan islanders' lives, that engagement at different times with the islanders might reveal different facets of their lives and that each ethnographer engaged with different aspects of teenage-hood. The ontological grounds for the argument are moved here from a realist perspective (that the world exists) to a relativist perspective (that there is not one single version of the world available). The epistemological basis for the ethnography also shifts. In place of questions regarding the accuracy with which the ethnography represents reality (including questions of who has the authoritative account of events) come suggestions that each of the ethnographies reports an aspect of the social life of the islanders. This provides a constructivist epistemology as a critique of a realist ethnography. Instead of a single, knowable reality providing the basis on which to assess an ethnography, there is a range of distinct views (for example, from different ethnographers, islanders and colonialists) that might provide a basis for considering the ethnography (see 'Reflexive ethnography' section below).

In this debate it could be argued that the islanders themselves provide an important means to assess the validity of the research. A similar point can be expressed in relation to organizational ethnography where members of the organization can form an important group who may express views on the ethnography. This can be treated in a more or less realist fashion. Members' views of the ethnography can be utilized to assess the (realist) accuracy of the ethnography (for example, do members feel that the ethnographer has made the same sense of the organization that they have, see exemplar seven) or members' views can be utilized as part of the (socially constructed aspects of the) research (for example, members' views of the ethnography expressed in an early phase of the research can be treated as data to be engaged with in later stages of the research, see exemplar fourteen).

47

Critical realism

Realism is not a singular entity. In order to introduce, briefly, an alternative to the realist suppositions of Mead and Malinowski's work, I will present some of the arguments of Dellbridge's (1998) factory floor analysis. In this ethnography of Japanese models of manufacturing exported to UK contexts, Dellbridge rejects positivist assertions that social science research can and should propose hypotheses to be tested, in order to produce predictive laws, based on assumptions that there is a world out there to be studied which is governed by logic (this critical, realist and non-positivist stance is mirrored in other ethnographic work, see for example, Jordan and Yeomans, 1995). Instead, Dellbridge approaches the world as a social product of the interactions which go into and maintain its production. However, unlike reflexive social constructivists (see 'Reflexive ethnography' section below), Dellbridge argues that his approach should be considered as a form of critical or theoretical realism.

> This research is actually founded on a form of 'theoretical realism' … this position regards social action as occurring within relatively enduring social–structural conditions which do not determine those actions but do constitute a form of 'objective reality' within which those actions take place. (Delbridge, 1998: 17)

Ontologically, Dellbridge's work suggests that there is a real social world out there to be investigated and that this social world is the outcome of ongoing social interaction. Social reality further provides for particular structural relations that do not then necessarily fix or determine social outcomes, but social actions are outcomes through which we can see that particular structural relations may have played a role or may provide a tendency towards a particular outcome. Epistemologically, Dellbridge's work provides for a tentative means to assess the validity of ethnographic claims. He argues that forms of data collection are subject to bias and forms of interpretation entered into by the researcher, but this should be treated as a challenge rather than a problem which undermines research. Epistemologically, the challenge is to open up the ethnography for readers to assess the validity of the claims being made.

> The way I see this challenge is thus: the researcher is responsible for persuading the reader that the work is worthy of their time and consideration, rather than rendered useless due to the biases inherent in collection, interpretation, and presentation of the data. (Dellbridge, 1998: 18)

In Dellbridge's work we can begin to see the complexities of titles such as 'realism'. The title can be used (just about) to cover an array of differing approaches based around a premise that a social reality is available for analysis. That premise, however, provides the grounds for the development of a distinct range of ontological and epistemological positions (Dellbridge's work only provides for one alternative version of realism; further versions can be found in exemplars seven and thirteen).

Narrative ethnography

I will use the term 'narrative ethnography' in this section to group together ethnographies which involve an account that is developed through relations between an ethnographer and one important research participant, sometimes called a key informant. I use the term 'narrative' in the absence of any more recognized term for grouping these studies together. Key informants can often also act as gatekeepers for an ethnographic study, enabling the ethnographer to access the field-site being studied. Such key informants and gatekeepers often proceed to constitute much of the narrative of the ethnography. They are sometimes the best story-teller in the tribe (see, for example, Smith, 1981), are someone who is particularly interested in the process of ethnographic research (see, for example, Harper, 1998; exemplar one) or hold a particular position in the group being studied which enables them to offer a particular kind of narrative of the group. The latter type of relationship can be seen in the work of Whyte (1955; exemplar three). Whyte developed a relationship in the field with a key informant, Doc, whom Whyte suggests is the leader of the street corner gang he is studying. Whyte also acts as something of a gatekeeper, taking an interest in Whyte's work and introducing Doc to various areas of street corner life (from Saturday night bowling to competing for the attention of local girls).

This form of narrative ethnography and the relationships it involves, raise particular questions of ontology and epistemology. Frequently, narrative ethnographies are predicated upon relativist ontology. The claim is often put forward that the narrative is an account among many possible accounts of the nature of the particular world in focus. This need not be seen as problematic. If the aim of an ethnographic study is to study CEOs' views of the world of corporate branding, it may be quite conceivable that these worldviews would be distinct from other members of the same organization without such difference undermining the valuable insights provided into CEOs' worldviews. The same can be said of Whyte's (1955) study. The production of a detailed analysis of Doc's view of street corner life is very different ontologically from contemporary media representations of the area where Doc lived. In place of a media version of the street corner world based on numbers (for example, crime rates, population statistics, rates of poverty) and scandals, Whyte provides an ethnography based on the detail of everyday life. Whyte suggests that through ethnography, in place of numbers, come lives.

Exemplar Three

W. Whyte (1955) *Street Corner Society* (University of Chicago Press, Chicago)

Whyte's study of street corner society in 1930s' Boston provides an example of an early sociological foray into the field of ethnography. It is a product of the Chicago School of Sociology and has its own particular brand of practical politics. The study of street corner life was designed to counter the then contemporary media and political accounts of life on a street corner:

> Through sight-seeing or statistics one may discover that bathtubs are rare, that children overrun the narrow and neglected streets, that the juvenile delinquency rate is high, that crime is prevalent among adults, and that a large proportion of the population was on home relief or W.P.A. during the depression. In this view, Cornerville people appear as social work clients, as defendants in criminal cases, or as undifferentiated members of 'the masses.' There is one thing wrong with such a picture: no human beings are in it. (1955: xv)

Whyte's approach did not just advocate getting close to the street corner, he also sought to provide a picture of the mundane, ordinary, everyday aspects of street corner life. This ordinariness was an important feature of the study – to counter spectacular stories about crime, unemployment and so on, Whyte wanted to show how street corner life is mostly banal. The importance of this study for considering organizational ethnography is that it provides a form of narrative approach to the methodology, it offers important insights on field relations and becoming a member of the collective being studied, it provides detail on ways to represent complex social relations, and it says something of the fragmentary and changing features of social organization.

An introduction to narrative forms of ethnography

'Narrative' can be used as a term to group together a particular epistemological approach to ethnography. By epistemological approach I mean the approach to knowledge which the author takes in observing and writing about observations. Narrative approaches to ethnography are based around a particular key informant who provides much of the narrative of the group or organization being studied. In traditional anthropological studies of tribes in far-flung places there was often a particularly good storyteller, willing participant or gatekeeper who provided much of the insight into what went on in the tribe. This is equally the case for ethnographies closer to home. In Whyte's study of street corner society, Doc is both the key informer and gatekeeper for the study. Doc enables Whyte to find a position within the men whose lives are based around various activities on the street corner and Doc provides a great deal of the narrative about their lives (from explanations of bowling and social status to the group's occasional interest in girls).

Narrative ethnographies involve epistemological questions regarding the account offered by the key informant. For Whyte, the account offered by Doc is available to be assessed in realist terms (that is, how accurately the account portrays street corner life). However, not all narrative ethnographies take this stance. Whyte uses Doc's narrative to build up a history of street corner life (through Doc's tales of his childhood) and to provide a context within which street corner life unfolds (through Doc's tales of what goes on elsewhere, what histories others bring to the street corner, where people's families come from and so on).

Access

Accessing street corner life is made possible by Doc acting as a gatekeeper for Whyte. Through this relationship access is relatively straightforward. However, such an access story can still be investigated for what it tells us about the organizational details of street corner life. Whyte is brought into the street corner through Doc. Doc represents himself as the toughest guy on the street corner and suggests others defer to his judgement (or even seek his judgement at particular times). Doc suggests the consequences of not acting in line with Doc's expectations are nearly always a fight or at least the threat of violence. Doc represents himself as the best fighter on the street corner. Not listening to Doc is akin to asking to challenge his position and challenge him to a fight. Being introduced to the other members of street corner life by Doc is therefore like being introduced by the chief of a tribe. To question the introduction of Whyte would be to ask for a fight.

Although it might seem an unlikely comparison to make between the self-professed toughest guy on the street corner and what might happen in a modern corporate organization, there are parallels to be drawn. The organization can be investigated for the ways in which status might be made and maintained and differentiated between members. The ethnographer might want to reflect on their own status in relation to other members of the organization. If the ethnographer's access is predicated on one particular gatekeeper, their position within any notional organizational hierarchy might be considered. While for Whyte's study the hierarchy is made and maintained through fighting, a wish to avoid fighting and the need to emphasize 'respect', modern corporate organizations can also be studied to investigate the ways in which status is actively achieved. An ethnographer's status may relate in complex ways to the status of the member who introduces them into the organization (see sensibility three).

Becoming a member

Although Whyte uses Doc to gain access to the collective activity of street corner life, this is not the same as saying he has become a member. Becoming a member, attaining the status of accepted and regular, ordinary participant in the group requires more than access. In Whyte's study, ten pin bowling becomes an important activity for demonstrating and achieving status. Whenever Doc, Mike and Danny (those Doc perceived to be of highest status) were bowling against Alec and Joe (those Doc perceived to be lower in the social hierarchy), it was no longer just about bowling but establishing and maintaining social order. Doc suggested that when bowling, Alec or Joe could not win:

> They wouldn't have known how to take it. That's why we were out to beat them. If they had won, there would have been a lot of noise. Plenty of arguments. We would have called it lucky – things like that. We would have tried to get them in another match and ruin them. We would have to put them in their places. (1955: 21)

Whyte uses the bowling as an example of the way street corner life is stratified and organized. What Whyte also reveals is the extent to which he became a member of

51

the organization. It seems that he was always held somewhat at arm's length from the group. In the bowling competition Whyte was asked to participate after one of the regulars had to pull out. Whyte went on to win the competition, but received none of the pressure (noise, catcalls, pushes) that others received when trying to bowl. Doc explained this activity as follows:

> We didn't want to make it tough for you, because we all like you, and the other fellows did too. If somebody had tried to make it tough for you, we would have protected you. ... If Joe Dodge or Alec had been out in front, it would have been different. We would have talked them out of it. We would have made plenty of noise. We would have been really vicious. (1955: 21)

What Doc's account of the bowling demonstrates is that although bowling was the key arbiter of social status, Whyte's bowling didn't count. He was effectively allowed to win (at least in not being put off each time he attempted to bowl), because his winning would not threaten anyone's group status. In this sense Whyte had access to the organization, but only partial membership. This partial membership, however, and close relationship with Doc enabled him to produce a detailed account of the organization of street corner life.

Organizing and representing data
Whyte's study of street corner life, although depending a great deal for its narrative content on a key informant, introduces the reader to numerous characters, activities, locations and forms of social ordering. To make sense of this array of detail, Whyte deploys a diagram (1955: 13). This diagram represents the entangled relations of the group and the hierarchical social status relations developed through fighting, threats of fighting, bowling, associations with girls, and so on. This kind of diagram, as with any form of simplified representation in ethnography, is difficult to accomplish. Ethnography bases many of its claims to robustness and relevance on being close to the action and providing significant detail on that action; a visual representation of names in boxes with lines drawn between them risks reducing ethnographic closeness and detail to a (relatively) simple picture. Whyte overcomes this difficulty by not employing the representation as an end point. In no sense is the diagram the thing to take away from the study. Instead, the diagram provides the reader with a way of navigating through the ensuing text so that names, activities and relationships can be understood as related to positions.

Organizations
Whyte's study of street corner society provides an opportunity to reflect on the orderly and disorderly within organizational forms. While the bowling provides a means to structure social order, it is predicated upon making sufficient noise and threatening violence to those deemed lower down the social order. When some members of the group begin seeing girls from a group called the Aphrodite Club, this again raises further forms of order and disorder. Doc proclaims himself to be the greatest lover (which the other members eventually accept), maintaining a sense of the stratified order of the groups' relations. However, some of the groups' members associate with girls who exclude or are rude towards other members of the group. This threat of re-stratification through non-members of the group leads to some disorder (and some members

leaving the street corner life). These forms of order and disorder, stratification, re-stratification, membership and partial membership can provide a rich backdrop of ideas for organizational ethnographers seeking to understand the way corporate organizations work.

What kinds of epistemological claims does such a narrative approach involve? The claims to knowledge that narrative ethnography can make are intricately involved with the relationships established between ethnographers, informants and gatekeepers. For Whyte, the relationship with Doc enables him to produce what he claims is a detailed and accurate account of street corner life. Whyte is quite happy for this account to be assessed epistemologically for its accuracy in realist terms (see Whyte's follow up to *Street Corner Society*, 1993). However, critics of Whyte have suggested that further exploration is required of the principle relationship between Whyte and Doc (see, for example, Boelen, 1992). These critics suggest that Whyte may have failed to adequately explore the ethics of his relations with Doc, particularly in terms of whether or not Doc gained as much from the (1955) study as Whyte. In place of realist assertions of accuracy, come ethical assertions of the correct way in which to carry out research (see sensibility four for more on field relations and sensibility nine for more on ethics). Further criticisms of Whyte's (1955) work have suggested that Whyte's realism is predicated upon an outdated mode of realist epistemology which ignores more recent ethnographic moves to clearly address forms of subjectivity (see 'Reflexive Ethnography' section below, and for detailed criticisms see Jermier, 1991; Denzin, 1992).

Reflexive ethnography

This section will introduce the principles of reflexive ethnography. Different versions of reflexivity can be understood as more or less radical. I will begin with what I perceive to be the less radical orientations of reflexivity before giving consideration to more radical, reflexive textual experimentation. I will argue that these forms of experimentation can be useful in helping us to think through some of the principles which might underpin our ethnographic research.

In a general sense, reflexivity suggests that members of the world are (reflexively) engaged in making sense of and producing (a version of) the world. The world is not independent of reflexive efforts to make it make sense. Further, ethnographies fit into this sense-making practice and ethnographers are reflexively engaged in the production of sense through their ethnographies. In its less radical orientation, this leads to reflexive questions of the author: how is the author involved in the production of the ethnographic text? These questions are given slightly different emphasis in confessional and auto-ethnographic modes.

Confessional ethnography

The principles of confessional ethnography (Van Maanen, 1988) are a detailed study of a particular ethnographic setting incorporating much reflection on the role the ethnographer has played in the setting. The way the ethnographer has entered the setting, become an adequate member of the setting and formed particular relations with members of the field become features of ethnographic analysis. This is not particularly different from other forms of ethnographic study. However, under the confessional mode, as the term suggests, greater space is devoted to potentially problematic issues involving the researcher. The epistemological approach focuses on making available information on the ways in which the ethnographer has been closely involved in the setting. The strength of this kind of knowledge claim lies in allowing readers to assess the reliability and rigour of the ethnography presented and the problems the ethnographer may have experienced.

Auto-ethnography

Auto-ethnography and confessional ethnography fulfil much of the same function. However, the emphasis in auto-ethnography can be a little different. In place of an ethnographic study, which incorporates an analysis (or confession) of the moves made by the ethnographer, auto-ethnography is based around the story told by or through the ethnographer. In a similar manner to an auto-biography, an auto-ethnography (more explicitly than a confessional ethnography) is focused on the life experiences of the ethnographer in doing ethnography. The emphasis in auto-ethnography is often on the 'cultural study of one's own people' (Rosen, 1991: 4), rather than on the exotic cultures of foreign tribes. The reflexive engagement in auto-ethnography can be as much about the ways through which the ethnographer makes sense of themselves and their role in the world as it is about focusing on a particular group, location or organizational form. Richardson (2000: 923) suggests that writing in this mode of research acts as a way of 'finding out about yourself and your topic'. The epistemological grounds for making knowledge claims in this kind of ethnography depend on emphasizing the value of subjectivity. The ethnographer situates themselves as having a standpoint from which to express valuable insights into their own experiences. This can lead to jokes, such as that retold by Marcus (1994: 393), in which the native says to the ethnographer 'that's enough about you, let's talk about me'. Readers can find more detail on auto-ethnography from the work of Ellis and Bochner (1996, 2000; Ellis, 2004) and Reed-Dehaney (1997).

In the next section I will argue that confessional and auto-ethnographic modes of study are not as radical as other orientations of reflexivity. I suggest this is primarily because they do not ask as many questions of ontology. Although both modes of ethnographic engagement suggest that the ethnographer is reflexively engaged in the production of the ethnography, this is not always taken further into questions of the status of the setting in which the ethnographer is engaged. For example, while confessional ethnography might devote an amount of space to the author's reflexive position, participants in the study might be treated in conventional realist terms. The author's role might end up constituting more of the ethnography than the interaction between members of the ethnographic setting or might be given more consideration than the interaction between the ethnographic text and reader (see next section). In this sense, reflexive epistemology can be combined with realist ontology or questions of ontology can remain absent.

More radical orientations of reflexivity

For more radically reflexive ethnographers, such auto- and confessional approaches are more about reflection (on, for example, the role of the researcher) than about reflexivity. To some extent the questions posed in confessional and auto-ethnographic modes are not very different from standard research questions regarding researcher influence. To restate, reflexivity suggests members of the world are reflexively engaged in the production and maintenance of the world as a more or less ordered phenomenon. Ethnography is itself involved in this ongoing reflexive production. Latour and Woolgar (1979) offer a more radical orientation of these questions of reflexivity in relation to ethnography. In studying scientists, Latour and Woolgar (exemplar four) reflexively engage with what it means for scientists (and the objects of science) to be reflexively engaged in the ongoing production of a more or less ordered science. The ethnography therefore involves investigation of what they as ethnographers are doing in attempting to ethnographically reproduce science. A central point of contention (like confessional and auto-ethnography) remains the role of the researcher in this ongoing reflexive production. However, scientists are being studied reflexively reproducing science and readers are invoked as engaging in a reflexive production process in reading the text. Reflexivity (in this sense) is not merely focused on reflection on what ethnographers do, but involves an analysis of a series of relationships, some of which are in principle unknowable (for example, what the reader will make of the text). This can provide for an unsettling experience. Rosen (1991) suggests that being analytical about the reflexive constitution of exotic cultures (that is, the way natives go about making sense of going about) is more comfortable than being reflexive about our own activities (that is, questioning the taken-for-granted basis for the way we go about making sense of going about).

Exemplar Four

B. Latour and S. Woolgar (1979, 2nd edn, 1986) *Laboratory Life: The Construction of Scientific Facts* (Princeton University Press, Princeton, NJ)

Latour and Woolgar's (1979) work is noted as being among the first in-depth ethnographic studies of the work scientists do to produce science. This ethnographic work shifted emphasis away from philosophers' concerns with the nature of scientific knowledge. Philosophers had focused on, for example, scientific knowledge as distinct from social scientific knowledge, or on the means by which scientists' advance knowledge (through, for example, Popperian falsification or Khunian paradigms). The ethnographic approach to the work of science and scientists also moved away from contemporary emphasis of social science approaches to natural science. In place of a focus on scientific error or mistakes, Latour and Woolgar pursued a symmetrical approach to the study of scientific knowledge. Normal, ordinary science was as much a focus for study as fraudulent, mistaken or incorrect science. This study was central to the development of the newly emerging field of science and technology studies, providing one means to raise questions regarding prevalent views on the nature of scientific knowledge and how scientists went about producing that knowledge. However, what is the significance of such a study for those doing organizational ethnography? I will argue in this brief summary that reflexive ethnography, ideas of social construction, social construction entangled with ideas of materialization and circumstances, and a focus on producing order from disorder can all be thought-provoking challenges for organizational ethnographers.

Reflexive ethnography

Unlike realist ethnography (where the world is assumed to exist as a knowable entity, from which an ethnography can abstract observational material, which can then be judged according to how accurately it represents the world out there), reflexive ethnography engages in a thorough and detailed analysis of the ethnographer's attempts to make sense of the world while those being studied are making sense of the world.

> By reflexivity we mean to refer to the realisation that observers of scientific activity are engaged in methods which are essentially similar to those of the practitioners which they study. (1986: 30)

The ethnographer is reflexively engaged in making sense of the world and pays attention to their own methods of making sense, while also comparing ethnographic means of making sense with the sense-making methods of those studied. In this sense, it is more difficult to say that the world straightforwardly exists independently of the ethnographer and that observations can be collected from the world and judged according to how well they represent the world. In place of such an approach, the reflexive ethnographer enters into an analysis of the means of producing the ethnographic study. Thus, instead of an assumption that the world exists outside the ethnography, the world is made apparent and rendered available through the ethnography. However, rendering the world available through ethnography is not straightforward – the reader of ethnography enters into a crucial relationship with the text, making sense of the world represented through the ethnography.

This introduction to reflexive ethnography suggests there are three principle elements to take into account (although these are not easily separable and are by no means a step-by-step guide to reflexivity). First, the world does not straightforwardly exist independently of efforts to make sense of the world. Second, ethnographers are as caught up in this sense-making as are those being studied through the ethnography. Third, ethnographies thereby make available a description of participants' ways of making sense of the world, ethnographers' ways of making sense of the members' methods for making sense of the world, and make these available for readers to make their sense of the ethnography. For organizational ethnographers this is something of a challenge. How and in what ways does an organization (and an organization's membership) make sense of itself? How does the ethnographer make sense of the organization's attempts to make sense of the organization? Should the ethnographer be concerned about the ways in which readers might make sense of the text?

For Latour and Woolgar, such questions are treated as principles of research to be engaged in the process of researching and writing. They are not deemed relativist problems which result in ethnography (or any other social science pursuit) being unable to say anything about anything. Treating such issues as principles rather than problems entails incorporating them into the research project. This incorporation is on anthropological terms. A scientific laboratory is approached in much the same way as a tribe, with an in-depth, detailed, observational account of the setting made available through the ethnography. Making observations in particular settings is pursued in order to avoid making general statements about the nature of science or relying solely on scientists' own accounts of science. Latour and Woolgar employ the anthropological principle of strangeness in engaging with the field (in order to render everything available for analysis, emphasizing that much scientific work depends on a great deal of mundane, routine activity, not moments of dramatic revelation). In place of concern with what readers might make of the text, they suggest 'It is the reader who writes the text' (1986: 273).

For Latour and Woolgar, reflexivity involves applying ethnographic scepticism or strangeness to the ethnographic text itself, making available an analysis of the ways in which the ethnography has been put together. Or, as Latour and Woolgar have it in their slogan: '…reflexivity is the ethnographer of the text' (1986: 284).

'Social' construction

This reflexive approach to ethnography introduces several further challenges for those undertaking organizational ethnography. The first of these is the notion of 'social' construction. This term was originally used by Latour and Woolgar to convey the idea that 'facts' were not straightforwardly available in the natural world to be collected and reported on by scientists. Instead, facts were constructed through multiple activities. They were 'social' in the sense that they were constructed through multiple, ongoing processes. However, the 'social' aspect of social construction was deemed problematic by Latour and Woolgar. Social was used by other researchers of science as a binary opposition to natural or technical. Such an approach does not fit comfortably with the symmetrical approach to science, treating everything with equal scepticism/interest. Introducing researchers' own caveats and binary oppositions effectively dismantles any possibility of symmetry as some things are now to be treated as belonging to the category of social, and some technical, according to decisions made by the ethnographers. Science, it is argued by Latour and Woolgar, is not made up of social features on the one hand and technical or natural features on the other. Instead, science is made and maintained through a series of actions (see next section). Latour and Woolgar summarize this as follows: 'So what does it mean to talk about "social" construction? There is no shame in admitting that the term no longer has any meaning' (1986: 281).

What is the relevance for this loss of meaning regarding the 'social' for organizational ethnographers? Often organizational research can get caught up in elaborating the importance of social or cultural variables or factors. Much time can be given over to defining the social or cultural, to distinguishing it from other factors, to measuring, observing, understanding or analysing the social or cultural factors which might play a role in shaping an organization. What Latour and Woolgar argue is that the social (and indeed the cultural) should not have a category of its own. Instead, the organization (of the laboratory in their case) is the product of a range of activities. Through focusing on these activities, ethnographers can provide a nuanced and reflexive account of the organization and the myriad means which make and maintain the organization. Definitions, sub-categories, factors and variables relating to the social and cultural are something of a distraction in this approach. So what does make and maintain the laboratory as an organization?

Construction through persuasion, materialization and circumstances

Although Latour and Woolgar are keen to shift attention away from social and cultural variables, by what means do they argue the laboratory is constructed? They suggest 'it is through practical operations that a statement can be transformed into an object' (1986: 236). These practical operations, through which a fact is constructed, involve convincing others that they have not been persuaded, that materialization provides evidence of the fact and that circumstances have never played any role in the apprehension of the fact.

> The result of the construction of a fact is that it appears unconstructed by anyone; the result of rhetorical persuasion … is that participants are convinced that they have not been convinced; the result of materialisation is that people can swear that material considerations are only minor components of the 'thought process'; the result of investments of credibility is that participants can claim that economics and beliefs are in no way related to the solidity of science; as to the circumstances, they simply vanish from accounts, being better left to political analysis than to the appreciation of the hard and solid world of facts! (1986: 240).

Order from disorder

These multiple processes of construction translate disorder into order. Although reflexive ethnography has been criticized for taking a stance which, it is claimed, is overly relativist (suggesting that things can be understood in multiple ways and therefore that anything goes, in a postmodernist sense), Latour and Woolgar emphasize that the 'transformation of a set of equally probable statements into a set of unequally probable statements amounts to the creation of order' (1986: 244). Through processes of construction facts are produced and refined, other possibilities are eliminated, outcomes are reduced down to (often) a single point, and science, the laboratory and a particular fact are achieved. The value of this approach for organizational ethnographers lies in its avowed and determined scepticism. Nothing is left as assumed or taken for granted. Everything (including the ethnography itself) is made available as a point for further consideration. If applied to organizational settings, such an approach to construction would introduce the following questions: By what means is the organization produced and maintained? Through what processes are organizational facts constructed and talked about? What analytical utility do ideas of persuasion, materi-alization and circumstance have for organizational analyses? (These questions will be dealt with in more detail under sensibilities four and eight).

Questions of ontology and epistemology become more complex in this approach to reflexivity. For Latour and Woolgar, the appropriate question to ask is not, does the world exist independently of the ethnography? Instead, given that the subjects of research and researchers are reflexively engaged in the ongoing production of a more or less ordered version of what's going on, the question becomes, how can this be captured within a written text? Furthermore, what is the reflexive relation that readers will then enter into in reading the text? In this approach to reflexivity, reading is an active process of making sense of the text. Ontologically speaking, the world (in text) does not exist independently of readers' work to make it make sense. Epistemologically, the forms of knowledge claims made in such radically reflexive ethnographies involve forms of constructivism (I resist here using the term 'social constructivism', as Latour and Woolgar argue that it is difficult to draw a boundary around a specifically 'social' set of factors to set them apart from some other set of factors to be accorded a different category). Epistemologically, constructivists argue that the world does not exist independently of efforts which make and maintain (construct) the world and ethnographies are one such way of making sense of the world.

Other radically reflexive texts propose experimentation with the form of ethnographic writing itself. The PhD thesis of Ashmore (1989), for example, is a thesis focused on doing a thesis. In place of a single 'author' there are multiple voices incorporated into the text and the reader is invited to take an active part in making sense of Ashmore's thesis construction. I think the value of such textual experimentation is to shake up the ways we take for granted the formal expectations, structures and conventions for writing, for authorship and what normally constitutes an ethnography. What Ashmore's reflexive thesis accomplishes is a destabilizing of where and who the ethnographic author is and what the relationship should be between text, author and reader.

Although I cannot lay claim to such radical underpinnings for my own work, I find particular value in these reflexive orientations in my organizational research. First, these more radically reflexive texts do not leave anything set-tled. They demonstrate how far ethnographers can go in questioning what gets taken for granted. This is a primary principle in my own ethnographic work. Second, questioning the position of authorship opens up further possi-bilities. In place of a conventional ethnographic relationship, where the ethno-grapher does the research and writes the research, we can think of alternative sets of relations which might help produce a text. In exemplar fourteen I set

59

out the ways in which my own work has involved handing over some of the authorship of the ethnography to members of the organization. Third, reflexive texts open up questions of readership. In place of assuming that readers will make the same sense of the text that ethnographers have when writing the text, reading becomes an active process of sense-making. It is possible to ask these questions and loosen the imagination of readers and writers in a variety of different ways (see Watson, 1994). In organizational settings I have found it useful to give research participants my ethnography to read as a way of generating further ethnographic conversations. Thus, although I have presented these reflexive experimentations as radical, their destabilizing of conventional ontological and epistemological premises can have utility for organizational ethnography.

Organizational ethnography and knowledge claims

The preceding discussion has argued that questions of knowledge are an important feature of ethnographers' attempts to engage in research. It has suggested that particular ontological and epistemological approaches come with particular commitments which might shape the direction the ethnographer is to take in doing their research. In this sense, giving consideration to questions of knowledge can help ethnographers to further develop their ethnographic strategy (see sensibility one).

An implicit feature of this discussion has been that claims to knowledge are likely to be assessed quite differently by different audiences. For example, what might be considered academically rigorous, might not be considered to have utility for a particular organization taking part in an ethnographic study. Claims regarding the validity of ethnography depend on who is assessing the ethnography.

Rigour and academic assessment
Each of the approaches to ethnography presented, in carrying particular epistemological commitments, also have implications for the ways in which the research should be regarded as academically rigorous (or not). Thus realist ethnographies can be assessed on the grounds of whether or not they accurately portray the reality of the setting studied, and reflexive ethnographies can be assessed for the lengths to which the ethnographer has gone in being reflexive (is there a constructed, reflexive stone that they have left unturned?). It follows that each of these approaches to ethnography can be interrogated from alternative epistemological standpoints. Rigour is perhaps best seen as an accomplishment. A recent development which alleviates some of these issues is modest ethnography (see exemplar ten). 'Rigour', in modest ethnography, involves considering the partiality of research – ethnographers are partial (rather than impartial) and ethnographies are partial

(rather than complete). Such modesty involves inviting readers to assess the strengths of the arguments presented and inviting ethnographers to pursue questions left unanswered by the study (as recommended by Malinowski in exemplar two).

Utility and organizational assessment

What counts as useful information in an organizational context can be complex (see, for example, the Conclusion of this book). However, epistemological claims that knowledge is useful, valuable and has integrity (through appropriate ethnographic methodology) can be as much about process as about the content of the claims. Ethnographers can utilize the time frame for ethnographies (see sensibility five) to make an early presentation of ethnographic data in the field setting. Such presentations can be occasions for organizational members to be invited to make something of the data. Responses from organizational members can lead to the development of new ethnographic avenues for the research. Discussions can then form a part of the ethnographic process, with follow-up presentations forming further occasions for the development of the knowledge claims being made (these issues will be taken further in sensibility four). The epistemological responsibility for knowledge claims is then shifted in these discussions from being the sole preserve of the ethnographer to being shared among contributing participants to the study. Within organizational settings I have found this kind of approach useful for enhancing the status of the ethnography, the number of participants willing to take part and the extent to which ethnographic findings are considered valuable. Such ethnographic manoeuvres should also keep in focus that observations which counter what members of organizations want to say can have utility (see sensibility four).

Combining utility and rigour

This separation of the grounds on which the knowledge claims of an ethnography can be assessed appears to rule out the possibility of combining academic rigour with organizational utility. However, this need not be the case. In subsequent discussions (see particularly sensibilities seven and eight), we will go through the grounds on which rigour and utility can be combined. We will also go through managing the different demands which organizational utility and academic rigour can make (in terms of access in sensibility three and in terms of time in sensibility five).

Recommended reading

Ashmore, M. (1989) *The Reflexive Thesis* (University of Chicago Press, Chicago)
Blaikie, N. (1993) *Approaches to Social Enquiry* (Polity Press, Cambridge)
Dellbridge, R. (1998) *Life on the Line in Contemporary Manufacturing* (Oxford University Press, Oxford)

3

$\triangleright\triangleright\triangleright\triangleright\triangleright$Sensibility Three
Locations and Access

Introduction

Under the previous sensibility the complex areas of epistemology and ontology in ethnographic research were discussed. Moving on to questions of locations and access for ethnographic research might initially appear to involve more straightforward practical concerns (such as getting in and getting on with research). Although there are many practical concerns regarding locations and access (and I will go through these), such concerns cannot be easily separated out from considerations regarding the development of an ethnographic strategy and questions of knowledge. Questions of ethnographic location and questions of access, I will argue, can be important for shaping the kind of study we do, the kinds of claims we make as a result of that study, and can form an important contribution towards ethnographic observations made during the study.

We will begin by looking at questions of location. First, I will highlight the importance that location plays in ethnographic research, analysing both single field-site ethnographic research and the newly emergent area of multi-site ethnographic research. I will suggest that multi-site ethnography, although providing some new terminology and interest in the field of ethnography, contains some familiar methodological questions. I will also argue that multi-sited ethnography does not necessarily provide more rigorous ethnographic research than traditional single-sited approaches. This section will end with a discussion of the (sometimes) different epistemological underpinnings of single and multi-site ethnography. Second, I will look at the difficult issue of getting access to a particular field. Convincing an organization of the benefits of allowing an ethnographer to spend a long time in their organization can be a challenge, but I will suggest that this challenge can provide something for the ethnography. It is in negotiating access that a great deal about the organization (and the ethnographer's engagement with it) comes to light. This discussion will conclude by emphasizing the utility of access negotiations for ethnographic research.

Location: single-site ethnography

Ethnography has traditionally involved the selection of a single field-site that will become the location for the ethnographer to enter, research, become a member of and write about. In the exemplars we can find several different sorts of location which have provided bounded field-sites for the completion of ethnographic research. In exemplar four, Latour and Woolgar (1979) study the work of scientists in a scientific laboratory and in exemplar seven Graham (1995) studies life in a car manufacturing plant. As we can see in the exemplars, these studies were conceived for very different reasons and set out to address very different types of question (for example, Latour and Woolgar addressed questions of the nature of scientific knowledge while Graham addressed the absence of unions in a car manufacturing plant). Selecting an appropriate field-site is heavily dependent on the development of a research question (see sensibility one). Attempting to figure out the ways in which CEOs of US corporations deal with conflict (exemplar thirteen) establishes a fairly narrow possible range of field-sites to consider (and introduces some difficult access questions, see section on 'Access' below). Examining the possibility of using ethnography to analyse the internet (see exemplar ten) does not set the same kinds of restriction.

I have always worked with the possibility of location as an organizing principle for doing ethnographic research. By this I mean that I have always given thought to the kinds of questions I want to address and constructed several possible locations for doing ethnographic research. Some of the questions which arise in considering locations are practical matters which will be taken up in the 'Access' section of this discussion (such as: What is my likelihood of access? What can I do to increase my likelihood of access? What do I want to ask the organization to let me study? What will the scope of the study be in terms of time – how long? – and type of participation – which areas of the organization do I want to participate in and in what role?). These practical concerns can help shape the research in quite important ways.

Other questions can help establish the direction of the research. Considering whether or not an ethnography will be an exploratory piece of research or will answer a tightly defined research question can help establish the relevance of particular organizational settings for doing the research. Addressing questions such as why a particular organization is relevant and whether or not other organizational settings are more or less relevant to the study can help set the question of location into the developing ethnographic strategy (see sensibility one).

Once these questions have been addressed and prior to considering questions of access, it is important to note that the ethnography has already started. While most ethnographic textbooks emphasize the importance of observations collected at the first point of entry into an organization, I have always found that the observations gained prior to entry are equally insightful. Keeping notes on the way in which I first became aware of an organization, on the kinds of things colleagues, friends or family may have

63

said about the organization and the kinds of preconceptions I have about the organization have each featured at the start of my ethnographic field diaries (see sensibilities six and eight for more on diaries and ethnographic writing). These observations can be useful for setting later observations of the organization in context and for keeping in mind that there may be several versions of the organization's identity (from those outside and those who have different perspectives inside the organization). These forms of observation come with the same caveat as all other forms of ethnographic observation – there is no guarantee that they will be incorporated into the final ethnographic write-up (see sensibility eight). The utility of these observations lies in their potential for addressing an ethnographer's initial view on the organization, on where the boundaries of the organization start and stop, and an initial justification for why the particular organization in focus is a relevant choice.

Exemplar Five

C. Geertz (1973) *The Interpretation of Cultures* (New York, Basic Books)
Particularly focusing on Chapter 15: 'Deep Play: Notes on the Balinese Cockfight', pp. 412–53

Balinese cockfighting may seem an incongruous choice for an exemplar of organizational ethnography. What on earth could Balinese cockfighting tell us about the way organizations work or about how people are organized? Surely we have already had an introduction to anthropological approaches to ethnography (exemplar two) and surely cockfighting is predicated upon quite different principles from the modern corporation? This may be the case. However, I will argue that Geertz's study of cockfighting can provide ethnographers with a broad range of illuminating insights relevant to the study of organizations. I will also suggest that elements of cockfighting might not be so different from the modern corporation.

An introduction to thick description

'Thick description' is the term coined by Geertz to describe his ethnographic writing style. Unlike other ethnographic forms of writing, the style is deliberately not focused on simply collecting, organizing and reporting on observations. Thick description involves drawing together detailed observations of particular events (such as cockfights, see below), with literary allusions, political events, particular uses of metaphors (as illustrations of, for example, social order), folk narratives from the field (such as natives' stories about themselves), and history and religion made relevant through the observations. Thick description neither limits itself to the observations nor attempts to situate the observations within a traditional sense of context. Instead, the observations and connections that are drawn together to illustrate the observations are the context.

Access

Geertz's entry into Balinese life provides for an access story so compelling it can act as a reference point for all ethnographic access stories, whatever the setting. The ethnographer arrived with his wife in the late 1950s at a remote Balinese village:

> We were intruders, professional ones, and the villagers dealt with us as Balinese seem always to deal with people not part of their life who yet press themselves upon them: as though we were not there. For them, and to a degree for ourselves, we were nonpersons, spectres, invisible men. (1973: 412)

This ethnographic invisibility generated problems: how could village life be understood if no one was willing to talk? How could Geertz become a member if no members were willing to acknowledge his presence? Geertz notes:

> People seemed to look right through us with a gaze focused several hundred yards behind us on some more actual stone or tree. Almost nobody greeted us; but nobody scowled or said anything unpleasant to us either, which would have been almost as satisfactory. (1973: 412)

Stones and trees had a greater resonance in village life than the invisible ethnographer. Even insults (which might have revealed something of the membership of the village and why the ethnographer was not welcomed) were hard to come by. After ten days in the field this invisibility had not diminished.

The event which marked access to becoming a member was unexpected. In Bali in the 1950s most forms of cockfighting were illegal. However, Geertz discovered that cocks and cockfighting were integral to Balinese village life. Cockfighting was a matter of status, of social interaction, of community and familial identity. Cockfighting provided the focal point for ordered and organized social life. Its illegality meant that cockfights were subject to police raids. During Geertz's first attendance at a cockfight, a truckload of policemen raided the fight, swinging (although not firing) guns while the crowd dispersed rapidly:

> On the established anthropological principle, 'When in Rome,' my wife and I decided, only slightly less instantaneously than everyone else, that the thing to do was run too. ... About halfway down [the street] another fugitive ducked into a compound – his own, as it turned out – and we, seeing nothing ahead of us but rice fields, open country, and a very high volcano, followed him. As the three of us came tumbling into the courtyard, his wife, who had apparently been through this sort of thing before, whipped out a table, a tablecloth, three chairs and three cups of tea, and we all, without any explicit communication whatsoever, sat down, commenced to sip tea, and sought to compose ourselves. (1973: 415)

When a police officer turned up at the compound, Geertz was surprised at the detail and passion of his host's defence of their presence. It turned out the villagers knew all about the ethnographers, why they were there, that they were to write a book about Bali for Americans and that the villagers were all taking part. As the police officer looked astonished, the host claimed they 'had all been there drinking tea and talking about cultural matters all afternoon and did not know anything about any cockfight' (1973: 415). The cockfight and run from the police signalled acceptance:

> The next morning the village was a completely different world for us. Not only were we no longer invisible, we were suddenly the centre of all attention ... everyone was extremely pleased that we had not simply 'pulled our papers' (they knew about those too) and asserted our Distinguished Visitor status, but had instead demonstrated our solidarity with what were now our covillagers. (1973: 416)

65

Membership

This access story can reveal a great deal about village membership. Not siding with the police was politically important (at this time the police were Javanese, not Balinese, and were engaged as colonial management). Acting in the way the villagers acted demonstrated a willingness to participate (they were not just there to observe). Having a story to tell of shared experiences became a useful ethnographic action (each of the villagers in turn wanted to hear the story and this in turn provided a means to hear villagers' own stories).

Geertz goes on to use cockfighting to illustrate features of Balinese life. Cockfighting was not just a focal point through which to become a member, but a means through which membership, the characteristics of members, the ways in which the social life of members is made and maintained, could be made apparent. What is useful for organizational ethnographers to consider here are Geertz's descriptive techniques. First, the cockfight is used metaphorically as a way of grouping together a broad array of features of the organization. Second, the importance of the cockfight is described in great detail (pp. 425–41) and then shortened to a summary list (in half a page on p. 441). Simply providing a list would mean excluding much of the ethnographic detail; providing the short list and the detail enables Geertz to deliver a comprehensive account and an accessible representation of cockfighting. Third, betting on cockfights is used to highlight the ways in which social status, identity and interaction are organized (this is taken up in the next section).

Organization

So what can cockfighting tell organizational ethnographers about organizations? Betting in cockfights is a form of social order in Balinese village life. However, cockfighting for the Balinese is not only about winning money – as the financial exchange of betting is seen as a regular redistribution of money rather than an end-point (I may lose this week and you may have the money, but I may win next week and then I will have the money). To be able to take part in cockfighting and betting is a demonstration that one has sufficient wealth (in monetary and status terms). Taking part in important fights (both owning the cocks and betting on outcomes) is a sign of one's status. Only placing small side bets, not entering a cock into a fight, only being able to play in the small stake games outside the cockfighting ring, are all symbolic demonstrations of a lack of status.

This description of betting reminds organizational ethnographers that understanding an organization, its rationale and the reason for members to be part of the organization, is not always reducible to a single explanation or even to something like a rational economic choice. What comes to be seen as a 'rational choice' may be derived from the observations, but the ethnographer should not impose such a rationale. Hence, it might seem straightforward to assume Balinese are betting to win money (and they are), but it is also important for the ethnographer to enter into a detailed analysis of the observational material to see what else is going on. It is not just that the Balinese are trying to win money, they are also trying to demonstrate status and their position within the social order, contributing to making and maintaining the social order and holding other members of the village to account for the ways in which they are involved in producing the social order. By approaching the observational material in this way, what might appear initially to be a chaotic world of betting, cockfighting, violence and (animal) death, can be understood as complex and orderly, organized activities. The modern corporation can be thought of in much the same way with (what might appear initially to be) an array of complex interactions, people, technologies, locations, prices, demands, battles, and so on, that are made to make sense at particular times and through particular activities (such as marketing and branding, annual reports or board meetings, or through business journalism).

Ethnographic strangeness

Geertz's analysis of betting acts as a vivid demonstration of the principle of ethnographic strangeness (see sensibility two) – the ethnographer suspends their own rationale for what might be going on in order to hold up everything for analysis, to see what the observations provide by way of a rationale for describing what is going on. To emphasize: the observations provide the rationale for describing events, not the ethnographer (this is illustrated further in sensibility six).

How the organization talks about itself

One final point I will highlight from Geertz's work, which can contribute to organizational ethnography, is his emphasis on the ways in which the organization (in this case Balinese village life and in particular cockfighting) talks about, understands and relates to itself. When talking of betting on cockfights, Geertz suggests:

> What sets the cockfight apart from the ordinary course of life … is not … that it reinforces status discriminations … but that it provides a metasocial commentary upon the whole matter of assorting human beings into fixed hierarchical ranks and then organizing the major part of collective existence around that assortment. Its function, if you want to call it that, is interpretive: it is a Balinese reading of Balinese experience, a story they tell themselves about themselves. (1973: 448)

How an organization makes available a detailed version of itself, through its members, through visibly (or textually or electronically) available sources, provides organizational ethnographers with a potentially rich source of ideas for thinking through the organization under study. An organization's website, publicity, logo, branding, employees' uniforms and so on can each provide a version of what an organization says about itself. For the organizational ethnographer the challenge is to consider how what an organization says about itself relates to what the ethnographer might observe inside the organization.

In sum, traditional single-site ethnographies involve the selection of a more or less bounded setting which can be ethnographically investigated in order to address a more or less open research question. In choosing a single location, I have always considered a range of practical questions (which will be analysed in greater depth in the 'Access' section below) and questions regarding the shaping of the study. These 'shaping' questions include: Will this be an exploratory ethnography or will it seek to answer a tightly defined research question? Why is this organization relevant? Are there alternative organizations I could choose? Addressing these practical and strategic questions does not stop prior to entry into the field. I hang on to the possibilities of location as an organizing principle in carrying out observational research. Once 'in' the organization I ask whether or not I am where the action is taking place, where else the action might be taking place, whether there are any comparisons I could draw with other potential field-sites and what these comparisons might enable. This is where the recently emerging field of multi-site ethnography can prove useful.

Locations: multi-site ethnography

The relatively recent emergence of the term 'multi-site ethnography' (Marcus, 1995) has reinvigorated discussions of ethnographic field-sites. The term multi-site ethnography, however, is used in two slightly different ways. First, multi-site ethnography is used to talk about ethnographies which involve more than one field-site. This might sound like an obvious statement. However, this approach is distinct from a second use of the term multi-site ethnography, which looks at the role of the ethnographer in moving through and between field-sites.

Multi-site ethnography: more than one field-site

In Vallas's (2003) study of management prerogatives in corporate settings, he uses multiple ethnographic field-sites to produce a comparative picture of what goes in four paper mills. The comparison is used partly to empha-size the validity of research findings – that the situation he details differed from place to place and having those different pictures can help us to understand more about the nature of managerial hegemony (a central fea-ture of his argument). Those features of the research which appear to hold true across the research settings are noted by Vallas as particularly robust features of his argument – they occur in more than one place and so can be seen as more rigorous.

To what extent is such an approach to ethnography multi-sited? Hovland (2005) suggests that some ethnographers who claim the epithet 'multi-site' do little more than incorporate into their ethnographic research more than one field-site. This is slightly problematic as it is nothing new. The early development of anthropological ethnography often involved more than one field-site. Thus the work of Malinowski (1922/2002; exemplar two) incorpo-rated studies of several islands and the exchange relationships that occurred between them. We can also see notable examples of having more than one field-site in exemplar three (where Whyte (1955) moves from street corner to pool hall, among other places) and exemplar nine (where Leidner (1993) moves from McDonald's University to a McDonald's fran-chise), neither of which make claim to be 'multi-sited' ethnographies. It would appear strange, then, to herald having more than one field-site as something which asks new questions of the ways in which ethnography takes place. Hovland (2005: 1) suggests that:

> at its most fruitful and provocative and promising, multi-site ethnography is not a question of carrying out fieldwork in 2 or 3 or 4 sites instead of one. Multi-site ethnography is not simply something that helps us to add perspectives ... but instead it forces us to change perspective.

Changing perspectives suggests that multi-site ethnography is as much about developing a particular kind of ethnographic attitude as it is about developing more than one location in which to do research. In Hovland's (2005) ethnographic studies of policy, this entails moving from place to place and studying the ways in which policy is understood differently in each place. What might appear to be a single policy is the focal point for very different forms of social organization in each site. Hence the ethnography is not just about moving from one place to another but investigating the ways in which policies move and change and form a central discussion point for different local forms of organizing. Marcus (1995) uses this sense of movement to establish a distinct approach to multi-site ethnography.

Multi-site ethnography: maintaining a mobile orientation

In place of focusing on the development of more than one research field-site (where each site might in itself be construed as a traditional, bounded, field-site, combined with other sites for comparative purpose), Marcus (1995) emphasizes a form of multi-site ethnography based on movement between – and connections established between – field-sites. Marcus sets out five ways of engaging with this movement and connection between and across field-sites.

First, Marcus (1995) suggests 'following the people'. This involves selecting a group of participants in the study who will be studied in their moves from place to place. The ethnographer can trace the connections between places and map out the ways in which organizational activity occurs in each place. Marcus suggests that such a study is a fairly traditional form of ethnography in that various ethnographers have studied the movement of groups. However, Marcus emphasizes a reflexive orientation to this movement, with the ethnographer analysing their own moves and how these contribute to the observation of people on the move.

Second, Marcus discusses the possibility of 'following the thing'. In exemplar one, the work of Harper (1998) emphasizes this kind of approach. Harper follows documents within the IMF in order to engage with the ways in which documents form a focal point for organizational activities and, as documents move from one part of an organization to another, the sense made of those documents can alter. Following the thing can provide a means by which the 'thing' is studied (what is made of the thing, how it is understood and used, how this changes from place to place) and allows the organization in which the 'thing' operates to be analysed (by observing the organizational practices around the thing).

Third, Marcus looks at the possibility of 'following the metaphor'. This advocates a discourse-oriented approach to ethnography. In place of following things or people, the ethnographer would follow a particular form of discourse as it is used in different settings within the same organization or within different organizations. Gilbert and Mulkay (1984) use this kind of approach to analyse the talk of scientists and the ways in which they use different forms of discourse to talk to different audiences (for example, colleagues or the media) and to talk about different experiments (for example, experiments which were more or less successful). Corporate examples of this include talk of 'flexible-working' (Whittle, 2005) and talk of 'strategy' (see exemplar fourteen).

Fourth, Marcus discusses 'following the life/biography'. In this approach, the ethnographer is not just called upon to make connections between different spaces, but also between different times. Exemplar six and the work of Hirsch (1992) provides a good example of this kind of study. The family is observed in its use of technologies in different places and how these technologies are understood differently across time. This exemplar also demonstrates how each of these approaches overlaps. The technology in Hirsch's study could also be thought of as 'following the thing', and the family as 'following the people'.

The final multi-site ethnographic approach which Marcus considers involves 'following the conflict'. Conflicts form sites which draw together a range of different, competing views about the 'same' phenomenon. The ethnographer has the opportunity to move between points of view and analyse the ways in which the 'same' phenomenon is argued over and disputed. At times this adds a social policy dimension to ethnographers' work. For example, Wynne (1996), in studying disputes over the Chernobyl accident's nuclear fall-out, provided a sense of the competing perspectives on the accident which were not at that point being incorporated into policy discussions.

To the list that Marcus (1995) provides, I would like to add 'following the story'. In exemplar ten, Hine (2000) uses the story of a British nanny accused of murder to trace connections between various online and offline media (in exploring the possibility of using ethnography to study the internet). Although this approach might be subsumed under 'following the conflict', there appears to be many aspects of Hine's study which are not conflict-oriented. That is, considerations of 'conflict' do not provide a satisfactory term to cover all aspects of what is going on.

There are two final points which make this typology of multi-site ethnography slightly more complex. First, some ethnographic research is based in a single site but draws in other field-sites through the ways in which the members of one site talk about other field-sites. This can be a useful source of observations for ethnographers who find that talk of 'other' settings by members of one organization sheds light on the identity of the organization in focus. The inclusion of further sites does not necessarily require the ethnographer to go to those other sites. Indeed, a study of a single site can often use this talk of other sites as a way of positioning the single field-site into a broader set of relations (but see the caveat below). Second, I should also point out that it is possible to experiment with ways of doing ethnography. I have recently been involved in an ethnographic study of airports. In this study I encouraged each of my students to become an ethnographer when going through an airport. It produced a form of ethnography which involved one kind of field-site (airports) being understood from multiple perspectives (ten different ethnographers). One of the useful features of multi-site ethnography is that it opens up ethnographic methodology to the possibility of this kind of experimentation.

Locations and epistemology

Returning to the questions discussed in sensibility two, what kinds of knowledge claim can be made from the different approaches to multi-site ethnography? Each multi-site ethnography appears to make a claim for its epistemic validity based on its multi-sitedness. However, the basis for these claims differs. Hence Vallas (2003) argues that his observations of paper mills are particularly valid because they can be compared across settings and some of the findings persist across each of the settings. The validity claim here lies in the pervasiveness of the observations (these are things we can all see in most paper mills). Marcus (1995), on the other hand, provides a different direction for his claims to knowledge. Marcus argues that the validity of his multi-sited approach stems from being able to trace movements. People and things are increasingly involved in global circulations and multi-site ethnography might provide an opportunity to trace some of those movements. This point is emphasized more strongly by Freidberg (2001), who suggests that her ethnography is multi-sited and therefore more able to deal with the newly globalized corporate world – corporations involve relations spread across the globe and it is only through moving between and studying these connections that we can hope to ethnographically engage with this world.

These alternative takes on multi-site ethnography involve making knowledge claims. Marcus (1995) is clear that his approach to multi-site ethnography is about testing the methodological limits of ethnography. Marcus is keen to explore the questions posed to ethnography by multi-site ethnography (such as, can multiple sites be dealt with in the same detail as single sites?) as well as using multi-site ethnography to address questions (such as, how do things move and how can we as ethnographers trace those movements?). Epistemologically, his knowledge claims are more modest than those of Vallas (2003), who provides a realist ontological basis for his findings. For Vallas, the world exists independently of the research and his multi-sited findings can be analysed according to how accurately they represent that reality. The multi-sited aspect of his research, he claims, bolsters the likelihood of its accuracy. For Marcus, multi-site ethnography provides an opportunity for engaging with testing methodological questions and involves the ethnographer engaging in detail with the ways in which they move between and construct versions of the settings they study. Marcus thus provides a constructivist ontology.

Exemplar Six

E. Hirsch (1992) 'The long term and the short term of domestic consumption: An ethnographic case study', in Silverstone, R. and Hirsch, E. (eds), *Consuming Technologies: Media and Information in Domestic Spaces* (Routledge, London), pp. 208–26.

This exemplar is derived from the recent anthropological study of consumption and draws on the established tradition of anthropological approaches to exchange (see, for example, the work of Malinowski, exemplar two). Through its focus on the day-to-day activities of a family's use of technology in the home, this exemplar provides a variety of useful ideas for ethnographers engaging with organizations. This brief summary will focus on ideas of multi-site ethnography, ideas of consumption and exchange, Hirsch's approach to the moral economy, the ways in which technology can be treated by ethnographers and the complexities of ethnographic time. I will suggest that each of these areas can tell us something useful about studying organizations.

Multi-site ethnography

This ethnography takes as its focus one particular family living in North London (among several families incorporated into a broader study). Hirsch follows the family's use of technology through the various settings in which they live, work and interact. The family spend time both socializing at home and, to a degree, working at home. They also have more than one house (one in London and one in a more rural setting in Cornwall) and have a boat on which they spend an amount of time each summer, sailing. Use of technology does not occur solely in one location. Hirsch moves between sites, studying the family's relationship with technology and providing detail on how technologies are understood differently by different members of the family (the sons use the computer to differing extents and for different purposes than the daughters) and form the focus for different sets of relationships (working, domestic, socializing with friends or being alone) in different spaces. However, this spatial differentiation is complex: it is not simply the case that the family relate to technology differently and are involved in one set of technological relationships in London and another set of relationships in Cornwall. Even within the domestic spaces of the family home in London, technology is understood differently. For example, the television upstairs (for the kids when they want to watch something) is treated differently from the TV downstairs (for occasions when the family come together to watch TV). What Hirsch demonstrates is that what can appear to be the same material artefacts can be used, understood and form the focus for different social relationships in different settings. The multi-site ethnography can help ethnographers to figure out what stays the same between locations, what changes, and how those changes are important for the subject under study, which in this case is the consumption of technology.

Consumption and exchange

Hirsch ties this study of technology into the recent development of the anthropology of consumption and the long-standing tradition of anthropologists studying exchange. Both notions of consumption and exchange can be primary principles for organizational activity. Hirsch argues against the idea that consumption is straightforwardly about buying something and consuming that thing until it is used up: 'So although consumption in many cases appears to be about the destruction of things, it is really about a process of reincorporation into the social setting in which things were either produced or acquired through exchange' (1992: 209).

Exchange is not merely about swapping one good for another. Instead, exchange involves the active appropriation of goods into the setting in which they are used, understood, related to and so on (in this case in the family domestic setting). This sense of consumption opens up the area for ethnographic study: just what do, for example, families do with, relate to and how do they develop an understanding of technology in domestic settings? Furthermore, this can open up our consideration of organizations: through what means are an organization's products consumed and what products are consumed in what ways by organizations?

Treatment of technology

This questioning of consumption provides the basis for asking questions about how technology should be treated by organizational ethnographers (see exemplars one and ten for more on approaches to technology). For Hirsch, technology does not determine a particular set of social relationships. Bringing a television into the home does not introduce a fixed notion of how that technology will be used and understood. Hirsch argues that the technology represents a set of potential relationships to be explored by the ethnographer. Interaction with forms of technology makes visible particular sets of moral and temporal relationships between members of the family. Applied more broadly to organizational forms beyond the family, this suggests some fertile ground for ethnographic enquiry; particularly recommending questions of what relationships can be seen through the use of technology and how can particular uses of technology be seen as characteristic of organizations and organizations' members.

Moral economy and ethnographic time

Hirsch emphasizes moral aspects of family life in his ethnography. As this is not an issue focused on by any of the other ethnographic exemplars, it is worth considering. In this study the moral aspects of family life are treated as those moments where members set out (and thus make ethnographically available) what they perceive to be the right and wrong correct and incorrect ways in which things should happen, ways in which technology should be used, and which relationships should occur in which spaces. This elaboration of moral features of family life concentrates on ideas of social obligations (how family members should relate to each other) and constraints (ways of encouraging, limiting, or possibly attempting to control uses of technology).

> It is these constraints and possibilities which work themselves out over time given the 'moral economy' in which the relationships exist. Each household strikes its balance between relatively individualistic behaviour and a locally constructed … order. The point I am trying to make here is that there is a 'moral economy' predicated on specific relations between persons and things. (1992: 210)

The moral order of the household, for Hirsch, is closely involved in a particular approach to time (see sensibility five for more on ethnographic time). Families operate a kind of 'moral-temporal structure' (1992: 210) according to Hirsch, which is centred on moral short-term and moral long-term social interactions. The short-term interests of the family might lie in an expressed desire for acquisition (in this study, the family is considering buying a new VCR), but this needs to be considered in relation to the expressed longer-term principles of the family (the parents are not keen on the children watching too much TV). The short term and the long term are brought together through the parents' eventual decision to buy a VCR so that they can record their children, who are due to appear on TV. This moral management of short-term and longer-term interests provides a fantastic exemplar for considering the interests, ideas and motives of organizations and their members. It demonstrates the relevance and interest of questions such as: What do members articulate in relation to short-term, long-term and moral interests? How are these managed across an organization? How are conflicts in these interests resolved?

Multi-site caveat

In this section we have presented two forms of multi-sited ethnographic research. The first involved the more or less straightforward addition of further field-sites beyond the traditional anthropological single field-site. However, it was suggested that such an approach was nothing new and may not require a new terminology of the multi-sited. The second involved the ethnographer making moves, connecting and sometimes crossing conventional boundaries and using that movement to shape the ethnographic study. This movement has also been termed mobile ethnography (see exemplar ten).

From this analysis it should not be assumed that the first form of multi-site ethnography is inappropriate as a research strategy. Although not a new method, it does not always follow that methodological innovation is the most appropriate way forward. I think the second version of multi-sited or mobile ethnography is an interesting new avenue for ethnographers to explore. However, there are many occasions where a more traditional approach to the bounded ethnographic field-site (whether there is one site or many) is a useful way to do research. For example, Leidner's (1993) work (exemplar nine) involves more than one location, but each location is treated as a more or less traditional, bounded, ethnographic field-site. Treating the field-sites as such is important for the study. It is the dislocations between McDonald's University and what actually goes on in McDonald's franchises that provide some interesting insights for readers. The different locations do not always work together in ways that the corporation expects. Communication between the locations is closely channelled and controlled, but McDonald's University does not manage to standardize every aspect of moment-to-moment activity in each restaurant. Treating the field-sites as traditional, bounded locations is a useful way of providing insights into the way the corporate organization operates.

A second point I would like to make in this caveat is to emphasize that although multi-site ethnography presents some interesting options for ethnographers, a single-site ethnography with a detailed analysis of a particular setting can provide rich and illuminating observations that address research questions in particular ways. For example, Geertz's (1973; exemplar five) study of Balinese cockfights uses the cockfights to illustrate the enormously detailed operation of Balinese culture. And the work of Graham (1995; exemplar seven) uses a US factory to explore workers' day-by-day experiences of the Japanese model of manufacturing. It is not clear that incorporating multiple sites into these studies would add anything extra to the ethnographic observations being made. Rich and detailed single-site ethnographies can be as valid, insightful and rigorous as multi-site ethnographies.

Access

Issues of access provide for a variety of practical discussion points. These discussion points only make sense in relation to each ethnographic setting entered. There is little in the way of a guidebook which will help predict how each individual organization will respond to an ethnographer's request for access to do ethnographic research. In this section I will set out the kinds of questions I (and other ethnographers) commonly experience in attempting to gain access to organizations and will then suggest that access negotiations can be useful for ethnographic research. (Each of the following discussion points is predicated on the assumption that the research will be overt, see sensibility nine on ethics for more on overt and covert ethnographic research.)

Recognizing an organization

An important first consideration for ethnographers can be the moment when they first encounter an organization. In selecting an appropriate location for addressing their research question, ethnographers may come into contact with an organization's advertising, branding or other promotional material. As mentioned previously, this can be the start of the ethnography. The very first contact with a form of the organization can tell the ethnographer something about the identity the organization wishes to portray. For example, in some recent research on waste management (Neyland, Wong and Woolgar, 2006), my first point of contact with national waste initiatives was UK government websites. These websites suggested that waste management involved a complex management structure involving local, regional and national government bodies (along with private firms). The websites provided sufficient informational access to these organizations to allow me to put together a series of suitable possible locations where I could research their activities, a set of initial questions I might ask and an angle I could work to gain commitment to the research. Each group was committed to national government guidelines on transparency; I assumed this could be used to discuss research access.

Assessing relevance

In most ethnographic research it is possible to draw up a list of potential organizational settings for addressing a research question. These can be assessed in terms of their relevance. How do the organizations fit with the initial ethnographic strategy mapped out? How easy will they be to access? What kinds of obstacles might they put in the way of access (for example, would studying police officers require that the ethnographer does police training or would entering a classroom mean the ethnographer has to acquire a variety of clearances that might take time)? How practical will the organization be in terms of access: is the organization in another country or on the other side of the country and is this a problem? For the waste management research, it turned out that a local city council could form an initial entry point into waste research. This location was both practical (local) and open to an initial meeting (at least to discuss possibilities). From this location I then followed connections (Marcus, 1995) in figuring out how waste moved from place to place and was subject to control by different authorities.

Approaching an organization

Having encountered (even through an organization's website) a seemingly appropriate organization, or perhaps a series of appropriate organizations, and having assessed the likelihood and practicalities of gaining access, a decision needs to be made about approaching the organization. Who would form the most appropriate point of contact? Would they be best approached by e-mail, by phone or by letter? In what ways could this approach be enhanced (for example, by using university-headed stationery)? Is there anyone who could facilitate access, such as a gatekeeper known to the ethnographer or to friends, family or a colleague, who may go on to play a role in shaping the study (see sensibility four)? I have always found that negotiating an initial meeting to discuss the possibility of research is a useful opportunity to find out more about the organization and to give members of the organization an opportunity to find out something about me as an ethnographer. In the waste management research, an initial meeting with local city council managers revealed that members of the council were keen to find out what local residents actually did on a day-to-day basis with their waste and why more residents were not recycling. This provided a viable route into promoting the advantages of an ethnographic study of waste.

Initiating negotiations

Having set up a meeting to discuss the possibility of research, negotiating access can be a complex process. There is a balance to be struck here between offering something that the organization would find useful and over-committing to something that the ethnography will not be able to deliver. It is important in these initial negotiations to figure out what expectations there are for using ethnographic data. Will the organization want to read (or edit) findings before they go beyond the organization? Does the organization expect verbal presentations of the data at some point during the research? Is the organization concerned about the commercial value of the ethnographic material, and what sort of agreement might they want in place to guard against commercial problems? I gained agreement with the city council to go out and study waste and recycling collectors' actions, and aimed to incorporate local residents' views on waste into the study. I established a time frame for the research and agreed with the city council to provide an anonymous report of results. This appeared to establish a mutually beneficial arrangement.

Getting an agreement

Access negotiations can be used as a means to shape the initial ethnographic strategy. Once again, I have found it useful at these moments to strike a balance between using negotiations to shape the strategy (for example, by altering the strategy as I learn more about the organization) and allowing the organization to establish the direction of the strategy (by setting out which parts of the organization will be available to be studied – of course these may not be the same areas deemed relevant under the original strategy). The ethnographer needs to figure out when to stubbornly stick to a strategy and when to go along in possibly interesting other directions offered by the organization. Getting an agreement that particular areas of the organization will be made available, for a particular amount of time, can be important for later parts of the study, where the ethnographer's presence may be called into question (see sensibility four on field relations and sensibility six on observing). Writing into the agreement

77

that, at certain points during the ethnography, ongoing findings of the study will be presented, can be a useful way of gaining feedback (see sensibility six). For some ethnographic studies it may be worth building into an agreement opportunities to review the agreement as the study progresses, or as the relevance of different areas of the organization become apparent, or as new directions for the research become appropriate. I developed a verbal agreement with the city council regarding access, time and the provision of results of a study of waste management with a member of the city council. She agreed that her stressful job was insufficiently resourced to carry out such a study. Having gained this agreement, she then took long-term leave from the council, due to stress. This left the results of the study in an ambiguous position – having lost the principle supporter or gatekeeper for the research, it was not clear that the city council ever used the research results (Neyland, Wong and Woolgar, 2006). Verbal agreements can be precarious for ethnographic research.

Utility of access

Although each of these discussion points might seem difficult (and each is necessarily vague as different organizations require different means of access), I have always found them a useful part of ethnographic research. A question I ask in doing ethnographic research is: What do these access negotiations tell me about the organization? Negotiations may say something about the identity of the organization, which areas of the organization are sensitive and which are not, and who or what is considered important in the organization (see Watson (2001) for an analysis of how managers talk about managing and talk about organizations). A second question I ask is: What ideas do these access negotiations offer me in developing the study? For example, negotiations may unveil parts of the organization I was unaware of, organizational principles I had not heard about or organizational initiatives which now appear to offer the potential for ethnographic engagement. In addition, I always try to hold on to the principle that first contact with an organization is the point at which most things about the organization appear strange. It is in these moments that I find it easiest not to take things for granted, that everything is up for potential analysis, that everything is ethnographically interesting. As ethnographies progress and features of the organization become routine, this opportunity for treating things as strange decreases (or at least involves more work). Capturing in detail these moments of strangeness are vital for shaping the eventual writing of the ethnography (see sensibility six on observing and sensibility eight on writing). Although this addresses the practical discussion points of gaining access, these are only first steps in getting into an organization and getting on with ethnography. As the next discussion will demonstrate, successfully cultivating research relationships can be an equally important part of developing ethnographic research.

Recommended reading

Liebow, E. (1967) *Tally's Corner* (Routledge and Kegan Paul, London)
Marcus, G. (1995) 'Ethnography in/of the world system: the emergence of multi-sited ethnography', *Annual Review of Anthropology* 24: 95–117
Mead, M. (1928) *Coming of Age in Samoa* (William Morrow, New York)

4

▷▷▷▷▷Sensibility Four
Field Relations

Introduction

In the last sensibility I suggested that selecting a location (or locations) for doing ethnography and negotiating access to that location are complex and challenging features of ethnographic research. In this discussion we will see how such challenges form the start of a series of field engagements. Engaging with members of the ethnographic field-site provides a further sensibility for orienting research. Ethnographers can use field relations as a way of gaining observational material, reflecting on such material, assessing the coverage of the organization being studied (are there areas or people within the organization not included?) and developing a reflexive understanding of their own role in the organization. First, we will analyse the ways in which ethnographers go about the business of managing field relations. Second, this analysis will be used to consider the importance and difficulty of developing trust through field relations. Third, we will consider the potential difficulties posed by being too close to research participants. Finally, consideration will be given to the ways in which field relations can form a useful focus for ethnographic investigation. The ways in which the researcher makes and maintains relations in an organization can be useful in thinking about how members of the organization interact.

Managing field relations

Insiders and outsiders

Perhaps the most difficult aspect of managing field relations is striking a balance between being sufficiently close to organizational members (being an insider) to figure out what is going on in the organization and retaining sufficient distance from members of the organization (being an outsider) to produce an ethnographic analysis. Junker (1960) introduces a schema for describing this balancing act, looking at the four different types of position the ethnographer can occupy. These range from complete participant, through participant as observer, observer as participant, to complete observer. The complete observer and complete participant position are not recommended ethnographic research roles. Being a complete participant would mean (to use an ethnographic term) 'going native'. This would result in the ethnographer having no distance from the organization, and indeed having little sense that what they were doing would contribute to an ethnography. No ethnographer should aim to be a complete participant or to go native if they want to produce an ethnographic study. At the other extreme, being a complete observer simply means having no participation whatsoever. This is also an unlikely position for an ethnographer to occupy. How could one be in an organization without in some way participating? It may be feasible to study settings via video recordings (see sensibility seven), but relying only on video would rule out interactions in the field which can produce much of the ethnographer's research. The two positions in between the extremes are intended to convey a sense in which some ethnographers are more observer than participant (see exemplar thirteen) and some are more participant than observer (see exemplar seven). However, it should be noted that neither of these exemplars involved complete observation or complete participation.

This management of positioning between being an insider and an outsider is not reducible to a physical sense of being in the field at some times and out of the field at other times, although times outside the field can be important for writing up observations and attempting some form of organization of observations (see sensibilities six and eight). The management of positioning is also about moving in and out of being a member of the organization. The work of Geertz (1973; exemplar five) can be useful here for thinking through what it means to be a member. Geertz's entry into membership, moving from being treated as invisible to being treated as a member of the community, provided a clear sense of what it meant to be a member and why being a member was important for the study (no-one would tell Geertz anything until he was recognized as a member).

Other exemplars give different insights into this balancing between outside and inside. Hirsch's work (1992; exemplar six) on familial use of technology is not predicated upon any expectation that he would become a member of the family. Instead, being 'inside' for Hirsch is about being with the family as they go through their usual routines of family life and family use of technology. In this sense he is more of an observer-participant. The work of Harper (1998; exemplar one) is predicated on a different set of field relations. Again, there is little sense in which the ethnographer is a traditional member of the organization being studied (in this case the International Monetary Fund), but instead the ethnographer is there to produce work that is of use to the IMF. Harper is thus accorded a temporary and utilitarian membership of the organization. Graham's work (1995; exemplar seven) offers an alternative stance on this insider–outsider balance. Her covert research (see sensibility nine on ethics) positions her as more of a participant than an observer. Making observations in this kind of fieldwork becomes a practical problem, as note-taking is not the standard activity of organizational members. For Graham, managing her identity as a member, as far as her colleagues knew, involved doing little which is expressly ethnographic. Alternative stances on the balance between insider and outsider are provided by the work of Suchman (1987; exemplar eight), who is an active participant in a work setting established to test technology (where one of the forms of assessing the tests is ethnography) and the work of Leidner (1993; exemplar nine), whose ethnographic identity is known to some research participants (McDonald's managers) and not others (McDonald's customers). The balance between being inside the organization and being outside the organization results in a productive tension. Stepping out of the organization (even conceptually while still in the building) can provide a means of reflecting on who members are, what they are doing and how the ethnographer themself is successfully cultivating a membership identity. Making the most of being a member, like Geertz, who used his honorary membership to strike up long and detailed discussions that no-one was previously willing to have, seems to require an element of trust (this will be taken up below).

Emic and etic

Developing close relations in the field can be one way of understanding how our engagement in the field setting we are studying can be assessed. This sounds complex. However, there are two principal criteria we can draw on for assessing our understanding of our relations in the field. The first of these is the emic perspective and the second is the etic perspective. Emic perspectives are those developed and maintained by members of the field-site we are studying. If we are interested in using emic criteria for assessing our field relations and observations of field relations, we could choose to present some features of our research to the organization we are studying (see particularly sensibilities six and eight). Alternatively, we could work hard in establishing close field relations in order to have a good understanding of the ways in which the organizational members talk about the organization. If we develop a detailed understanding of how different members of the organization talk about the organization in different ways, we may be close to developing an emic perspective of the organization. This perspective may be helpful for revealing features of the organization that are held to be important or meaningful by members of the organization.

Alternatively, we might look to bring in external criteria for assessing our field relations. These would be etic criteria and might include methodological principles (such as assessing our field relations through forms of sampling or questions of reliability and rigour), research questions (assessing our field relations according to what they reveal about a particular question or how successfully we are getting to the heart of the matter that we want to address) or some form of assessment criteria (such as a form of measurement). Traditionally, emic criteria have been the focus for ethnographic analysis and etic approaches have been associated with 'scientific' attempts to provide neutral, objective facts about a situation (see, for example, the work of Headland, Pike and Harris, 1990). However, we can also think about emic and etic criteria more broadly as part of the debate regarding inside and outsider perspectives. Drawing ideas of emic and etic criteria into this debate suggests that questions should not be limited to whether or not we are physically inside or outside a location or whether or not we are actually a member of an organization, but should also include consideration of the perspective utilized in assessing our engagement in the organization (for example, is the picture we are producing of organizational activity predicated on an emic or etic perspective or a combination of both?).

Gatekeepers and key informants

Thus far we have considered the ways in which we, as ethnographers, can be at once inside and outside an organizational setting and can bring in different criteria for understanding our field relations. Ethnographers also frequently take into consideration very particular field relations. It is not the case that ethnographers will always develop the same kinds of relations with all members of a field setting. A particularly striking example of the ways in which ethnographers engage in establishing very close relationships with particular members of an organization is through ethnographic gatekeepers or key informants. Although not every ethnography involves a gatekeeper or key informant, consideration of this relationship can provide us with ways of thinking through the problems and benefits of close field relations.

Perhaps the most famous example of an ethnographic gatekeeper and key informant is Doc, in the work of Whyte (1955; exemplar three). Doc enables Whyte to access various features of the street corner activity at the centre of the ethnography, enabling Whyte to gain access to different locations (such as the local bowling alley). However, Doc also enables Whyte to become a member of those particular settings, speaking on behalf of Whyte and assuring various members of the street corner setting that Whyte is someone who should be allowed to take part in street corner activities. Furthermore, Doc also acts as a commentator on these activities, providing a history of members of the street corner (where they come from, the basis for status differences between members) and explanations for why some members act in certain ways (because of competition with other members) and why some actions are particularly important (like winning at bowling as an arbiter of group status). Doc is both an important gatekeeper and informant and it is clear that Whyte's study would be poorer in Doc's absence.

83

However, such field relations can also be problematic. First, these close relations can raise ethical questions regarding the possibility that people like Doc might be exploited by the ethnographer (although this is by no means certain, see sensibility nine on ethics). Second, entering the membership of an organization through connection with a particular member can carry significant connotations not necessarily welcomed by other members. For example, in the work of Malinowski (1922/2002; exemplar two), we find the ethnographer requiring local missionaries and colonial administrators as gatekeepers to gain access to a setting. However, Malinowski treats this relationship as a practical necessity and is keen to throw off the shadow of the gatekeeper as soon as possible. For Malinowski, not being associated with the gatekeeper offers the best prospects of becoming a member of the setting. Such problematic connections emphasize the difficulties involved in using particular organizational members as gatekeepers and hint at the problems of using such members as key informants (for example, Malinowski would have produced a very different ethnography using colonial administrators as informants). The same may hold for senior management in organizational settings. Third, Van Maanen (1979) presents the problem of ethnographic truth; how we might know whether one informant is (deliberately or accidentally) providing misleading information. Van Maanen argues that the only way to figure this problem out is to draw in multiple members of any setting and to avoid leaving a single voice from the field as the arbiter of 'truth'.

Exemplar Seven

L. Graham (1995) *On the Line at Subaru-Isuzu: The Japanese Model and the American Worker* (Cornell University Press, London)

Graham's study of a Subaru-Isuzu auto plant in the USA begins by raising questions regarding the shifts in recent years of Japanese ways of working into other employment settings. Graham seeks to ethnographically study the 'Japanese model' in the USA, to ask questions about the workers' day-to-day experiences of the model, the relationships built into the model and to question the extent to which recent management research on the model matches up to experiences of the model. Graham argues that the recent literature on the Japanese model as either benefiting (for example, increasing worker control and co-operation in the workplace) or creating problems for workers (for example, undermining unions) is often characterized by an absence in the kind of detail of day-to-day activities that an ethnography can provide. Although a dense initial literature review can slow the pace and interest for readers of ethnography, Graham employs a strategy to cut through such limitations. Graham skilfully situates her study within a set of established literature, while also using that literature to justify and focus her research questions. Graham sets out her ethnographic interests as follows:

> This book contributes to the current debate by directly examining worker responses to the Japanese model. It is based on a long-term, covert, participant observation study of work experiences in a non-union Japanese automobile transplant. … This research identifies patterns of behaviour that emerge among workers and between workers and management in their day-to-day experience. Such an analysis contributes enormous insights into the nature and dynamics of labour relations in a non-union transplant under the Japanese model.
>
> Without including the worker, the debate over the Japanese model remains somewhat speculative and superficial. (1995: 4)

The covert aspects of this research may invoke ethical questions regarding the relationships established between the researcher, research participants and the text (see the next section and sensibility nine for more details). This quotation also places emphasis on union issues. Graham is clear that this is an area of personal interest for her. She suggests that while working at a previous factory 'I became a staunch union advocate' and felt personally responsible to represent women in the workplace. 'We believed that if we were unsuccessful, it would not only be a personal failure, in that era when women were beginning to break into traditionally male jobs, we felt that women were depending on our ability to stick it out' (1995: 14).

This declaration of personal interests in advancing women and unionism in the workplace might appear to question the validity of Graham's research; the researcher appears to provide an angle on the research prior to entry into the field. However, given ethnography's tradition of openness and invitation to readers to actively make sense of and assess the ethnographic text, this need not necessarily be the case. Graham's personal declaration of interests could be seen as an important part of the ethnographic text to be made available to readers, in making an assessment of the ethnography. This brief summary will focus on two central components of Graham's work: field relations established during the study and the composition of the ethnographic text.

Field relations

Graham had few problems in becoming a member of the Subaru factory. Given her previous factory experience and that many of the other workers had attained a reasonable level of higher education, she felt there were few cultural or experiential barriers to membership. For Graham, this was as much a hindrance as it was an advantage. Treating the setting as strange is an important feature of ethnographic fieldwork, ensuring that nothing is taken for granted or left unanalysed as simply being the way it is. With Graham's familiarity with the setting came a need to work harder to treat aspects of the setting as strange.

Graham engages with the potentially problematic aspects of covert research in the following ways. She argues that a covert ethnographic methodology was important for four reasons. First, entering the field covertly meant she gained quicker access to what was going on and did not need to wait for approval for access or risk getting turned down. Second, Graham argues that covert research is least disruptive to the 'natural course of events' (1995: 16), in that the ethnographer is treated in the same way as other members and an ethnographer's experience is likely to be similar to that of other workers, if not treated as a researcher. Third, Graham suggests that the ethnographic method enabled her to develop field relations in such a way that she could ask relevant questions in the field, while being a member of the field, providing a 'means to identify categories of behaviour as they emerge in their natural contexts' (1995: 16). Fourth, Graham argues that her ethnography enabled her to observe quite subtle forms of resistance to the factory in everyday actions. A practical problem which characterized these covert field relations was how to record observations while engaged in factory work. Graham managed to move into a position in the factory where she could carry a clipboard (and thus write down observational notes) and augmented these through frequent bathroom breaks where she could scribble down more observations. These were typed up at the computer each evening after a factory shift.

A particular aspect of Graham's field relations in her study of the factory was that she carried into the field particular commitments. She was interested in the potential for unionization and possible problems faced by women in the workforce. These concerns are given focus in her detailing of health problems faced by workers in the field, where women were (according to Graham) criticized for developing problems that men might not have. Graham speculates on the development of non-union, temporary workers who could be hired and fired as required, without regard for their long-term health. Graham also offers detail on the potential for racial divisions of labour to evolve on the factory floor. Graham recounts examples of black workers and female employees who were refused possible promotions to team leader status through their own team leader's refusal to allow particular employees to sign up for leadership training. The ethnographer's field relations in this study could be seen as an example of a politicized ethnography where the ethnographer's presence in the field is designed (by the ethnographer) to address particular kinds of questions.

One way in which Graham attempts to shift the burden of these political field relations away from her own personal commitments is through returning to the field to get feedback on what her fellow factory workers thought of her study. Although this broke the bounds of covertness, it is not reported that workers were particularly distressed by the revelation that they had been working with an ethnographer. It is also not the case, however, that those involved in the follow-up interviews who read the study were wholly supportive of Graham's claims. Graham's first concern in returning to the field was to assess whether or not her time in the field was representative of other periods on the factory floor:

> I feared that the events documented here might be anomalous, arising from kinks that had to be worked out during the first year of production. It was important to discover if my findings were relevant to people currently working in the plant. (1995: 129)

A second concern was to figure out the extent to which workers agreed with the substantive arguments of the text, that women and black workers were sometimes denied opportunities and that unionization would benefit the workforce. For both concerns the reactions were mixed. These ranged from employees who wholly supported the ethnography, to others who were mildly surprised to find themselves the subject of a book, to others who disagreed about the value of unions. Incorporating these comments into the text provides readers with further opportunities to assess the relevance, interest and value of Graham's arguments. The comments provide an opportunity to shift the weight of ethnographic argument from the ethnographer to the participants in the ethnography.

The ethnographic text

Graham's revisit to the field provides one of several points of interest for ethnographers interested in building an ethnographic text from the study of an organization. Alongside the revisit, are five points which organizational ethnographers might want to consider. First, the author incorporates direct quotes from her fieldwork into the text. This opens the opportunity for readers to enter into an assessment of the arguments being presented and differs from other ethnographic accounts (see other exemplars) which use a singular, unbroken narrative to report on the study (see sensibility eight for more on the conventions of ethnographic writing). Second, Graham produces diagrams in the text of the field (setting out positions for people and technology) to give readers a chance to look at the spatial dynamics of the relationships she is discussing. These differ from the kinds of relational diagrams offered in, for example, Whyte's (1955) work (see exemplar three). Third, all ethnographers will inevitably have more observational materials than they can possibly incorporate into a single write-up. Graham selects her observational material by providing a focus (for example, one section is entitled 'A Typical Day'), through which a particular set of observations (what has happened that day) can be situated within a broader set of observational experiences (how those happenings relate to the happenings of other days). Fourth, Graham's work offers a further example of a realist epistemological stance (see sensibility two for more on realism). Fifth, Graham's conclusion is not restricted to a picture of 'what was going on' in the field, but provides a broad based advocacy for solidarity among workers in the workplace (with an implied criticism that the Japanese model does not necessarily support such solidarity). This approach to ethnography, providing something of a political conclusion, is unusual. Although such politics might provide for an uncomfortable lack of neutrality for some readers, it should be noted that each of the exemplars incorporates a specific aim (for example, methodological development in exemplar ten, establishing ethnography in exemplar two, or uncovering information on marginalized groups in exemplar three).

Developing trust in the field

Much of the focus thus far in this discussion has been on the difficulties of maintaining a balance between closeness and distance to the ethnographic field-site through the management of field relations. One way to think about the development of these relationships in detail is to use concepts of trust. Social science research provides for a variety of ways of dealing with trust (see, for example, Garfinkel, 1963; Barber, 1983; Shapin, 1994; Misztal, 1996; Luhman, 2000). Garfinkel (1963) suggests that social order involves a multitude of trust expectations and accountability relations which characterize mundane, day-to-day interactions. For example, in a conversation the first speaker will hold to account the second speaker's response, assessing the extent to which the second speaker has demonstrably understood the first speaker, displayed this understanding in their response and thus accomplished the expectations of the first speaker. Such mundane expectations are forms of trust and such forms of trust hold the social order together. Garfinkel (1963) argues that at moments where expectations break down, further assessments of trust are initiated and repair sequences are entered into in order to get the interaction back on track.

This approach to trust can be helpful in thinking through questions to ask in the field. For example, what are the ordinary, ordered ways in which members of the organization under study go about doing their day-to-day activities? How does the order provide a range of expectations among members regarding how members should act? Once an ethnographer has got some sense of the routines, rituals and everyday expectations that members maintain in the organization, they may consider asking: How can my ethnographic enquiries fit into that order? One means of managing these attempts to figure out expectations in the organization while also studying it is to adopt the position of the acceptable incompetent (Lofland, 1971). The acceptable incompetent may make organizational 'mistakes' but through forms of trial and error they come to navigate their way through (and in the process learn) organizational expectations and routines (for more on this, see Hammersley and Atkinson, 1995: 99).

Garfinkel (1963) is noted, however, for not sticking to such a limited range of tentative enquiries on trust. He conceived of a series of breach experiments to disrupt the normal ways in which people might go about their everyday activities. It was in the breach that we could see what expectations were, how strongly expectations were held and what repair sequences were required to get interactions back on track. Although there is a certain bravery required from ethnographers to try to constitute a breach in the expectations of members of an organization (and this may raise ethical considerations), entering into detailed consideration of organizational expectations, what would break those expectations and how those expectations might be repaired can tell us much about the members of an organization and what holds those members together.

How close is too close?

There is no definite rule to guide how close ethnographers should get to their participants. However, getting too close can bring problems. First, there is the danger (mentioned previously) of going native. In these situations the ethnographer loses any sense of ethnographic distance and may even lose the sense that they are carrying out an ethnography. Second, getting too involved in research can result in the researcher directly or indirectly manipulating what is going on in the organization. Drawing on Garfinkel's (1963) work, this kind of intervention can be useful if treated reflexively. In the absence of such reflexive treatment, such researcher involvement can problematically change the direction of the research. Third, in working closely with a key informant, consideration needs to be given to how the informant's stories will be used. As we saw in sensibility two, Mead's (1928) choice of informants later came under scrutiny and criticism for providing a distorted account of life in the society Mead was studying. Such problems can be managed by dealing with key informants' accounts as one possible way in which a story of the organization can be told and comparative perspectives can be sought from other members of the organization (for more on this, see Van Maanen, 1979; Burgess, 1984). Fourth, some ethnographers have been incredibly close to their participants (for example, several ethnographers report on having sexual relations in the field, see Coffey, 1999). Decisions on what counts as too close need to be taken in the field.

Field relations as an ethnographic focus

Although in this discussion I have suggested that there are tensions involved in doing ethnographic research between being an insider and an outsider, risking getting too close to research participants and going native, I would like to end the discussion by emphasizing how important field relations are for ethnography. Negotiating through these tensions, attempting to be as 'inside' as possible at times while withdrawing at other times to produce an ethnographic, distanced perspective on events, is vital. Figuring out who the gatekeepers might be, who might act as useful informants, what the regular routines are of the organization, how these can be engaged to develop trust and how each of these considerations can be managed while also maintaining an analytical ethnographic stance can be difficult. Utilizing the reflexive sensibility introduced in sensibility two can be an important way of ensuring that everything in the field is kept available for analysis. Taking into account, in detail, the ways in which the ethnographer moves through the organization, develops relations in the field, begins to produce some sense of the organization and the criteria being used to assess that sense of the organization, all need to be at the forefront of analysis. Discussion in the next sensibility will emphasize that the only sensible way to manage this complexity is through time.

Recommended reading

Boelen, W. (1992) 'Street corner society: Cornerville revisited', *Journal of Contemporary Ethnography* 21(1)

Headland, T., Pike, K. and Harris, M. (1990) *Emics and Etics: The Insider/Outsider Debate* (Sage, London)

Junker, B. (1960) *Field Work: An Introduction to the Social Sciences* (Chicago: University of Chicago Press, Chicago)

5

▷▷▷▷▷Sensibility Five
Ethnographic Time

Introduction

Under the preceding sensibility I emphasized the value and difficulty of establishing research relations in ethnographic field-sites. Part of the difficulty in establishing good field relations is that they take time. In this discussion I will argue that ethnographic time should be treated as a further sensibility to guide and orient research. Although questions of time introduce some practical matters, ethnographic time also requires a particular way of thinking about doing research. Traditional ethnographic research is slow, expensive and laboriously detailed. I will suggest that these are all advantageous aspects of ethnographic time. We will begin by first looking at the tradition of lengthy ethnographic immersion in the field. Second, the tension between organizational and ethnographic temporal demands will be analysed, investigating whether thick or quick description is most appropriate. Third, we will look at the ways in which time can become a problem in ethnographic research. Finally, the discussion will conclude with a defence of ethnographic time.

Ethnography: the long haul

Early anthropological ethnography often involved researchers developing career-long interests in particular ethnographic regions. In some universities, it is still a requirement to gain a tenured anthropology position that the researcher has a 'region' in which they specialize. However, with the growth in ethnographic studies of organizations, does this still hold? For example, would an ethnographer devote themselves to a career spent studying McDonald's? This is unlikely, although there are ethnographers who have devoted a significant proportion of their career to working with a particular organization (see, for example, the work of Suchman, 1987, exemplar eight). Also, there are still ways in which organizational ethnographers might develop long-term interests in particular areas. For example, ethnographers may specialize in studying organizations of a particular geographical area (for example, Japan; see, for instance, Bestor, 2004), a particular type of organizational activity across several ethnographic studies (for example, the work of Leidner (1993) on organizational standardization in the fast-food and insurance industries; see exemplar nine), or a particular type of organization (such as marketing organizations; see, for example, de Waal Malefyt and Moeran, 2003; Moeran, 2005).

In these ways, ethnographers can still commit to the long haul. However, it should also be noted that many ethnographers simply complete one ethnographic study and then move on to another in a substantively different area, addressing different issues and sometimes for different purposes (for example, in my own work I have analysed forms of organizational strategy and then forms of informational usage and privacy; Neyland, 2006a, 2006b). Despite this movement between substantive areas, it should not be assumed that ethnographic research suddenly gets any quicker. Smith (2001) suggests that the average time taken for academic ethnographic research from the start of fieldwork to the point of publication is 8.14 years, or for anthropological researchers, 10.7 years. This sounds terrifically slow, particularly as UK academics are assessed for their publication outputs every five or six years. Jeffrey and Troman (2004) suggest that ethnographers often aim to spend around a year in the field (although this is not always possible, see next section). Assuming it then takes a year to write some papers and a year to get published and assuming that not all papers are written at exactly the same time, academic ethnographers should be in a position to publish reasonably regularly (perhaps several times annually). It is difficult to find substantial evidence to support or refute the work of Smith (2001) or Jeffrey and Troman (2004), but in looking at my own work, I publish more than one academic paper from each ethnographic project. On occasions my ethnographic projects run concurrently and I end up publishing a few papers per year. (On the other hand, I should also note that a book I started in 1997 was published in 2006, adhering to Smith's average.) One conclusion we can draw from this is that academic ethnographic research takes time. However, in doing organizational ethnography, we should also keep in mind the demands of the organization with whom we are working. How long are organizations willing to wait? The next section will look at the tensions between ethnographic and organizational time.

Ethnographic versus organizational time

Bate (1997) suggests that demands made on organizational ethnographers' time can be understood in relation to two modes of research operation: thick description and quick description. Thick description is a term coined by Clifford Geertz (1973; exemplar five). Thick description involves long-term immersion in the field setting, the development of incredibly rich, detailed and (con)textured observations, the establishment of close relations with those studied, and the incorporation into the ethnographic text of numerous reference points (Geertz draws a broad range of sources into his thick description of Balinese cockfighting from myths to historical texts and works of art; see exemplar five). Thick description is not tied into any sense of organizational utility – it is not designed as ethnography *for* the organization – but can be understood as exemplifying the principles of academic anthropological study. Rosen (2000) suggests that thick description and thin description can be distinguished through descriptive adequacy. Rosen suggests that if two boys are sitting in a classroom and are closing their right eye rapidly, a thin description would straightforwardly provide this detail. A thick description would analyse the possibility that the boys were engaged in the cultural tradition of illicit winking. However, for Geertz, this would be the thinnest of thick descriptions.

On the other hand, quick description can be understood as brief immersion in the field, often directed towards achieving a specific and sometimes quite narrow goal. In this sense, quick description is closely tied to a utilitarian aim. Bate (1997) suggests that quick description often involves flying visits to several locations and the presentation of findings. It is closer to 'yet another business case study or company history' (1997: 1150) than the richly detailed tradition of anthropological research. In Bate's terms, it is clear that thick description is more genuinely ethnographic than quick description. Hammersley and Atkinson's guide to ethnographic research also warns against quick ethnography, suggesting that researchers need to spend time in the field to understand what is going on (1995: 58).

This duality between quick and thick ethnography may be somewhat misleading. It is not always the case that ethnographers will have to make a stark choice between one or the other. A variety of ways have been proposed for navigating the tension between thick and quick in organizational ethnography that do not necessarily involve opting for either extreme. Some of these options are more recommended than others. First, it is possible to do ethnographic research in what Jeffrey and Troman term 'a compressed time mode' (2004: 538). This involves spending up to a month in a particular setting, completing some directed research (perhaps based on a single theme or deliberately based on a small aspect of organizational activity). Second, Jeffrey and Troman also look at the possibility of doing ethnography in 'a selective intermittent time mode' (2004: 540) and in 'a recurrent time mode' (2004: 542). The former involves devoting some time to doing the research (perhaps two years) but only spending part of that time immersed in the field. The latter involves deliberately setting out to do observations in organizational settings at fixed, repeated and patterned times (for example, studying monthly board meetings or the production of annual reports). Third, such movement in and out of the field has connections with Burawoy's (2003) work on ethnographic revisits. Such revisits can be completed across an ethnographer's career, enabling some reflexive engagement with the ethnographer's changing understanding of the field under study over the years. Alternatively, revisits can involve refutation of other ethnographers' findings or can build on the observations that other ethnographies provide. Each of these strategies might enable the ethnographer to move away from a single, long-term immersion in the field.

These are not the only means available for ethnographers to move outside the traditional focus on long-haul ethnographic research. Fourth, Millen (2000: 280) looks at 'time deepening strategies' for ethnographic research. Strategies can involve narrowing the field of research by zooming in on important activities, using multiple observational techniques to try to uncover important activities quickly, selecting key informants who can offer a great deal of data rapidly, and using computerized techniques to code and analyse observations. These strategies are designed to focus ethnographic research on the needs of the organization (see next section). However, we should be careful in assuming that such needs are necessarily the most appropriate way to guide research. Figuring out what might be 'important' about an organization for an ethnographer is not easy. What might be interesting for an academic piece of ethnography might not be useful for an organization, what might be unusual activity from an ethnographer's perspective might be a commonplace expectation for a manager, and an interesting informant for an ethnographer might be considered an unreliable story-teller by members of the organization (see sensibility eight for more on appropriate ethnographic writing).

Lynch (2004) argues that researchers need to step out of these demands for utility on occasion to give themselves the space to develop an analysis of the research in which they are engaged. In order to understand what might be important and who might be reliable and interesting takes time and many, successive interactions with multiple members of the organization. This process of taking time involves similar moves to those presented in sensibility four; ethnographers need to be attuned to being both inside and outside the organization they are studying. In terms of taking time, ethnographers need to be both aware of the organization's demands and keep a sense of their own temporal ethnographic requirements (such as the time it will take to address questions and the organizational areas, activities and issues they want to incorporate into their study). In order to maintain the principal aspects of the ethnographic strategy that has been developed, the research questions to be addressed, the field-site locations to be incorporated and the field relations which need to be developed, ethnographers may have to take into account some of the features of ethnographic time that are frequently deemed problematic.

Problems with ethnographic time

One of the chief stumbling blocks for organizational ethnography is often said to be time. It is claimed that ethnography is slow and thus expensive. It takes time to engage in observational work and further time to produce an analysis of those observations (this argument is outlined in Bate, 1997). It is further argued that, for example, product development or organizational change operate on a speedier basis, thus rendering ethnographies' slow findings less relevant to organizational settings; products and organizations have moved on by the time ethnographies produce results (see, for example, Millen, 2000). Often it is said that for all its time and expense, ethnography produces results which are narrow (for example, they are sometimes focused on one particular aspect of organizational activity) and out of line with organizational expectations (that is, they are not written in the same style or format as other organizational reports, but often rely on a thick analytic description that is not easily accessed by busy corporate types; for more on this see sensibility eight on writing). Finally, it is said that academic funding bodies are wary of supporting ethnographic research because of a perceived lack of utility in relation to its costs (this argument is set out in Jeffrey and Troman, 2004). These arguments against ethnographic time are important, not necessarily because they are correct, but because ethnographers may need to engage in these arguments to defend ethnographic time.

Exemplar Eight

L. Suchman (1987) *Plans and Situated Actions* (Cambridge University Press, Cambridge)

I selected Suchman's ethnography as an exemplar for organizational ethnographers for three reasons. First, it provides a detailed ethnographic study designed to address a particular theoretical question. The question to answer is this: given increasing amounts of human–machine interaction, how can we engage with the question of mutual intelligibility in such interaction? Second, Suchman's work is carried out in a particular organizational context: an organizational space for technology (in this case, a photo-copier) development. This provides a challenging basis for asking questions of what the technology will be (as it is, to an extent under-development) and how people will interact with the technology. It introduces methodological questions regarding how we can ethnographically capture this kind of interaction. Third, Suchman's work combines both practical and theoretical questions. The work was carried out in and for a technology development organization. The study also raised questions regarding the most appropriate means to draw together disparate social science approaches to human–machine interaction. This combination of practical and theoretical questions offers insights for organizational ethnographers interested in ethnography *of* and *for* an organization. This summary will offer detail on each of these three areas in turn.

Research question

Having a research question provided Suchman's work with a particular focus (relating back to sensibility one, the question formed the basis for developing what I have termed an ethnographic strategy). Suchman's question was to figure out a way of conceptualizing mutual intelligibility in human–machine interaction. That is not to say that such interaction was definitively characterized by mutual intelligibility. Rather, the aim was to figure out what form the interaction took, the extent to which this kind of interaction could be considered mutually intelligible and the possibility that problems with mutual intelligibility might provide an explanation for problems with (photo-copier) technology use. Suchman sought to challenge the design orthodoxy for inter-active machines which designed a plan into the machine. These plans would reify 'certain premises about purposeful action' (1987: 4) through the machine. That is, 'designing in' to the machine a particular plan would result in designing particular assumptions (that people plan interactions and that a plan-based model of interaction is appropriate) about users into the machine. In place of carrying assumptions into the research, Suchman sought to study particular situations and the actions that made up those particular situations, which would provide detail on users' interactions with machines.

> Specifically, if we are interested in situated action itself, we need to look at how it is that actors use the resources that a particular occasion provides – including, but crucially not reducible to, formulations such as plans – to construct their action's developing purpose and intelligibility. (1987: 3)

However:

> … the coherence of action is not adequately explained by either preconceived cognitive schema or institutionalized social norms. Rather, the organization of situated action is an emergent property of moment-by-moment interaction between actors, and between actors and the environments of their actions. (1987: 179)

Studying such situated actions required the development of a particular form of ethnographic engagement in the organizational setting.

Organizational setting

Suchman's study began with 20 hours of observations of users interacting with a particular photo-copier. Within the organization it had been reported that users were confused by what the designers thought was a relatively straightforward machine. Suchman began her ethnographic study by noting observations using a pencil and paper. However, Suchman found that the users' confusion was matched by her own. She had material which gave a detailed portrayal of confusion, rather than any insights into what might have provoked particular instances of confusion. Suchman sought a detailed way of capturing particular situated actions, without imposing an a priori order on those situations:

> What the description should look like – what its terms should be, what its structure should be, what of all that goes on it should report – is an open methodological question. If, in order to put some constraints on the description, we set out with a template that asks for a list just of what the actions come to, then what counts as

> 'an action' is prescribed ahead of time as 'its outcome', and the list format prescribes the structure of the description. Only that part of the activity that fills in the template will be recorded. The action's structure, in other words, will be decided in advance, and the method employed by the scientist will ensure that that structure is what is found. (1987: 112)

Suchman decided to video-tape particular situated actions in order to provide a record which could be replayed and studied again and again to produce initial ideas of what was going on and then return to the video record to assess those ideas.

> The point of departure for the study was the assumption that we lack a description of the structure of situated action. And because the hunch is that the structure lies in a relation between action and its circumstances that we have yet to uncover, we do not want to presuppose what are the relevant conditions, or their relationship to the structure of the action. We need to begin, therefore, at the beginning, with observations that capture as much of the phenomenon, and presuppose as little, as possible. (1987: 114)

Suchman set up the video sessions in the following way. Users were asked to interact with the photo-copier for the first time in pairs. Although photo-copier use might conventionally be done alone, such situations enabled each user to talk extensively to their pair about what they were doing, what they had just done, how they understood the machine and their task. This provided a video-based data set which could be analysed without any required prejudgement by the analyst. In Suchman's study, video was used to manage a particular problem of ethnographic time. In user testing of photo-copiers, actions occurred quickly and although Suchman could take notes, she was concerned that what was noted was only a partial and rapid documentation of what had happened. Video enabled a suspension and replaying of users' actions which Suchman could then study in more detail (for more on the use of video, see sensibility seven).

Practical and theoretical orientation

Closely involved in these methodological questions were a series of theoretical and practical organizational questions. Theoretically, social science provides a variety of ways of thinking about, conceptualizing and analysing forms of interaction. Studies of mutual intelligibility have been based, according to Suchman, on person-to-person, not person-to-machine, interaction. Suchman argued that designers of machines had taken little account of social science research and were mostly based on assumptions that interaction was planned. Instead, Suchman argued that one way to conceptualize the interaction between users and photo-copiers was to suggest that photo-copiers were designed with particular plans 'built-in', while users related to plans in a variety of ways. Users could attempt to navigate their way through plans, orienting their actions as best as they could to what they perceived to be the task at hand, using the plan as a series of interpretable instructions (each time their use of the photo-copier appeared to fail, users might return to the plan and try to produce a new interpretation). Other times users would engage with plans and instructions as a way of rationalizing their actions after using the photo-copier; the plans became a way of making sense of what had gone on. This augmentation of theories of human–machine interaction also introduced practical organizational considerations. If it was the case that machines were plan-based and users took up plans in a variety of ways, this could provide an initial set of ideas on the possible problems users were having with photo-copiers. Suchman suggests that the copiers only had limited access to what users were doing. For example, if users pressed one of the buttons on the copier, the copier could only register this interaction. The copier could therefore only offer a narrow range of responses as the copier did not have access to all the negotiations, interpre-tations and discussions taking place between users which led to the pressing of the button. Suchman was able to provide a detailed analysis of these negotiations, thereby providing both theoretical insights into human–machine interaction and practical organizational insight into what went wrong in users' interactions with photo-copiers.

For organizational ethnographers this exemplar provides: a frame of reference for considering practical problems with observational work and the need to develop ways to engage in this work (in this case through video); insight into the augmentation of social science theory (in this case through questions of human–machine interaction); and the development of these theoretical positions into practical recommendations (in this case that photo-copier design may be predicated upon narrow versions of human–machine interaction).

Defending ethnographic time

Several of the supposed 'problems' with ethnographic time can be seen as advantageous aspects of ethnographic research. First, it has been suggested that ethnographic time does not fit in with organizational conventions. However, providing research which does not fit in with organizational expecta-tions can provide a new perspective on commonly held assumptions or produce counter-intuitive outcomes which offer an original and challenging way of con-sidering organizational activity (for more on the counter-intuitive, see Woolgar, 2002c). At the point of negotiating access to an organization, emphasis can be placed on the length of time ethnography will take (see sensibility three for more on access negotiations). Such negotiations can involve discussion of ways to make best use of time by enabling access to particular parts of the organization or through discussion of appropriate strategies for time usage (see previous section on ethnographic versus organizational time). These time negotiations can be revisited as ethnographic research develops (as an ethnographer demonstrates some utility in initial feedback, organizations may be willing to allow more access for more time).

Second, although it can take time to develop close field relations with some groups who are particularly difficult to access, ethnographic details on such groups can be organizationally valuable (for example, technology developers may be keen to know, and find it difficult to figure out, how teenage girls use mobile technology, but ethnography can provide ideas; see March and Fleuriot, 2005). It should be noted that providing such information to organizations requires careful ethical consideration (see sensibility nine). Third, it is often claimed that ethnography is slow and therefore expensive. Although ethnographic time might operate on a slower scale than some organizational activities, it does not follow that it is necessarily expensive. Useful ethnographic findings can often be provided at less expense than management consultancy. Fourth, it is said that ethnographic time is too slow for specific organizational actions, such as product development. This does not seem to have hampered many notable ethnographic projects which have engaged in product development (see, for example, INCITE, as described in the work of Wakeford, 2003). Furthermore, if the aim of the ethnographer is to engage in a very specific form of organizational activity (such as product development), which has its own time scales, the purpose of initial access negotiations could include discussion of precisely what the ethnography might be able to contribute to that activity.

In sum, these discussions of time can emphasize once again the value of modest ethnography. No study can ever include everyone and everything and continue indefinitely; the limits of ethnography (as with any form of research) need to be incorporated into the analysis. In the next sensibility we will look at the ways in which ethnographers use their time in the field to go about participating in and making observations of organizational activity.

Recommended reading

Burawoy, M. (2003) 'Revisits: an outline of a theory of reflexive ethnography', *American Sociological Review* 68(5): 645–79

Jeffrey, B. and Troman, J. (2004) 'Time for ethnography', *British Educational Research Journal* 30(4): 535–48

Smith, V. (2001) 'Ethnographies of work and the work of ethnographers', in Atkinson, P., Coffey, A., Delamant, S., Lofland, J. and Lofland, L. (eds), *Handbook of Ethnography* (Sage, London), pp. 220–33

6

▷▷▷▷▷Sensibility Six
Observing and Participating

Introduction

Ethnographers have the opportunity to treat observing and participating as sensibilities to orient their research; questions such as what to observe, how to participate and how to understand what is going on in relation to previous observations, can each be used in navigating a way through organizational research. Yet in most ethnographic textbooks, more text is devoted to issues of participation than to the actions of observation. Those interested in ethnography are often told that the only way to learn how to do observation is to go and enter a field-site and engage in the practical action of that location (see, for example, Hammersley and Atkinson, 1995: 175). Meanwhile, ethnographers are offered a great deal of information on the potential complexity of participation, featuring, among other things, issues of ethics (see sensibility nine), time scale (Bate, 1997), role adoption (Burgess, 1984) and field relations (Jorgensen, 1989). Thus far this book has been no exception. Up until this point the would-be ethnographer may have been left with the impression that the art of observation itself is something that they will be left to discover (or not) once in the field. However, I have often found 'doing observation' to be one of the most perplexing aspects of ethnographic research. Hence, we will begin with a brief summary of the modes of participation featured in preceding discussions before going on to address questions of what to observe, how to observe and ways of organizing observations. The discussion will end with an analysis of the value of feeding observations back to the organization under study.

Forms of participation

In the preceding sensibilities we have given participation a great deal of consideration. This section will provide a brief summary. First, participation was considered in relation to developing an ethnographic strategy for engaging with the organization (see sensibility one). It was argued that ethnographers should map out potential ways in which they might engage in the organizational setting prior to initial entry into the field. Second, in the development of a particular field-site or set of interconnected field-sites (see sensibility three) it was suggested that ethnographers should consider the kinds of roles available to them in those sites (that is, how will they participate) and what those roles might enable (that is, what will they be able to contribute to the ethnography through participation). Negotiating access to field-sites can be a means of shaping future participation. Third, field relations formed the focus for discussions of the ways in which participation in the ethnographic setting might develop (see sensibility four). Questions addressed here included how participation could be used to foster trust, how ethnographers might maintain a stance at once both inside and outside the organization and what would count as too close participation in the field. Fourth, participation was considered in relation to time (sensibility five). Time formed a focus for considering the length of participation, the tension between ethnographic and organizational demands (which ethnographers might need to negotiate through participation) and ways of mounting appropriate defences of lengthy participation in particular field settings. Each of these sensibilities provided detail on the complex issue of developing a role or form of participation in the ethnographic setting under study. However, these sensibilities did not provide significant detail on the practical and theoretical task of 'doing observing'.

What to observe?

Observe everything

The principle I employ in ethnographic research is a form of scepticism. This has a long ethnographic tradition dating back to early anthropological fieldwork. Ethnographers entered field settings in remote places and were confronted by a range of unusual, uncomfortable and occasionally unsettling activities. Everything for early ethnographers was treated as strange. To some extent this treatment of colonial outposts as 'strange' has been criticized (see Burgess, 1984, for a discussion) for its western-dominated viewpoint on what should count as normal. However, this treatment of ethnographic strangeness has utility for organizational ethnography. When asked the question 'what to observe?', the answer for ethnographers should always initially be 'everything'. That is, nothing should be taken for granted and nothing should be assumed to be uninteresting. The organization should receive the traditional ethnographic treatment of strangeness. Holding everything up for potential analysis can result in revealing something of the organization which others (even members of the organization) are unaware of or have not considered in detail. Choosing not to observe or take note of something early in the ethnography can be effectively choosing not to include something in the study (see Plath, 1990). Decisions on narrowing observations can be made more effectively as the research progresses (see the section on 'Utilizing familiarity' below).

Working on strangeness

This treatment of strangeness is difficult to maintain. The longer the ethnographer remains in the organization the more things, activities and people begin to seem familiar. Initial stages of ethnographic fieldwork are thus more likely to reveal most about the organization and provide the moments where ethnographers find it most straightforward to treat the setting as strange. After initial engagement in the organization, ethnographers need to put in more effort to make things strange, to try to ensure that they are not taking things for granted. There are a variety of strategies available for maintaining strangeness. First, ethnographers can take a staggered approach to their fieldwork (Burawoy, 2003). Taking time out of the field may help to make things appear strange once again. Second, returning to ethnographic field notes to check activities observed now with previous observations can help refresh our sense of what it is we have been observing (see the section on 'How to observe?' below). Third, ethnographers have the opportunity to supplement their ethnographic observations with other methods in order to refresh their perspective (see sensibility seven).

Fourth, it might be possible to take more extreme action. The ethnomethodologist Harold Garfinkel (1967; see sensibility four) famously ran a series of breach experiments which were designed to disrupt the normal and conventional ways in which people might go about their daily activities. These breach experiments were designed to reveal something about the taken-for-granted assumptions involved in mundane and orderly, ordinary action. For example, Garfinkel asked his students to act as lodgers in their own family homes and observe the consequences (some students abandoned the experiment very early – it caused some arguments between family members trying to make sense of students' strange behaviour and so on. In short, the experiment involved shaking up – and making available for analysis – taken-for-granted aspects of family life). Ethnographers should be careful in attempting such breach experiments, particularly in relation to ethical considerations (see sensibility nine) and the impact such experimentation might have on the ethnographer's role in the field (upsetting too many members of the organization might lead to an early exit; see sensibility ten). However, modest forms of breach experimentation might be appropriate.

The value of playing the acceptable incompetent (Lofland, 1971) in organizational settings is often emphasized. In such a role the ethnographer engages with members of the organization on the basis that they know very little about the ordinary actions of organizational members. The ethnographer emphasizes their incompetence in order to justify asking more questions (hence revealing more ethnographic information) than other members of the organization would normally be permitted to ask. This is a gentle breach of convention in that the ethnographer is not acting in the same way as ordinary members of the organization. How long the ethnographer will be accepted as incompetent requires close attention from the ethnographer; continually asking questions may eventually antagonize organizational members (this kind of approach is not available to covert researchers; see sensibility nine).

Utilizing familiarity

An alternative stance to working hard on maintaining the 'strangeness' of an organizational setting is for ethnographers to utilize their growing familiarity with a particular setting. This can work as follows: in a previous ethnographic study (Neyland, 2006b) I was interested in figuring out the ways in which closed-circuit television (CCTV) camera systems were being introduced to particular towns in the UK as part of a package of investments in town-centre improvements. I spent some time with the staff watching how they operated the camera equipment and became interested in the kinds of things they spent their time watching (as many people assumed CCTV had nothing to do with town-centre investment and was narrowly focused on cutting crime). As I became more familiar with the kinds of things CCTV staff observed, I utilized this familiarity in order to start building a typology of the kinds of things that were watched. This typology became a means through which I could understand further observational material (as maintaining or questioning the typology, as a particularly good example of one aspect of the typology and so on). Using familiarity in this way requires some care: I had to constantly return to the choices I was making in comparing new observations with previous material and had to be careful not to reduce the complexity of the actions I was observing to a simple list. An important feature of this kind of approach is to report on and analyse the choices made in doing the ethnography to provide readers with a scope through which they can understand the ways in which the research was produced.

How to observe?

Writing field notes

Having given consideration to the question of what to observe, the next practical task facing the ethnographer is how to go about doing that observation. The principle means for gathering observational material is through ethnographic field notes. However, writing field notes is not always straightforward. In meetings where writing is part of the routine activity of the setting, ethnographers may find the time and space to write down observational notes at will. In the middle of a conversation with an organizational member, stopping to write down something the person has said may be the quickest way of ending that conversation. Also, ethnographers are faced with the problem of needing to make notes as soon as possible in order to retain all the necessary richness of the observations they have made. Ethnographers employ a range of tactics for overcoming these problems. First, ethnographers can scribble down as much detail as possible in a rapid shorthand and later write those notes up into something more coherent (see Emerson, Fretz and Shaw, 1995). Second, ethnographers can use a technological means to record the field (see sensibility seven). Third, ethnographers could rely on their memory to effectively retain all the relevant detail until such time that they are free to write detailed field notes. I have always found the latter an unsatisfactory approach to field notes, with memories providing an insufficiently detailed rendition of the complexity of a field setting. Fourth, ethnographers can attempt to make features of organizational activity work for them. As mentioned above, meetings can provide opportunities to write copious notes. Alternatively, ethnographers can occupy a role in the organization which enables them to carry with them the means to make notes (see exemplar seven and the work of Graham, 1995), or ethnographers can take numerous toilet breaks to scribble down notes or provide some other means through which to disguise note-taking (see Hammersley and Atkinson, 1995: 176). Whichever technique is employed, the ethnographer should develop keen sensibilities in the field to initially record everything and treat it as strange, to try to keep in mind other things that have been observed during previous visits to gauge the importance of pursuing particular events, and to attempt to develop relations with other members of the organization to further understand particular features of the organization.

Exemplar Nine

R. Leidner (1993) *Fast Food, Fast Talk: Service Work and the Routinization of Everyday Life* (University of California Press, Berkeley), particularly Chapter 3 'Over the counter', pp. 44–85

Leidner's ethnography of McDonald's asks how routinization is made and maintained across dispersed corporations such as global chains of fast-food restaurants. The question is a traditional concern of management research, investigating training, standards, management techniques, employee relations, customer relations, profits, marketing and professionalization. Leidner is clear in why she wanted to study McDonald's:

> McDonald's took a classic approach to routinization, making virtually all decisions about how work should be conducted in advance and imposing them on workers. (1993: 15)

Participation and observation

Leidner's participation was overt and sanctioned by the management of the organizations she studied. The staff involved in the research were also aware of her study. The only people who were not notified of her ethnography were McDonald's customers. Her observations involved more than one field-site:

> I collected information through interviewing and participant-observation. I examined routinization at two levels, First, I learned as much as I could about the company's goals and strategies for routinization by attending corporate training programs and interviewing executives. Next, I explored how the routines worked out in practice by doing or observing the work and by interviewing interactive social workers. (1993: 15)

This summary will investigate the utility of Leidner's work in using organizational ethnography to address questions of management research.

Management research questions and ethnography

Leidner provides an up-close study of routinization in action. Through detailed analysis of observational and interview material, we find a complex combination of professionalization, training, instruction manuals, videos and management techniques in the corporate fast-food setting of McDonald's restaurants. How does Leidner go about producing and organizing this detailed study? She begins by enrolling in McDonald's Hamburger University. This provides an opportunity to experience the ways in which McDonald's teach managers, franchisees and crew staff that there is a right (McDonald's) way to do everything and 'doing things differently means doing things wrong' (1993: 54). The university is compulsory for franchise owners and senior restaurant managers. Those attending courses must put in many hours of work preparing and achieving a certain standard of McDonald's qualification before they can attend the university. Once there, they are taught management techniques from increasing revenue and profitability, through managing staff relations, to the correct amounts, types, storage and handling of food stuffs (from burgers to ketchup).

Leidner immerses herself in the setting in order to experience being a McDonald's Hamburger University student. She purchases McDonald's merchandise from the shop (a french-fry necklace), she attends the courses, she takes part in the quizzes (designed to test product standardization knowledge among would-be graduates of Hamburger University) and she talks extensively to fellow attendees at the university. This only provides a partial view of routinization. What happens back in the restaurants? Leidner signs up to become a crew member in a particular restaurant and charts her shifts on french-fries and in serving breakfast. She notes here that training and the attitudes of managers do not always match up to the idealized, standardized version advocated at Hamburger University. She speculates and talks to employees about why they work so hard, for such little pay, with so little job security. She looks at the lack of training she is given for one job and the problems she has in getting useful support to help her learn the job she has been given. In relation to the latter she suggests: 'I went through this breakfast shift in a state of suppressed rage' (1993: 71).

Leidner concludes that routinization depends on multiple factors. Although the training at Hamburger University is important, it operates alongside close management supervision of employees (who keep them under surveillance in order to check standards are maintained), a team ethic among staff (where it becomes socially sanctionable to let down a team mate, giving them extra work to do), the need of staff for the job (they cannot easily find work elsewhere), mostly good relations between managers and employees (the latter felt mostly supported by the former) and sticking to routines was perceived mostly as the easiest way to do the job. However, Leidner also catalogued the moments when such routinization appeared to break down.

> Despite elaborate socialization and social controls, McDonald's stores do not, of course, carry out every corporate directive exactly as recommended. In the store I studied, managers did not always provide their workers with the mandated support and encouragement, crew trainers did not always follow the four-step training system, and window workers did not always carry out the Six Steps of Window Service with the required eye contact and smile. There were many kinds of pressures to deviate from corporate standards. (1993: 84)

Leidner's study provides a useful demonstration of the ways in which organizational ethnography can be utilized to analyse traditional management research questions. What the ethnographic methodology provides, which other approaches might not manage, is the detail and range of activities through which standardization is made and maintained, an understanding of the multiple locations through which standardization is achieved, an analysis of both the achievements of standardization and occasional notable failures.

Providing context

Alongside the detailed analysis of the successes and failures of routinization, there are several other useful points would-be ethnographers can take from Leidner's ethnography. In comparison with, for example, Geertz (1973; exemplar five), Leidner does not provide a context for McDonald's through observational details. Instead, she includes sections entitled 'McDonald's' and 'McFacts'. These sections outline a backdrop for following observations about the corporation. Placing the context upfront as a separate section from the observations and interview data provides an alternative style of presentation for ethnographers to consider. The ways in which the ethnographic write-up is put together are important in constituting a representation of the field, so ethnographers should not take decisions on writing-up lightly (see sensibility eight). Leidner's facts are presented as uncontested, mostly numerical representations of the organization under study. This representation suggests something of the size of McDonald's, of the extents the organization goes to in producing routinization and the impact McDonald's has on ways of life (including the number of customers who visit, how often, how much they spend and so on).

    While such a context can be a useful way of providing a backdrop to ethnographic observations, ethnographers should tread carefully. If every observation is treated sceptically and analysed through the lens of ethnographic strangeness, but introductory sections of the study simply present a mass of uninterrogated facts, the ethnographic write-up can seem a little unbalanced. Often, providing a context through the observations (such as an analysis of observations regarding the way the organization relates to itself, promotes itself, and interacts with other organizations) can provide a more nuanced ethnographic write-up.

Customers

A further area which may be of interest to organizational ethnographers is Leidner's treatment of customers. McDonald's, in common with many corporate organizations, is dependent on a steady stream of customers who can be encouraged to spend money, enjoy their experience in the organization and return to the organization at some point in the future to spend more money. However, particularly when studying an organization by becoming a member of staff, customers can be difficult to incorporate into the study. With most focus on other members of staff in the organization, how can customers' views be accessed, accumulated, gathered, organized or analysed? One means of achieving this is to collect the stories about customers from members of the organization. This can provide a wealth of interesting material on the way customers and customer relations are perceived. Leidner does this through her interviews with McDonald's staff members. However, there are other ways to consider incorporating customers into research. Although Leidner studies both corporate training and restaurant work, it would be possible to ethnographically engage with a company like McDonald's as a customer, observing the routines, rituals, expectations and so on with which one comes into contact. It may be possible to involve multiple ethnographers producing multiple accounts of customer experience in order to provide a broad view of customer experience (for more on this, see sensibility seven).

Organizational beliefs

Ethnographic studies of corporate settings have a relatively brief history. However, the history of ethnographic anthropological and sociological studies of particular settings can prove useful in considering the organization in focus. Leidner hints at this kind of approach when considering the kinds of beliefs which hold together or are common across multiple members of McDonald's staff.

> McDonald's extraordinarily elaborate training programs are designed both to teach McDonald's procedures and standards and to instil and enforce corporate values. Kroc [McDonald's founder] approached his business with a zeal and dedication that even he regarded as religious: 'I've often said that I believe in God, family and McDonald's – and in the office that order is reversed. (1993: 53)

This passage neatly draws a connection between organizational beliefs – the common shared views of organizational members and sometimes their reason for being a member – and religion, thus opening up the possibility for connecting organizational ethnography with traditions of religious ethnography and the multiple insights that the field provides in suggesting why people might become and remain members of a group. Drawing such connections between ethnographic areas of research can be an alternative way of situating the study of an organization.

What to include in field notes

Although the principle of attempting to record everything initially still holds, there are some further practical considerations I try to keep in mind when making field notes. As a basic prerequisite for future analysis, I record the date and time of ethnographic field notes (also see next section),

I make an attempt to record some details of the setting where the notes were taken, who was there and some contextual work I may have gone through. By the latter I mean that I try and keep note with what was observed, a record of the kinds of work I did to make sense of what was going on. This feature of field notes can be important for making sense of an ethnographer's developing understanding of the field. Further decisions need to be made regarding detail. For example, if an ethnographer wants to analyse the conversations of members of field settings, this will require some consideration by the ethnographer as to how such detail can be captured (one option is presented in sensibility seven). What is included and what is excluded, how the ethnographer pursues particular features of the organization to observe, and what level of detail the ethnographer manages to record need to be developed in the field. Although a member of a hi-tech corporation suggested to me recently that they use ethnographic 'cheatsheets' to guide their ethnographers through observational work, I think these are too limited to be applicable to a broad range of organizational settings.

The following excerpts illustrate some of these points (they are a detailed write-up of events scribbled down during the day). They are taken from my recent ethnographic study of recycling initiatives in the UK and were designed to figure out what households in the UK do with their waste. The first excerpt comes from my first day as a waste auditor, attempting to employ the local authority's (apparently straightforward) system for assessing recycling material left by householders for collection by the authority (the comments in square brackets are later additions I made for clarity).

Excerpt from field diary: day one

… Also confusing is the scoring system. [we are expected to give each house a score of: (1) – [recycling] box out and ready to be collected, (2) – box contaminated by incorrect material, weather, etc., (3) – box already collected, (4) – box not out, (5) – box not by kerbside, within a metre of kerb.] Although only 5 numbers there is just about infinite variety in what each number can be made to do. If a box is out, it should get a 1. But if it is just behind a gate, is this a 1 or a 5 (not by kerbside)? R [recycling manager] said in some places pavements are too narrow to put boxes out so they get a 1 from me, but do they get the same from [other] crews? And if a box is halfway back down a drive, is this a 1 or 5? Also if a box has paper on top, and is out, it should get a 1. However, what if there are things hidden beneath such as cardboard or plastic [which cannot be collected for recycling]? Should it then be a 2 (box contaminated)? Do I have time to check each box? As decisions have to be made really quickly to stay ahead of [i.e. not delay] the crew I try and apply my scoring relatively consistently, but this is very tricky. Not all pavements are the same width so in some streets I think residents should

have made more of an effort in putting the boxes out and so I give them a 5. Is this fair? Also it turns out some people stack cardboard next to their box – do they expect this to be collected and so should I give them a 2? Or is it rubbish and should I just focus on the green box and give them a 1? This is very confusing this early in the morning.

In the next excerpt we can see how quickly my concerns and deliberations over appropriate scores for recyclable materials declined in line with organizational expectations that I should get the job done quickly:

Excerpt from field diary: day two

In [this particular part of town] the most common score is 4 – box not out. This makes my job relatively easy. If I can't quickly see a box anywhere it is a 4. It is always possible that there is a box slightly hidden which would be a 5 (box not at kerbside) but I don't have time for such discrimination [as it will slow down the collectors who want to go home].

I used these notes to provide (one small part of) an analysis of the complexities of recycling and the likelihood of a mismatch between recycling collectors who want to get the job done quickly and the local authority who only want recyclable material collected. What the notes demonstrate is how rapidly I took on the rationale of those employed to collect recyclable material, the ways in which the strange became familiar and the usefulness of my initial confusion for highlighting the complexity of the system. It was at this early stage of the research that I was most able to play the role of acceptable incompetent and ask the local authority why they operated this system.

How to organize observations?

More will be made of the work required to translate field notes into analysis in sensibility eight. However, there are some basic principles which ethnographers can adhere to in collecting and collating field notes in order to make that writing more straightforward. First, ethnographers can organize their field notes in such a way that they make sense when it comes to analysis. Traditionally, ethnographers use a diary format (see previous excerpts) for collating field notes, organizationally structured by day and time of day. This makes for a relatively straightforward means to make field notes available for analysis. Ethnographers could also consider organizing notes in line with sections of the organization under study or in line with organizational members or according to field-site (if it is a multi-sited study). Second, I always find it useful to review notes and try to figure out possible ways of organizing them while still in the field. In this way, current observations can be understood in relation to previous observations and sometimes gaps in observational material can be made more apparent. Third, ethnographers can apply scepticism to their own field notes, asking whether or not field notes are useful, what kind of study can be made from the field notes, what other potential ways there might be for organizing notes from the field? This kind of sceptical interrogation of the organization of notes can be important for ensuring that time spent in the field is utilized fully.

Feeding back observations

In the preceding sensibilities (see sensibilities three and four) it has been suggested that the relations developed between the ethnographer and the organizational field-site can be a useful focus for assessing the ongoing development of research. Ethnographers can utilize relations struck up in field-sites to explore a variety of ways of feeding back observational material to organizational members. This can be useful as a means to assess the validity of the material for organizational members (do they make sense of the organization in the same way as the ethnographer?), to get organizational members talking (by provoking interest in the ethnographer's partially external view of the organization), and this can be used to develop further ethnographic research (things members say about the organization in response to a presentation of ongoing ethnographic work can say much about emic views of the organization; see sensibility four for more on emic and etic criteria). There are several different options available for ethnographers to feed observational data back to organizations. First, ethnographers can straightforwardly engage in conversation with members of the organization and test out various ways of understanding the organization. This is normally informal and on a small scale. Second, ethnographers can negotiate an opportunity to present some initial ethnographic observations during a meeting with members of the organization. Presenting observations at some time during the ethnography can be an important way of getting further feedback from members of the organization on the ethnography. This can help in fostering trust between organizational members and the ethnographer (see sensibility four). Third, ethnographers can negotiate an opportunity to present the results of the ethnography to the organization. This might be more formal and final and less focused on gaining feedback which might contribute to the study. Such a presentation can be discussed as early as the access negotiation stage and may be written into the ethnographic strategy. More detail on the content of these types of presentation will be offered in sensibility eight. In discussion of the next sensibility, we will engage with ways in which ethnographers can supplement their standard field observations.

Recommended reading

Garfinkel, H. (1967) *Studies in Ethnomethodology* (Prentice-Hall, Englewood Cliffs, NJ)

Lofland, J. (1971) *Analyzing Social Settings: A Guide to Qualitative Observation and Analysis* (Wadsworth, Belmont, CA)

Sanjek, R. (ed.) (1990a) *Fieldnotes: The Making of Anthropology* (Cornell University Press, New York)

7

▷▷▷▷▷Sensibility Seven
Supplementing

Introduction

Under the auspices of preceding sensibilities we have covered a great deal of ground relating to issues of observation and participation in organizational settings. In this sensibility I will suggest that a further way in which ethnographers can navigate their way through research is to take on the possibility of supplementing their observational work. Why would ethnographers want to supplement forms of participation and observation? It may be that there are locations within the organization under study which are not accessible to the ethnographer and so some other technique may be required to elicit views from members of the organization on those areas. Alternatively, it may be the case that some members of the organization are less involved in the ethnography than other members so their views may be sought. Instead, there may be particular members of the organization who are understood to be very useful informants, in which case it can be important to give those informants the chance to talk at length outside the usual confines of their day-to-day work in the organization. These are just a few of the kinds of notable absences that ethnographers may note during their research. Supplementation involves ethnographers continually considering whether or not there are notable absences in their ethnographic research, what might be a suitable means of engaging with those absences and what kinds of issues might be raised by those means. The discussion will focus on six forms of supplementation which I have found to be broadly compatible with ethnographic observation: interviewing, virtual ethnography, visual ethnography, documentary analysis, ethnographic diaries and using ethnographic teams. The discussion will conclude with an analysis of the grounds for not supplementing.

Interviews

Within the social science methodology literature there are whole texts devoted to the subject of interviewing (see, for example, Rubin and Rubin, 2004) and texts devoted to ethnographic interviewing (see, for example, Spradley, 1979; for a summary, see Sherman Hayl, 2001). This section will offer a brief introduction to the issues involved in doing interviews and combining interviews with a more traditional ethnographic focus on forms of participating and observing.

Why interview?

In the course of research, ethnographers may find that there are particular places or people in the organization under study whose activities are unclear or inaccessible to observation or there may be informants who seem to offer the potential for particularly interesting or informative accounts of organizational activity. Each of these concerns might recommend interviews as a form of supplementary activity. The ethnographer will need to decide whether or not these areas will ever be available for observational research and how compatible interviews will be with observations already completed (see 'Types of interview' section below).

Who to interview?

In sensibility four I suggested that ethnographers can strike up relations with key informants (although these relationships can be problematic). One option for integrating the views of key informants into research is to interview them. In this way, the informants are offered the opportunity to give a lengthy and detailed account of their views, which can form a backdrop for understanding other aspects of their observed activity (see Whyte, 1955; exemplar three). Alternatively, interviews can be used precisely because members of some organizational settings are particularly difficult to observe or their observable activities are less than clear (see exemplar thirteen and Morrill's (1995) interviews with CEOs whose day-to-day activity is difficult to straightforwardly observe). The same holds for Becker's (1973; exemplar twelve) study of marijuana users, which was mostly based on field conversations as interviews.

Types of interview

Interviews can range from structured, formal interviews where the researcher has a pre-prepared list of questions which they will follow, to unstructured, informal interviews (or field conversations) where the researcher may have a guide prepared, but during which the researcher may follow some points more closely than others, may choose to interject their own personal views and so on. In between these two forms of interviewing are semi-structured interviews, which usually involve the researcher having a set of questions or themes, but these are not slavishly followed (for more on these different types of interview, see Fielding and Thomas, 2001). Structured interviews in general are quicker and provide information which is comparable (as the same questions are asked). Less structured interviews are slower and data is less comparable but they are not so dependent on a set of questions designed by the researcher. In ethnographic terms, less structured interviews fit more comfortably with the imperative to explore a setting through the understanding developed by members of that setting.

A decision needs to be taken to interview in the ethnographic setting, while continuing to operate in the organization, or to separate interviews from daily activity either in a separate room away from daily organizational activity or away from the organization altogether. Unstructured interviews can operate something like a focused conversation (Spradley, 1979). These are useful for ethnographers attempting interviews in the field. Ethnographers have the opportunity to focus conversations in the field around particular themes on which they wish to discover more detail. These types of 'interview' are difficult to record (if they are to be kept as more or less natural conversations) and sometimes difficult to manage (in terms of keeping the interviewee on the same focus as the ethnographer wishes to develop). Organizing a more formal time and place (either inside or outside the organization) for an interview can make recording and focusing more straightforward. It does not mean, however, that such interviews have to be more structured. Often, for example, ethnographers can ask interviewees to talk at length about their working life or experiences in the organization, or their histories of engagement in the workplace (for more on histories, see Jorgensen, 1989). This kind of semi-focused interview may produce a great deal of information outside the scope of the study, but may also provide much in-depth data on issues that are unexpectedly relevant for understanding the setting.

Choosing a more structured interview approach may be quicker, but may provide information less straightforwardly compatible with ethnographic research. If, for example, the researcher's aim is to provide a representative sample of hundreds of factory workers' views on workplace conditions, this may be more straightforwardly accomplished through structured and comparable interviews, but more work might be required to integrate such data with ethnographic observations of such factory work. Such structured interviewing might require assumptions on the researcher's part as to the relevance of a particular set of questions and may be less focused on organizational members' own methods for making sense of what goes on.

How to interview?

There is no single guide or set of instructions that can prepare interviewers for the variety of interview situations in which they might become involved. Spradley (1979) offers a guide to the types of question ethnographic interviewers might ask. Spradley outlines descriptive questions (which simply involve asking for more detail on a particular subject), structural questions (such as, 'can you tell me how organization x operates?') and contrast questions (such as, 'what is the difference between middle managers and CEOs in organization x?'). Spradley suggests that interviewers should not be worried about expressing ignorance of a particular subject or asking to go back over a previous topic. Furthermore, Fielding and Thomas (2001) suggest that interviewers can help guide interviewees through prompts, forms of encouragement (such as expressions of interest) and through restatements (repeating what the interviewee has said as part of the next question). Also, as we have already discussed, interviewers can devote time to developing either an interview schedule (for structured interviews where a series of questions will be repeated across interviews) or an interview guide (for less structured interviews where the interviewer may use a set of themes in an attempt to shape a conversation).

Perhaps the clearest way to demonstrate the art of interviewing is to offer an example. In the preceding sensibility I discussed some recent ethnographic research I had completed on recycling. Having spent time with the local authority responsible for waste collection and disposal, and having spent time going out with waste collectors, I had plenty of detail on the organizational aspects of recycling. However, I knew little of householders' views and activities in relation to recycling. I chose to interview householders because they seemed to be notably absent from the study and it appeared difficult ethnographically to become a member of several different households. I selected households to interview geographically, broadly representing different demographic aspects of the city in which I was working. As my aim was to discover something about the kinds of things householders in the city thought about waste and recycling, I decided to use unstructured interviews. I produced a guide to focus these interviews (it included themes which could be further explored, such as 'take me through a typical week of the kinds of things you recycle'). This produced a series of conversations broadly compatible with other observational data.

Problems with interviewing

Problems associated with interviewing are similar to problems associated with doing ethnographic research. Questions of researcher influence, of becoming too closely involved with research subjects, the time and cost of interviewing, epistemological issues (such as how can we know that what is said actually relates to a person's activity) along with the gender, ethnicity, age and background of the interviewer each require careful management

(Burgess, 1984). This similarity of problems actually lends further compatibility to interviews and more traditional forms of ethnographic research. The types of data accumulated through unstructured interviews and observations require similar careful handling.

Virtual ethnography

In recent years many ethnographers have situated their research in online, electronic or virtual settings. Many of the issues involved in doing virtual ethnography are covered in the work of Hine (2000; exemplar ten). In addition, we should also note that other researchers in the area of virtual ethnography (or cyberanthropology as it is sometimes termed) have discussed issues of online objectivity, research strategies, reflexivity, field relations and data capture (summarized in Beaulieu, 2004) and issues of complexity and movement (Wittel, 2000). However, what are the issues involved in using virtual ethnography to supplement forms of traditional 'offline' ethnography? With increasing amounts of organizational activity seemingly focused on internet communication, virtual ethnography can contribute in a variety of ways to organizational ethnography. First, initial contact with an organization (see sensibility three on locations and access) can often occur through a website. Ethnographers should recall that the ways in which an organization is first encountered, the face the organization portrays to the outside world, can be an important constitutive element of an organization's identity. Ethnographers should carefully note their sense of the organization on first contact. Second, if first contact with the organization is made through some other means, an organization's website can still be analysed in much the same way as its other forms of documentation (see 'Documents' section, below). What does the website tell us about the organization? What information does it incorporate? What forms of communication with the outside world does it invite? How does this material connect to what we observe as ethnographers inside the organization? Third, ethnographers might pay attention to an organization's internal communications platform, such as an intranet. Intranets can provide a further virtual forum through which all kinds of organizational activities occur, from the publication of a meeting's minutes, through organizing work social activities, to offering profiles of organizational members. Intranets may provide a rich comparative source of activity for offline organizational activity.

Exemplar Ten

C. Hine (2000) *Virtual Ethnography* (Sage, London)

The internet has become a pervasive reference point for organizational activities. Engagement with the internet can range from an organization's primary point of contact with customers, through to a location for innovative forms of marketing. Hine's study provides a means of engaging with the internet ethnographically. Although other ethnographers participate in versions of ethnography of the internet, Hine's text is particularly useful as it takes methodological issues seriously. That is, for example, issues of what the internet is, how it can be ethnographically researched, and questions of epistemology, co-presence and virtual ethnographic field-sites are each given detailed consideration.

A brief summary of virtual ethnography

Hine's virtual ethnography took as its focus a topic rather than a location or a particular group or set of activities (see ethnographic strategies in sensibility one). The topic was the murder trial of a British nanny in the USA. Hine looks at the multiple websites that were constituted to support the nanny's case (and those that were not so supportive) and the ways in which the trial and the trial result were communicated via the internet. Hine used this topic to study the internet as culture (exploring the ways in which the case was discussed on dedicated websites and through newsgroups) and as a cultural artefact (the way the internet was talked about in relation to this particular case through other media, such as newspapers). The ethnography was developmental and explored successive connections that were made available through the case. In order to explore questions regarding the development of these support websites, Hine asked website owners to answer questions about what they did and why.

Why do virtual ethnography?

Hine is clear on her justifications for studying the internet ethnographically. First, she suggests that a great deal of research on the internet makes grand claims about changes across society as a whole, often linked to a particular idea of time. Thus we are told we are heading into the information age, a new era of technological exchange or a new decade characterized by revolutionary changes in the way we communicate. Second, Hine suggests that much of this research is characterized by a form of technological determinism, as if the technology once in place straightforwardly produces a set of (revolutionary) effects.

> The recipe is simple: take something with a material form; then argue that the same function can be carried out in virtual form; assume that the virtual form will (by force of its own logic) displace the material form; propose a dire threat to the industry that produces the material form and radical changes for the users of the old material form and the new virtual form. The trick depends upon stripping the material form of social significance and imbuing it with purely technical qualities. The equivalence of material and virtual form can then be declared, and the revolutionary prospects appear. (2000: 3)

In the face of such grand claims and forms of technological determinism, Hine argues that the internet requires detailed up-close study in order to look at how websites are developed, who is developing them, why websites might be developed and so on. Ethnography provides the means to get close to such developments.

> Ethnography is an ideal methodological starting point for such a study. It can be used to explore the complex links between the claims which are made for the new

technologies in different arenas: the home, the workplace, the mass media and the academic journal and monograph. An ethnography of the Internet can look in detail at the ways in which the technology is experienced in use. (2000: 4)

Principles of virtual ethnography

Hine, in common with most ethnographers writing about ethnography, suggests that there is and should be no single set of instructions on how to do ethnography. Instead, ethnography should be constituted in relation to each study and each setting being explored. However, Hine does set out ten principles for virtual ethnographers to consider. (1) Ethnographic engagement with the internet can treat use of the internet as problematic, as a question to be addressed (why, how, with what outcome, etc.?) rather than as taken for granted. (2) The internet can be conceived as an opportunity for ethnographers to explore the internet as culture and cultural artefact. (3) Virtual ethnography need not limit itself by ideas of field-site, but can explore a topic through mobile ethnography. (4) Rather than focus on a field-site, virtual ethnography can focus on flows of connective communication. (5) Boundaries (perhaps between websites, or users or virtual spaces) can then be explored through the ethnography rather than treated as taken for granted. (6) Virtual ethnography only involves occasional immersion in the field and is often fragmented temporally. (7) Virtual ethnography offers a partial account of what is going on (there may always be other ways of talking about what is going on). (8) Virtual ethnography can take mediated communication seriously. (9) Ethnographic engagement can be made in, of and through the internet. (10) Virtual ethnography is 'virtual' in the sense of being not quite (or only virtually) ethnography. The following sections will explore some of these issues in more detail.

The challenge of co-presence

Virtual ethnography poses something of a challenge for the anthropological tradition of ethnographic co-presence. What would co-presence mean in virtual field-sites? Hine argues that, although in some senses virtual ethnography is characterized by non-co-presence, the ethnographer can study the internet through engagement in the same experiences as users of the internet. That is, the ethnographer and users are not necessarily face-to-face in the same geographical location, but can be said to be in the same virtual location. Furthermore, the virtual location can be said to be the location where the users come into virtual co-presence – it is where they interact. Hine, however, suggests that her ethnography should also be conceived as 'virtual' in the sense of it being 'not quite' conventional ethnography. It is virtually an ethnography through investigation of online interaction. The boundaries between online and offline activity are blurred through Hine's requests for information from website developers about the ways in which they have constructed their websites. Although these requests are sent and responses received electronically, this is information which is not immediately available through an online environment.

> Face-to-face interaction, and the rhetoric of having travelled to a remote field-site, have played a major part in the presentation of ethnographic descriptions as authentic. A limited medium like CMC [computer-mediated communication] seems to pose problems for ethnography's claims to test knowledge through experience and interaction. The position changes somewhat if we recognize that the

ethnographer could instead be construed as needing to have similar experiences to those of informants, however these experiences are mediated. Conducting an ethnographic enquiry through the use of CMC opens up the possibility of gaining a reflexive understanding of what it is to be part of the Internet. (2000: 10)

Virtual ethnographic field-sites

Hine suggests that the field-site is something of a question for virtual ethnography. Given the absence of a sense of travel to an exotic location, given the absence of living in the field-site to gain full immersion into the setting, in what ways can virtual ethnography be said to have a field-site? Hine explores the possibilities presented by forms of multi-site ethnography (see sensibility three), in which the ethnographer moves between locations and studies the characteristics, connections, boundaries and movements made between multiple field-sites. For Hine, this approach is a useful starting point for considering virtual ethnography. However, the internet is not so neatly bounded as a multi-site ethnographic approach might suggest. Instead, Hine argues for the relevance of mobile ethnography:

> Ethnographers might still start from a particular place, but would be encouraged to follow connections which were made meaningful from that setting. The ethnographic sensitivity would focus on the ways in which particular places were made meaningful and visible. Ethnography in this strategy becomes as much a process of following connections as it is a period of inhabitance. (2000: 60)

Adaptive ethnography

Hine suggests that ethnography should always be in a process of adaptation, carried out by the researcher, in relation to the particular setting in which they are working. For Hine, her adaptations were experimental and carried out in exploratory engagement with the internet. Her approach to virtual ethnography was as much about considering ways to engage with the internet through ethnographic methods (and the advantages and issues raised by such an approach) as it was about the specific study, in which she investigated the case of the British nanny accused of murder. Hine suggests that it was not just a question of methodological adaptation where she sought to figure out ways of collecting data on the internet. The themes of the ethnography were also the focus for adaptation: issues of time and space, and authenticity and identity, became the focus for her virtual ethnography. However, Hine argues that issues of gender, of lurkers on internet sites and of the transformation of the internet through different forms of use, could each have become the focus of ethnographic study. Hine argues that ethnography (and ethnographers) needs to be adaptive in this sense, to be open to the possibility of change, new directions, new ways of engaging with the field of study and new themes for exploration. In this way ethnography is always partial as there is always the possibility of further studies, forms of engagement and questions which can be asked.

Visual ethnography

Attempts to engage with visual aspects of field-sites has a long tradition in visual anthropology, focused mostly on film (and more recently video) and photography. Anthropologists have used camera equipment in attempts to capture visual records of field settings and bring those visual materials 'back home' for analysis. However, visual anthropology has been associated problematically with the idea that a film straightforwardly 'tells the world as it is' (for a discussion, see Rory, 1996; Grimshaw, 1997, 2001; Ruby, 2000; Ball and Smith, 2001), as if anthropological films simply picked up parts of the world and replayed them elsewhere. Visual anthropologists, along with other social scientists such as ethnomethodologists (for a summary, see Mondada, 2003), have more recently moved to actively discuss exactly what films can tell us about a particular setting. Pinney (1992), for example, suggests that film can be an overpowering medium, with the combination of visuals, image selection and commentary forming a difficult source to counter. To address such issues, Martinez (1992: 134) argues that fairly open films that present a range of ideas rather than a fixed narrative can 'empower viewers by allowing them spaces to negotiate meanings in a more dialogic, interactive way'. The problem then becomes how should films, for example, be left open to interpretation? Pink (2001: 138) suggests that 'video is not simply a "data collecting tool" but a technology that participates in the negotiation of social relationships'. In this sense, visual data from the field is similar to field notes (in that field notes can be thought of as reflexively engaged in the business of making sense of a particular field-site) and requires all the careful treatment, analysis, consideration and questioning afforded to that material (see sensibility two on knowledge claims and sensibility six for more on the treatment of field notes).

Many visual anthropologists are engaged in producing visual accounts to be shown to audiences. What challenges might the ethnographer face in using visual methods to supplement more traditional ethnographic research? First, many of the same problems arise. Ethnographers should not assume that a video straightforwardly tells a factual account of what has gone on in the organizational setting. Videos are open to numerous interpretations (Livingston, 1987; Neyland, 2004) and require careful handling so that readers are informed of the ways in which the video has been collected and analysed. Second, video and photography can quickly begin to involve the collection of masses of data. Ethnographers might need to assess, prior to entering into visual methods, why they might want to capture videos or photographs. For example, it might be the case that a particular area of organizational activity (in exemplar eight, how users might use new equipment; see Suchman, 1987) requires the kind of close attention that the repeat playing of a video can allow. Third, ethnographers need to think carefully how visuals can be used for analysis. It is still the case that most ethnographic outputs are textual, hence ethnographers will need to think about how videos, for example, fit into such an output. Videos and photographs might contribute background information, be a source of information to be frequently replayed during analysis or provide material to use during presentations of the ethnography.

Documents

Forms of documentary analysis have a long and noble tradition in the social sciences, being traceable through the works of Durkheim, Marx and Weber (for a brief summary, see Macdonald, 2001). Organizations also continue to produce texts at a rate, defying the possibility of the paperless office (Sellen and Harper, 2001), in addition to producing an ever-increasing number of electronic texts (see 'Virtual ethnography' section above). In seeking to supplement organizational ethnographic work through documents, several questions need to be addressed. First, what are the types of document available within the organization and what can these types of document usefully tell us about the organization? Burgess (1984) highlights differences between primary and secondary sources (documents produced at the time for the time and documents produced which reflect on those times), public and private documents (for example, newspaper reports or internal company memos) and solicited and unsolicited documents (provided for research purposes or not). Each of these distinctions can be useful for organizing collected documents. However, second, alongside typologies for organizational documents, how easily available are these documents? Some documents may only be available to be read, some may not be accessible at all, some may attain a mythical status due to their apparent absence (in an ethnography of university strategy documents, I found that in one university a strategy committee had spent five years not producing a strategy; Neyland and Surridge, 2003), while other documents are straightforwardly collectable from the internet. The accessibility of documents might suggest something regarding their use and value in the organization. Due to the mass of organizational documents that are sometimes available, ethnographers may have to make decisions over whether or not to collect available documents and how such documents could be organized (on first entering a field-site I have always found it best to collect everything and discriminate later). Third, ethnographers might need to assess the validity, authenticity or credibility (Macdonald, 2001) of the documents that have been collected. Ethnographers may have to do some detective work within the organization to figure out the provenance of particular documents. 'Authenticity' should not be considered an absolute determinant of the value of a document; a 'fake' document can be an interesting organizational object (such as false passports in airports) and a 'genuine' document which no one ever notices or ever uses can also be of organizational interest.

Having collected a body of documents, ethnographers might then be faced, fourth, with the question, how should they be analysed? A straightforward ethnographic means of analysis is to simply follow the ways in which a document is used in the organization (see exemplar one). This approach emphasizes the ways in which documents are made to make sense through work in the organization. An alternative approach is to analyse the content of documents. For example, media sources are often analysed by social scientists in order to reflect on the ways in which the structure of a document provides an understanding of a text. Lee (1984), in analysing newspaper stories of Hell's Angels, suggests that the newspaper texts provide an order through which readers can discover who the innocent victims and evil doers are in the story. A similar approach is taken by Smith (1993), who investigates the ways in which one young woman is textually positioned as being mentally ill. This type of approach to documents is known as textual analysis. The basic premise of textual analysis is disarmingly simple: the analyst should look at a text and provide a reading of the text (that is, what story the text is telling) and then assess why that reading is possible (that is, what elements of the text – titles, phrases, quotes, etc. – recommend that sort of reading). I have found it particularly useful to try these forms of analysis with groups of students who are asked to provide a reading and then account for why that reading should be followed as opposed to another. This kind of analysis can be performed on a range of organizational documents, such as promotional material which attempts to convey a sense of organizational identity (even an organization's website is useful for this), or meeting agendas that try to organize the way in which meetings will operate, or reports which attempt to persuade readers of a particular set of arguments. I have found supplementing observation and participation through documentation a useful way to provide a backdrop to observations, to analyse features of organizational identity and to follow ways in which particular bits of information are used in the day-to-day lives of organizations. The problems involved in documentary analysis are the mass of potential sources which could be collected, how these can be clearly linked to observational activity, and the ways in which an ethnographer's reading of a document may or may not match up with the ways in which those documents are used on a day-to-day basis in the organization.

Diaries

Diaries provide a further means for supplementing ethnographic research. Although other people's personal diaries have formed the subject of social science analysis (see Burgess, 1984; Hammersley and Atkinson, 1995), I am only focusing here on what I term 'participants' diaries'. These are diaries given to participants in the research to record their daily or weekly activities. Burgess (1984) suggests that diaries were useful in a classroom setting because teachers (and presumably students) did not always feel comfortable with the presence of another adult. Burgess gave teachers an unstructured diary in which they could note down their thoughts with a brief suggestion of the kinds of things they should record (this was mostly a form of encouragement to write the detail of their actions): 'I used diaries to get access to events in classrooms. Here I asked teachers ... to keep diaries of what occurred within their classrooms' (1984: 129). An alternative here would be to provide a structured day-by-day diary with more detailed instructions on the kinds of things to write down. However, Burgess was interested in spontaneity, detail and a chance to explore what teachers thought and did. Burgess eventually collected diaries and interviewed participants based on their diary entries.

This approach to diary entry might be particularly useful for giving participants a clear voice in an organizational ethnography (by using their words), getting to know what a range of participants do on a day-to-day basis over a period of time and for providing a detailed backdrop for ethnographic observational work (some of the observations can make sense through the diaries). Diaries provide a further way through which members of organizations, whose activities might not be immediately accessible for observation, can be brought into the research. The problems with such diaries are giving people sufficient encouragement to write, compiling information across a range of different responses to the diary exercise, and the need to figure out if the researcher's understanding of the diary entry matches that of the diary's author.

Ethnographic teams

A further way in which ethnographers might supplement their observations is to engage a team of ethnographic participants and observers. This appears popular in corporate uses of ethnography. For example, Arnould and Wallendorf (1994: 486) suggest that 'in conducting participant observation, access to different domains of meaning is fostered by including research team members with varying demographic profiles'. They suggest that mixed gender teams of ethnographers often provide a broader range of understandings of a particular topic (such as in their research on preparations for Thanksgiving). My own experiences of corporate organizational ethnography bear this out. One hi-tech corporation suggested to me that it is 'best' to use teams of ethnographers to do the observational work and a more select group of experienced ethnographers to analyse those observations. Such an approach to supplementation raises problems regarding the ways in which one ethnographer's observations might be compiled with another's, why one ethnographer should have better insights than another (and what would count as 'better') and why multiple sets of perhaps quite shallow observations are regarded as providing more insights than one set of in-depth insights.

In my own research, I was recently involved in carrying out ethnographic research on the organization of airport terminals (Neyland and Woolgar, 2005). I successfully negotiated access to airport check-in areas, departure areas and security, and this provided me with a great deal of insight into the spatial organization of these areas. I then engaged in numerous field conversations with members of the organizational setting (such as the terminal managers). There remained a notable absence: the passengers. What did they make of the airport? How did they understand the airport's space? I asked keen students at the university where I teach ethnography to provide me with an ethnographic account of their next trip through an airport (being an international student body, this was relatively straight-forward). This provided me with a range of detailed observational material. In order to avoid the same problems I had noted with the hi-tech corporation's approach, I got as many of the students as possible to take part in compiling and analysing their airport ethnographies. This enabled me to supplement my own observations, employ a team of ethnographers, but avoid problems I might encounter with simply imposing my views on other ethnographers' observations.

Summary

It is frequently assumed in the methodological literature (for a discussion, see Macdonald, 2001; and sensibility eight) that the accumulation of a broader variety of data is necessarily advantageous for research. However, there is a tension here between collecting an ever-broadening range of types of data and failing to provide sufficient depth to any particular area of the research. To do some observing and then some interviewing and then some visual analysis and then some virtual ethnography might lead to the development of a study where no particular part of the research offers an in-depth analysis of the organization. On occasions, an in-depth analysis of a specific feature of organizational activity can be more useful than an analysis which briefly touches on several aspects of the organization, each requiring a different methodology. I have always found that further methodological engagement (such as the use of interviews) raises additional methodological considerations (such as questions of epistemology and researcher influence) and further complexity in how to integrate data into analysis (attempting to draw together insights from observations and interviews can prove complex, with each providing quite different types of data; see sensibility eight on writing). I have always placed the emphasis in ethnographic research on the possibility rather than the necessity of supplementation. Much of what is ethnographically interesting might be engaged through traditional ethnographic means. As Emerson, Fretz and Shaw (1995: 140) remind us in doing ethnography, interviewing, for example, 'is not the primary tool for getting at members' meanings. Rather, the distinctive procedure is to observe and record naturally occurring talk and interaction'.

Recommended reading

Banks, M. and Murphy, H. (eds) (1997) *Rethinking Visual Anthropology* (Yale University Press, New Haven, CT)

Macdonald, K. (2001) 'Using Documents', in Gilbert, N. (ed.), *Researching Social Life* (2nd edn, Sage, London), pp. 194–210

Spradley, J. (1979) *The Ethnographic Interview* (Harcourt, Brace, Jovanovich Publishers, New York)

8

▷▷▷▷▷Sensibility Eight
Writing

Introduction

The discussion of this sensibility will follow on from preceding sensibilities on observing and participating and supplementing ethnographic observations, by focusing on how to translate ethnographic material into a written ethnography. Peculiarly, 'ethnography' refers to both the methodology (going out and doing ethnography) and the written text (the ethnography). This might begin to highlight the importance of writing in ethnography. Unlike quantitative and some other qualitative research, where data might be analysed and then written up, ethnography involves analysis through writing to a much greater degree. Through organizing the writing and doing the writing of ethnography, much of the ethnographic 'analysis' is completed. However, it should not be assumed that ethnographic writing is simply the end point of fieldwork. Ethnographers can be continually involved in the possibility of writing while doing fieldwork. That is, ethnographers can spend time with their observations while doing fieldwork, figuring out possible ways in which field notes can be organized, arguments structured and points made. Ethnographers may also reflect on possible problems with writing while still doing fieldwork, asking questions of the completeness of their data. In this sense, writing can hang over fieldwork like a dark shadow, raising questions such as: What on earth am I going to say about this organization? How am I ever going to organize all these observations into a coherent ethnographic text? How can I draw together all the different parts of my ethnography?

I have always found such questions useful for orienting my fieldwork and developing a particular writing sensibility for each ethnographic study. By the latter I mean that there are a variety of different styles of ethnographic writing, different ways of making claims about ethnographic material and different ways of organizing ethnographic texts (the exemplars begin to hint at this stylistic variety and sensibility two, on questions of knowledge, introduces some of the arguments on the kinds of claims ethnographers make about their data). In this discussion we will start by looking at ways in which ethnographic material can be organized in order to portray a particular field-site. Second, I will suggest that situating the organization is a particularly important and complex feature of ethnographic writing. Third, we will engage with the difficult question of ethnographic ownership: does the text belong to the ethnographer, the reader or the members of the organization studied? Fourth, we will look at ethnographic writing about writing and I will suggest that reflexivity is an important consideration in producing an ethnographic text. Finally, the discussion will conclude with an assessment of the kinds of conclusions ethnographers can make.

Translating observations into ethnographic text

Ordering notes and supplementary material

The primary and most complex feature of ethnographic writing is to translate ethnographic material (field notes and supplementary data) into an ethnographic text. In order to achieve this translation, ethnographers usually carry out a form of indexing. First, ethnographers need to organize their material into a coherent form. This might involve going through their field diaries of observations to make sure they make sense, transcribing interviews (if they have carried out interviews) and organizing any documents they have collected so that they make sense (that is, the ethnographer understands where they came from and what organizational role they played). Second, ethnographers then have to go through a laborious process of searching through field notes and other data again and again and again (some ethnographers I have spoken to even advocate sleeping with their field notes in case they wake in the night with an idea). My own approach to field notes has always been to try to produce possible themes for the notes while still in the field. I have then tried to test out these themes while still in the field to see if they 'fit' with my continuing observations of the field. I have then attempted to organize my observations into this scheme of themes. Third, ethnographers are presented with problematic material. What to do with material that doesn't fit the themes? Such problematic material can be used to reconsider the themes (are new themes required? Do the current themes seem reasonable?), can be ruled out of an ethnographic write-up (an ethnographer will only ever be able to include in an ethnographic text a small percentage of material collected), or can be managed (for example, they may be used as footnotes which provide counter examples to the main analysis). Fourth, the themes require further interrogation. What sub-themes might be usefully incorporated under themes? What can be said about each theme? What do the themes represent in terms of providing an argument, analysis or depiction of the organization? Also, the themes can be presented to members of the organization under study to ask what they make of the themes (see 'Whose ethnography is it?' section below).

For Spradley (1980), ethnographic argumentation involves ethnographers using the particular to illustrate the general. That is, through building up a specific series of observational incidents, ethnographers can then produce a broader argument about the type of activity that is being presented. Themes, then, can be used as the headings under which a mass of observational data can be presented as evidence to back up an argument made under that heading. For example, in my recent ethnographic research on recycling (see sensibility six for more detail) I amassed a great deal of observational material on the complexities of the accounting system the local political authority used to assess householders' recycling activities. This became a theme under which I could draw together and further organize the observational data (into sub-themes such as problems encountered by householders, problems encountered by recycling collectors, defiance from the local political authority, and so on). Analysing these themes and the evidence which could be placed under each theme led me to produce the argument that such accountability systems were problematic for accumulating knowledge (in this case, about householder activity which the local political authority sought). The argument moved from the particular (for example, the numerous examples of recycling collectors' activity) to the general (an argument about the problems of accountability systems). However, producing such an argument can be problematic.

Producing an argument

Producing an argument through an ethnographic text is primarily achieved through using ethnographic material as evidence. However, the production of an argument is not straightforward. Hammersley and Atkinson (1995: 240) argue that '[t]he world does not arrange itself into chapters and sub-headings for our convenience'. This is a point also made by Law (1994: 31), who suggests that '[w]riting is work, ordering work'. According to Clifford (1986), ethnographic writing is just one example of such ordering. For Clifford, 'what appears as "real" in history, the social sciences, the arts, even in common sense, is always analyzable as a restrictive and expressive set of social codes and conventions' (1986: 10). According to Clifford, ethnographic texts involve context (drawing from or creating a social order for the text), rhetoric (drawing on expressive conventions), institutions (either within or against which the ethnography is situated), contain generic features (texts are recognizable as a type of ethnography), politics (including contests of authorial responsibility) and involve history (how these features are understood as changes over time). So what kind of ordering should ethnographers do?

127

EAGLE LIBRARY
The University of Bolton
Eagle Campus

Arguments can be ordered to provide an ethnographic text that is useful *for* an organizational setting (see exemplar one). They can be designed as an insightful ethnography *of* an organizational setting (see exemplar seven), or to introduce a new set of methodological questions (see exemplar ten), question an existing methodology or body of knowledge (see exemplar four), and so on (also see sensibility two for more on argumentation). An important aspect of such ethnographic writing is making choices about how to illustrate the membership of an organization (for example, as a hierarchy in exemplar three, or as developing over time, as shown in exemplar twelve). These forms of argumentation and representation raise epistemological concerns.

The epistemological issues of ethnographic argumentation

Becker (1998: 9) refers to Geertz's view on ethnographic writing as a 'grand contraption'. Such a view suggests ethnographic writing is a mechanism for bringing together a variety of things: field notes, supplementary material, arguments predicated on ethnographic material, connections with other ethnographic texts and connections with other research more broadly. However, the contraption is not straightforward; there are a variety of ways to do the work of drawing things together and each of these ways involves particular epistemological standpoints. For example, Van Maanen (1988) identifies three approaches to writing: realist tales which involve the collection and retelling of events as they have happened; confessional tales which involve elaborate articulations of what people have said has happened (including the ethnographer); and impressionist tales which involve a creative articulation of the field through expressive texts which might draw their allusions widely (for example, making connections with poetry and other art forms).

The three styles of writing carry with them epistemological considerations. Does the world straightforwardly exist independently of the ethnography (realist)? Is a specific version of a part of the social world built through the representations of the text (confessional)? Can the reader be offered the opportunity to reflect on aspects of the social world provided by the ethnographer through positioning ethnographic material in a milieu of further creative works (impressionist)? We should not assume either that Van Maanen's (1988) three styles are all-encompassing. An alternative schema for applied forms of anthropology is offered by Brewer (2000), which incorporates an empiricist approach (collecting facts to inform policy), an engineering approach (identifying problems and solutions through ethnography) and an enlightenment approach (providing alternative ways of thinking about problems or alternative ways of addressing problems). Alternatively, Willis (2000) suggests approaching ethnography as a creative art. Similar epistemological questions can be asked of these approaches. One means for navigating these issues is to enter into explicit consideration of the ways in which the organization in focus will be situated and for whom the ethnography is written (this will form the focus for the next two sections).

Situating the organization

To reiterate, in building a text, ethnographers need to figure out what it is they want to say about the organization they are studying (using themes to make data coherent), how they want to put together that argument (producing sub-themes and using ethnographic material as evidence for arguments), the strength of claim they want to make through that argument (raising epistemological issues; see also the final section of this discussion), and who they want to address with that argument (see the next section). An important feature of this text-building is to decide how to situate the organization. Van Maanen (2001) suggests that organizational ethnographers no longer have the relatively straightforward job of presenting the field-site as some strange, exotic, other place. This is because

> [t]he natives of these tales are not ... the alien and exotic others of faraway lands put forth in the classic monographs of cultural and social anthropology but, rather, oddly familiar domestic others who might be our cohorts at work, our next door neighbours or even, gasp, ourselves. (2001: 233)

Exemplar Eleven

J. Orr (1996) *Talking about Machines: An Ethnography of a Modern Job* (Cornell University Press, New York)

Orr's work provides a useful example of ethnographic research into work practices. Through a detailed study of the day-to-day activities of photo-copier repair workers we see the ways in which office organizations are made and maintained, how service workers operate according to particular rationales and respond to particular situations, and are involved in particular relationships. The focus on practice is an important aspect for justifying this study. Orr argues that much research on 'work' looks at labour trends, capitalist exploitation, issues of employment and unemployment, and treats service work as predictably routine and standardized. Employing the anthropological principle of strangeness, Orr engages with 'work' as an area which requires study. He asks what constitutes work, what relations are involved in work, what moment-to-moment practices maintain work (while also maintaining photo-copiers) and looks at how moments of work are retold through stories of the field to colleagues. Such an approach resists treating the everyday activities of work as standardized and routine and instead analyses the ways in which work is actively accomplished. The form of writing moves from the particular – multiple instances of photo-copier repair – to the

129

general – the nature of work. A brief consideration of each of the principle areas of Orr's ethnography can prove illuminating for organizational ethnographers wishing to write about particular employment situations.

Work as non-rational

Orr is keen to emphasize the importance of getting close to the detailed practices of work:

> ... in common usage the word 'work' now refers to the relationship of employment much more than to either the doing or what is done, and that employment further skews our understanding of work by making what is said to be done part of a contest about reward and status ... this emphasis may omit vital elements of working practice. (1996: 148)

In place of a focus on work in the aggregate, as relating to trends, capitalism, labour forces, political movements, commodities, and so on, Orr looks at work as a moment-to-moment accomplishment. First, the daily practices (of photo-copier service technicians) form the starting point for analysis, not aggregate representations of workers or labour trends. Second, this focus is used to highlight the ways in which work (particularly in the case of service technicians) is neither routine nor standardized. Their work is characterized by multiple successive moments of decision-making about what particular problems might be, what a particular machine might represent as a problem, the relationship developed between users and the machine, the kinds of tasks the machine has been employed for, and the stories that colleagues tell in the field. Third, any particular repair can be seen as both an instance similar to other stories of repair told by colleagues (and can thus be reported to colleagues at a later date as such) or can be seen as a new or different variation on previous repairs. This moment-to-moment accomplishment of repair, the unpredictability of repair (organizations do not know when a photo-copier will break down), situating repairs within ongoing stories of other experiences in the field, and the frequent changes in technology result in repair being a non-standard, non-rationalized form of employment:

> ...individual machines are quite idiosyncratic, new failure modes appear continuously, and rote procedure cannot address unknown problems. Technicians' practice is therefore a response to the fragility of available understandings of the problematic situations of service and to the fragility of control over their definition and resolution. ... Work in such circumstances is resistant to rationalization, since the expertise vital to such contingent and extemporaneous practice cannot be easily codified. (1996: 2)

Orr's work provides organizational ethnographers with a useful example of the ways in which trends in research (such as assumptions regarding the treatment of work as an aggregate phenomenon) can be questioned through the use of detailed ethnographic observations to highlight features of employment which run counter to expectations.

Work through relationships

The repair of photo-copiers might initially appear to be a primarily technical job, often carried out by a lone service repair technician, and thus devoid of many of the social interactions conventionally at the centre of ethnographic research. However, Orr argues that the work of service repair technicians is accomplished through the building and maintenance of social relationships. First, there are relationships with other service workers. These relationships form an important component part of getting the job done. Through the discussion of stories of other repairs, service workers situate each task they complete within a range of other tasks and experiences services workers have had (see next section). Second, there are relations between technicians and customers. These relations are often characterized as slightly awkward: the technician is in the workplace because the machine has gone wrong, and getting the machine to work is not necessarily straightforward and may require calling in other technicians. The technician has the opportunity for both heroism, rescuing the customers from the perils of the copier not working, and irritant, through failure (albeit often temporary) to get the copier, the customers and the organization working again. Third, there are relations between technicians, machines, customers, the corporate entities to which they belong and the space of the workplace where the repair will be carried out. These complex and multiple relations are one feature of technicians' attempts to sustain control over the repair situation (see below). Fourth, however, the relations between technicians and machines should not be underplayed. Although a technical rather than a social relationship according to Orr, this still forms the focus for decisions regarding what tools to bring to the job, the need to display competence and the difficulties of maintaining a sense of control (see below). This technical relationship should not be seen as separate from the other relationships through which technicians accomplish their job.

Work through stories

Orr's detailed analysis of these relationships provides researchers interested in organizational ethnography with the opportunity to consider the ways in which apparently mundane and technical jobs are entangled in a range of relationships necessary for accomplishing the job. Orr argues that the relationships between technicians, machines and customers involve the building of narratives:

> The actual process of diagnosis involves the creation of a coherent account of the troubled state of the machine from available pieces of unintegrated information, and in this respect, diagnosis happens through a narrative process. A coherent diagnostic narrative constitutes a technician's mastery of the problematic situation. (1996: 2)

However, these diagnostic stories do not operate alone. Narratives diagnosing a problem with a particular machine can also feature in stories shared between technicians:

> The circulation of stories among the community of technicians is the principle means by which the technicians stay informed of the developing subtleties of machine behaviour in the field. The telling of these narratives demonstrates and shares the technicians' mastery and so both celebrates and creates the technicians' identities as masters of the black arts of dealing with machines and of the only somewhat less difficult arts of dealing with customers. (1996: 2)

Orr suggests there is a haphazard separation of stories of diagnosis (the building of narratives to form relations between technician, machine and customers) and what he terms 'war stories' which are told for entertainment or as a boast between colleagues. 'War stories' are an important feature of the development of relationships between technicians. Being able to tell a war story, as well as recognize and respond to one, is a central aspect of being and becoming a member of the community of technicians. This approach to narrative suggests one way for organizational ethnographers to approach the field setting. Orr uses organizational stories to reveal something of the characteristics of what constitutes the membership of the organization and the ways in which members display and respond to such narratives of membership.

Control

Orr's conclusion is that technicians' work is characterized by 'a drive to preserve order in one's work and to appear always to be in control of the situation' (1996: 144). Accomplishing working tasks for technicians and maintaining their identity as successful technicians involves constituting and maintaining order. This conclusion provides an endpoint for the ethnography. However, it is only one of several means available to ethnographers for concluding their research. As the other ethnographic exemplars demonstrate, conclusions can also feature further questions to be answered, a detailed presentation of a particular topic (see exemplar ten) or challenging epistemological assertions (see exemplar four).

Writing

Orr's work can usefully contribute to an organizational ethnographer's understanding of the possibilities available for writing ethnographic texts. Orr uses what he terms 'vignettes' to capture detail of the field and then provides a detailed commentary on each vignette presented.

> To preserve the flow of events and to suggest the complexity of the tasks these technicians have mastered, I first present the vignettes with minimal explanation, recognizing that the reader will find some of the detail alien. Following each vignette comes a section of commentary which includes necessary background information about the organization, the activities, and the nature of the machines. (1996: 14)

Orr's approach to writing has the advantage of incorporating into the text a great deal of uninterrupted observational material from the field. His subsequent commentary then provides an analysis of what is going on in the vignette and how this can help us understand the work being accomplished by technicians.

There are multiple options available to the ethnographer in positioning the organization. First, the organization can be presented as a particularly unique example of a phenomenon that has already been studied (in that sense, the close-to-home organizational location can still be understood as unusual, other or exotic; see exemplar twelve). Second, the organization can be presented as a normal example, representative of a broad range of similar examples (about which the ethnographers will say something different; see exemplar four). Third, ethnographers can position the ethnography as having utility for other similar types of organization (see exemplars one and eight). Each of these approaches requires the careful elaboration of a form of context. The ethnographer needs to describe the type of organization which is in focus, why this is (or is not) a typical example of that type of organization and what evidence there is for that typicality (perhaps also drawn from the ethnography). Such a presentation can draw on features discovered during the research (where members of the organization or organizational documents do work to position the organization), can use others' research (which might suggest a definition for a type of organization which can be referenced), or some other source of representation which details organizational background (such as media reports or other companies' reports). Providing such a background can begin to position the ethnography in terms of what is being said, about what type of organization, and address questions regarding the general applicability of the arguments being made.

Whose ethnography is it?

Although positioning the organization in the ethnography is important, this needs to be done in tandem with making decisions regarding ownership, responsibility and readership of the ethnography.

Ethnographers

Making suggestions that an organization is of a particular type and that claims within the ethnography should be understood as having a certain level of generalizability raise questions of the authority and responsibility of the ethnographer. Van Maanen (1988: 1) argues that ethnographic writing 'carries quite serious intellectual and moral responsibilities for the images of others inscribed in writing are most assuredly not neutral'. Furthermore, for Hammersley and Atkinson (1995: 253) 'In the construction of ethnographic texts we display implications of ethics and ideology. We display our implicit claims to authority' (see sensibility nine for more on ethics). The problem here is that often ethnographies involve a range of different participants in the study, but the ethnographer is the only voice heard in the final text. One means of dealing with this issue is to bring more voices into the text. Drawing on the work of Clifford, Hess (1989) suggests that ethnographers can incorporate multiple voices into the ethnographic text to reduce potential problems of having a single author provide a definitive account of what has happened in an organization: 'The result is a multi-authored, multi-vocal text with multiple implied readers and readings, an open text' (1989: 169). In organizational ethnography this can be achieved by drawing in members of the organization and also giving consideration to the 'authority' of the reader in making sense of the text.

The organization

Organizational members can be invited to participate in ethnographic writing in various ways. They can be offered the chance to attend a presentation of initial ideas from the ethnography, during which they will have the opportunity to feed back views on the ethnography (which may form a contribution to the final ethnographic text). Alternatively, a selection of organizational members might be interviewed during the ethnography to provide a detailed rendition for the final write-up of those members' views of the organization and the ethnography. Or some members might be invited to read a more or less final version of the ethnography to comment on (and comments could be included in an appendix). Finally, members could be invited to take an active part as co-authors in writing the text (although see the Conclusion of this book for the difficulties faced in such forms of co-authorship).

Often I have found that getting organizational members involved in such ethnographic endeavours requires some work by the ethnographer to convince members that this is a worthwhile practice. Strategies for encouraging members to take part include suggesting that the ethnography: will form a different or independent perspective (for example, those not usually heard might be given the chance to voice their views to management); will provide an expert perspective (that is, will collect together things already known in the organization, but under the terms of an accredited expert, or will provide an expert analysis of those things already known); will shed light on a different area of organizational activity of which not everyone is aware; will provide a counter-intuitive outcome (that is, will suggest that things that are taken for granted are not as straightforward as they seem); or will address a specific question.

Readers

Members of an organizational ethnographic setting form one type of reader for the ethnographic text. However, there are many more readers of such texts and the relationship between ethnographer and these readers is far less clear. Reflexive ethnographers have suggested that the reader writes the text (see exemplar four). However, the relationship between text and reader is not straightforward. As Golden-Biddle and Locke (1993) suggest, ethnographic texts are involved in various attempts to do the work of convincing readers of a particular argument through the text. They suggest that the process of convincing can be understood to involve three principal elements: authenticity, plausibility and criticality. In terms of authenticity, ethnographers appeal through their texts to readers to accept that they have genuinely been there in the field and have genuinely witnessed the events reported. Authenticity equates to being a reliable witness and can involve strategies such as providing masses of detail on everyday life, detailing the relationship between the ethnographer and the organization (including problems which arose) and emphasizing 'the disciplined pursuit and analysis of data' (1993: 595). Ethnographic plausibility, they suggest, involves attempts to convince readers that the argument which the ethnography addresses is a matter of common concern (it is a concern that the reader is invited to share). Recruiting readers can be a strategy for smoothing contestable assertions, normalizing unusual methodologies or paving the way for acceptance of unexpected research outcomes. Criticality involves ethnographic texts attempting to get readers to re-examine taken-for-granted assumptions about the plausible problem which they have just agreed to commonly recognize. Strategies for convincing through criticality involve positioning the unexpected as the valuable part of ethnography (for example, you may have recognized the rest of the ethnography as commonly held knowledge, but what about this new finding?), building dramatic tension (so that the reader to an extent knows something unusual is coming), or more straightforwardly encouraging readers to use the text to re-examine what they have taken for granted about a particular commonly held concern.

Writing about writing

In order to address the ways in which ethnographic writing might involve complex relations of authority and responsibility, Sanjek (1990b) suggests that there is a need for a kind of ethnography of ethnography. If ethnographers entered into an analysis of the way their texts were produced, this would allow readers to consider all the moves made by ethnographers in putting together their texts. Such an approach calls for a particular kind of reflexivity. We saw in sensibility two that reflexivity refers to the notion that members of a social order are continually engaged in the ongoing production of that order. Ethnographers are then engaged in participating and observing and writing about that order. Ethnographic texts are reflexive accomplishments in the sense that they are texts which produce (through providing a particular description of) a social order. What Sanjek suggests is a further reflexive orientation where ethnographers explicitly engage in an analysis of the ways in which they have produced a social order. This, Sanjek suggests, will make 'method visible' (1990b: 285) and available for consideration by readers. Readers can then make decisions about the convincing and reliable (or unconvincing and unreliable) aspects of the text.

Although there is not the space in this discussion to offer a detailed analysis of an ethnographic text, we can pause for a moment to read through again my introduction to this sensibility and look at the work done to position the reader (which is just one aspect of the ways in which texts might be involved in complex relationships of authorial power):

> In this discussion we will start by looking at ways in which ethnographic material can be organized in order to portray a particular field-site.

135

Second, I will suggest that situating the organization is a particularly important and complex feature of ethnographic writing. Third, we will engage with the difficult question of ethnographic ownership: does the text belong to the ethnographer, the reader or the members of the organization studied? Fourth, we will look at ethnographic writing about writing and I will suggest that reflexivity is an important consideration in producing an ethnographic text. Finally, the discussion will conclude with an assessment of the kinds of conclusions ethnographers can make.

What work does this text do to position the reader? It begins by suggesting 'we will start' (so readers are invited as the 'we' to take part in a journey), and then goes on 'I will suggest' (so the personal pronoun appears to demonstrate that I will take responsibility for the argument as author), before suggesting 'we will' (so personal responsibility is replaced by collective invitation), before continuing 'we will … and I will' (inviting readers once again to take part in the journey and suggesting I will take responsibility for that journey) and finishing with 'finally, the discussion…' (shifting responsibility for the final points to a neutral, objective authority). From this very brief analysis of one small aspect of the text I hope readers can see that the ways in which the text is put together involves complex features of audience-building and directing. Ethnographers should recognize that choices made in writing ethnography are important for shaping relations between the text and reader. However, none of this shaping means a great deal without the reader recognizing and taking part in that process.

Ethnographic conclusions

We have seen in this discussion a variety of issues presented in relation to writing ethnography, from ways of translating ethnographic material into an argument to the problems of authorship, readership and ownership of the text. Emerson, Fretz and Shaw (1995: 108) summarize this problem when they argue that 'members' meanings … are not pristine objects that are simply "discovered." Rather, these meanings are interpretive constructions assembled and conveyed by the researcher'. What does this tell us about the kinds of conclusions ethnographers can make in writing ethnographies? Once again, conclusions depend on whether ethnographic research is *of* an organization or *for* an organization. In the former, conclusions are often designed for a research audience. Hence conclusions might involve highlighting problems with previous research, augmenting previous research, addressing new questions or the possibility of looking at old issues in new ways. In ethnography *for* an organization, conclusions can often involve addressing a question negotiated earlier in the research, can involve a presentation of a picture of organizational activity (which may be recognizable to the organization or not), may provide new ways of thinking through issues or suggest further questions that the organization might wish to address. Often these conclusions can be produced in collaboration with members of the organization (see preceding section). In both forms of ethnographic research, ethnographers might need to think through how modest they wish to be in their conclusions and how this might fit in with organizational expectations. A modest ethnography might involve highlighting new challenges to pursue or questions to engage, while a less modest ethnography might be more directly critical of others' work (in terms of both research and work done in the organization) and use this as the basis for suggesting a more suitable alternative path. In the next sensibility we will pick up on these questions of responsibility as one aspect of ethnographic ethics.

Recommended reading

Clifford, J. and Marcus, G. (eds) (1986) *Writing Culture: The Poetics and Politics of Ethnography* (University of California Press, Berkley and Los Angeles, CA)

Golden-Biddle, K. and Locke, K. (1993) 'Appealing work: an investigation of how ethnographic texts convince', *Organization Science* 4(4): 595–616

Van Maanen, J. (1988) *Tales of the Field: On Writing Ethnography* (University of Chicago Press, Chicaco)

9

Ethics

Introduction

In the preceding sensibility of writing I argued that what gets included and what gets excluded in an ethnographic write-up, how the content is ordered and analysed, and what claims are made through the ethnography involve decisions which ethnographers need to make in navigating their way through ethnographic research. These decisions are ethical. Ethnographers have to take responsibility for what they have decided to include, exclude and the ways they have decided to represent features of the field. However, this is only one aspect of ethnographic ethics. Researchers also need to consider, among other things, types of ethnographic consent, publication, accessing sensitive organizational areas, negotiating ethics and methodological openness (Burgess, 1984). All social science research involves ethics of a kind, but due to the intensity of ethnographic field relations, ethics can be particularly important (and difficult) for ethnographers (Ellen, 1984). This discussion will engage with these ethical questions by first looking at different ways in which ethnographic ethics can be encountered. Second, we will analyse ways in which ethnographers can work through differing types of ethical system and the range of ethical questions they can encounter. Third, we will focus on one central question for the history of ethnographic ethics which has involved issues of overt or covert research (being open or not about research). Although covert research has become ethically difficult to sustain, ethnographers can still be questioned for the extent to which they manage to introduce and maintain overt methods. Fourth, the discussion will conclude with an analysis of the ways in which questions of ethics can contribute towards ethnographic writing.

An ethical typology

Ethnographers can experience ethics in at least three principal ways: ethics as rules, ethics as guidelines and ethics as an accomplishment. On most occasions I have encountered some combination of these ethical types. However, I will separate them out here for ease of presentation.

Ethics as rules

At the start of research, ethnographers should check their institutional ethical procedures (for example, their universities' ethical guidelines for research involving human subjects and check that these are up to date and in line with legislation), the ethical procedures of any professional association to which their research might adhere (such as the American Anthropology Association) and any ethical principles operated by the organization they seek to enter and research (these principles should be useful for shaping an ethnographer's approach as they offer clues about the kinds of work the organization might deem appropriate or inappropriate. Such principles are also, therefore, a potentially interesting ethnographic document; see sensibility seven). Some or all of these ethical documents might contain ethical rules. By ethical rules I refer to those kinds of ethical statements which straightfor-wardly (attempt to) determine the way research should be conducted. In my own institution, the ethics committee provides a checklist which ethnographers (alongside others doing research) should complete. The checklist asks straight yes or no type questions, such as:

10. Does the research involve the deception of participants?   YES/NO. (CUREC, 2006)

The checklist acts as a set of rules which attempt to reduce ethics down to straightforward YES/NO answers and reduce the possibility of ethics being complex, messy or confusing. If any answers fall on the questionable side of the YES/NO distinction, the researcher needs to enter into further processes (notably filling in an application to be submitted for ethical assessment). If all the answers fall on the correct side of the divide, there is no need for further action. Although this reduction of complexity might have organizational utility (if ethical complexity is reduced, so is the administrative burden of being ethical), it is not clear that ethics is always this straightforward. In the question included above, one could frequently say 'no participants were decieved', but how certain should one be? Might this change for different people during the research? Might different ethnographic projects involve more or less deception? Within the YES/NO schema, there is no space for such consideration. This has led to the development of ethical guidelines.

Ethics as guidelines

In order to cope with the possible complexity of ethics across ethnographic research, the American Anthropology Association (AAA) has drawn up a set of ethical guidelines (AAA, 2004). In place of a focus on rules which attempt

139

to restrict the possible complexity of ethics, these guidelines act as 'a framework, not an ironclad formula, for making decisions' (AAA, 1998: 1). The guidelines include avoiding harming the people and things (such as historical records), which might form a part of ethnographic research, understanding and protecting privacy (that is, figuring out what privacy means to those in a particular setting and respecting that) (see Burgess, 1984), providing anonymity and/or credit where requested, obtaining informed consent in a suitable manner (that is, consent does not have to be written, but suited to the field-site) and not exploiting research participants (see sensibility four on field relations and accusations against Whyte (1955; exemplar three; and Whyte, 1993, for a discussion of ethics) that he exploited his key informant). The AAA guidelines also suggest that ethnographers have a responsibility towards science and scholarship such that potential ethical issues are considered in advance of research, data is made available for others (when suitable) and research is conducted in a manner which does not harm the chances of future ethnographers doing research. The AAA guidelines are only one of many sets of principles, codes of conduct, guidelines or statements which may govern ethnographic research. They are a useful initial set of guidelines for ethnographers to consider as they are stringent and comprehensive and yet also flexible (see AAA, 2004; for more on these principles, see 'Ethical questions' section below). Flexibility is important for rendering guidelines suitable for the multiple situations in which ethnographic research might engage. However, flexibility can involve the ethnographer in a great deal of ethical work.

Ethics as an accomplishment

Unlike ethical rules, guidelines require interpretive work by the ethnographer. Guidelines may involve the ethnographer producing a report prior to research which sets out the ways in which the research will meet the demands of the guidelines (made suitable to that particular piece of research) and the report might require assessment by, for example, an ethics committee (according to institutional rules). Ethnographers may also need to demonstrate after the completion of fieldwork that they have met (a version of) ethical guidelines. This is a kind of ethical accomplishment; the ethnographer is called upon to demonstrate that they have understood sufficiently what the appropriate ethical considerations are for the research. However, such accomplishments are not restricted to occasions where ethics are demanded, for example, by heads of university departments. These ethical accomplishments might also feature on those occasions where there are few apparently visible ethical guidelines, for example in negotiating access to an organization which appears to have no particular policy on research. On these occasions it can be important to ask: 'What defines virtuous conduct in different contexts?' (Collier and Lackoff, 2005).

One straightforward means to provide a backdrop for such ethical considerations that I have found useful has been to quote an appropriate professional body's ethical criteria (such as the British Sociology Association or my own institution's rules) and demonstrate to the organization that my research will adhere to these criteria. This invocation of rules situates access negotiations within a professional context and is useful for accomplishing ethics at moments where there appears to be no particular ethical guidance.

Exemplar Twelve

H. Becker (1973) *Outsiders: Studies in the Sociology of Deviance* (Free Press, New York), particularly Chapters 3 and 4 'Becoming a marijuana user' pp. 41–58 and 'Marijuana use and social control,' pp. 59–78.

Becker's study of marijuana users was a key early text in the sociology of deviance. It established the need to get close to deviant subcultures in (and to some extent outside) mainstream society. Indeed, Becker suggested that his study was motivated by the absence of literature on the day-to-day detail of deviant practices. As Becker argued, 'there simply are not enough studies that provide us with facts about the lives of deviants as they live them' (1973: 166). Becker was also concerned by an absence in range of deviance studies: there were insufficient studies of different types of deviance. His study of marijuana users was important in its attempts to understand the formative social action of drug use. The study did not reduce drug use to a simplifying question of 'Why take drugs?' but instead focused on the taking of drugs, how drug users understood themselves and their actions in relation to a routine and somewhat ordered set of social activities. This may prompt readers to ponder the relevance of studies of drug use for ethnographic analyses of corporate organizations. I will claim in this summary that the means Becker uses to construct his arguments can be illuminative for studies of organizations.

Becoming a member

Becker provides one of the clearest studies of what it means to become a member of a socially organized setting. Just in the same way that an ethnographer can come to understand a great deal about an organization under study through analysis of the actions, identities, displays, knowledge and so on of the members which make up that setting, so Becker comes to understand the marijuana user through his or her movement into becoming a marijuana smoker. Becker argues that marijuana smoking does not just happen, but instead becoming a marijuana smoker involves actively participating in particular activities, coming to understand oneself and the object in focus (the marijuana) in particular ways, using certain forms of language and maintaining activities in ways that will enable marijuana use. Becker argues:

> No one becomes a user without (1) learning to smoke the drug in a way which will produce real effects; (2) learning to recognize the effects and connect them with

drug use (learning, in other words, to get high); and (3) learning to enjoy the sensations he perceives. (1973: 58)

The argument is made that marijuana users learn to feel the effects of the drug through social interaction as much as through smoking. Through social interaction, users are encouraged to smoke in particular ways, are encouraged to breath in particular ways and there is some reflection by new users on the extent to which they felt it necessary to take these ideas on board in order to feel high (so as to avoid looking inexperienced, a dumb punk or in order to look cool). Such social interaction is also involved in learning to perceive the effects of smoking where other social inter-actors might encourage the smoker to feel high, to relax, to feel the effect of the drugs. Becker argues, however, that new users still had to subsequently learn to enjoy the effects of marijuana (also through encouragement from experienced users that everything would be fine). 'In short, what was once frightening and distasteful becomes, after a taste for it is built up, pleasant, desired and sought after'(1973: 56).

Developing from initial experimentation or early or occasional use of marijuana to regular smoking, Becker argued, involved incorporating the possibility of marijuana into one's life. Thus parents or spouses, friends or employers who might disapprove of marijuana use would need to be related to in certain ways in order to maintain smoking. The user might have to work to avoid such potential disapproval when high or change those with whom they maintained regular social contact. Furthermore, given that marijuana smoking is subject to legal prohibition, users would need to handle interactions with law enforcement officers carefully and cultivate relations with marijuana sources which would not lead to trouble.

What Becker's study demonstrates is the complexity of becoming a member (as a marijuana smoker). A member's lifestyle, social relations, attitude, experiences, money, the way one understands oneself, home life and work life might each need to be reoriented towards regular use of marijuana. What can this tell us about organizational ethnography?

Organized social action
Marijuana use involves regular and somewhat routinized social action. It may not have the same characteristics as a large corporate organization, but its members relate to each other in routine ways, and activities are maintained in patterned and repetitive forms and can be studied as such. Marijuana smoking acts as a demonstration of the complex social interaction which can go into the making and maintenance of particular forms of social action. In the same way, being a member of an organization can involve orienting one's identity, language use, interactions with other members, claims to knowledge and experience in such ways as to demonstrate that one is indeed a competent member of the group. Such demonstrations are not one-off events. Maintaining such demonstrations can become an important feature of maintaining one's membership of the group under study. This is as true for CEOs as it is for factory workers on shop-floors and McDonald's employees and managers.

Deviance in organizations
A further aspect of Becker's study that might be useful for considering organizational activity is the idea of deviance. Although Becker is particularly focused upon deviance

as a subcultural activity at once partially inside and outside mainstream society (for example, being reported by the press, but not involving the majority of the population as active participants), in organizational ethnographic settings, deviance can be a more widespread phenomenon. Workers acting in ways which subtly reinterpret management prerogatives in order to generate more time, space and freedom for employees who are bored in repetitive and mind-numbing jobs is characteristic of many workplaces (from factories to universities). Indeed, it could even be that fellow employees or middle managers will place pressure on other employees to work more slowly in order that senior managers do not have raised expectations and demand more work (these forms of deviance are reported from the earliest industrial ethnographies onwards, for example in the Hawthorne studies of the 1930s, reported on by Schwartzman, 1993).

Ethics

Becker's study provides a nuanced and detailed analysis of the social basis of the making and maintenance of deviance. Translated into the workplace, such a study would raise ethical difficulties. Becker reflected on questions of ethics when discussing the difficulties of studying deviance. He identified two principle problems to studying deviance close-up. First, there were technical considerations:

> It is not easy to study deviants. Because they are regarded as outsiders by the rest of the society and because they themselves tend to regard the rest of society as outsiders, the student who would discover the facts about deviance has a substantial barrier to climb before he will be allowed to see the things he needs to see. Since deviant activity is activity that is likely to be punished if it comes to light, it tends to be kept hidden. (1973: 168)

Second, there were moral considerations:

> It is not a matter people take lightly. They feel either that deviance is quite wrong and must be done away with or, on the contrary, that it is a thing to be encouraged – an important corrective to the conformity produced by modern society. The characters in the sociological drama of deviance, even more than the characters in other sociological processes, seem to be either heroes or villains. … Both these positions must be guarded against. (1973: 175)

In studying organizational deviance (forms of action which appear to go against the guidelines drawn up by management, break the law, contravene the conventions to which particular work is expected to adhere), ethnographers should pay close attention to both these technical and moral questions. First, the technical question relates to what the ethnographer is able to observe. If there is what might be termed deviance in a workplace setting, how is that accessed by the ethnographer and on whose terms is it deviant? If the ethnographer considers that there may be more going on in a setting than they are able to view (forms of action which only a few members are entrusted with witnessing), then the ethnographer needs to consider what could be done to view these activities, what would such a view reveal, how important would viewing these activities be and would it ever be possible for the ethnographer to access such views?

143

Second, the moral question relates to what the ethnographer should do with observations which might be termed deviant? Making available detailed accounts of activities which contravene the law or guidelines of organizational expectations and conventions could lead to difficult questions for both participants in the study and the ethnographer. I recently completed an ethnographic study of speed cameras designed to hold to account drivers who broke the speed limit. I spent a great deal of time working with and talking to those regional partnerships which have the responsibility to put in and maintain such cameras. Counter to expectations, it turned out that each partnership set the cameras to a speed limit they deemed reasonable (many of which were way above the advertised speed limit). What this unexpectedly revealed was an alternative map of speed limits, of locations where drivers could drive faster or needed to pay more attention. This presented a moral question and put me in a position of responsibility whereby any publication of the data might raise questions of road safety. The detail of this aspect of the study remains unpublished. However (as this sensibility shows), issues of ethics and publications can be worked through.

Supplementation

A final point to draw from Becker's study is a note regarding his field method. Although in sensibility seven the subject of interviewing was tackled as a form of ethnographic supplement, much of Becker's data comes from conversations with marijuana users in the field. An argument could be made either way that this is a form of unstructured interviewing which takes place in a field setting or this is a form of ethnographic observation where the data comprises much talk by marijuana users of their actions. For Becker, the emphasis is clearly ethnographic: 'The researcher … must participate intensively and continuously with the deviants he wants to study' (1973: 168). This approach to observation and field conversation might be an alternative means for ethnographers to get close to forms of activity which are not easily explained by the visual alone, where the ethnographer needs to work to get participants to talk about and give an account of what it is they are doing.

Ethical questions

The preceding ethical typology initiated discussion on the types of question which ethnographers might consider in completing research. In this section I will offer a brief summary of the types of ethical question ethnographers might experience (like ethical guidelines, these should be made suitable for purpose). These questions often require a balancing between the interests of different parties (ethnographer, different members of the organization, readers, research community, etc.; see Ellen, 1984).

Consent

Although it is a common assumption among ethnographers that overt research (see next section for more on covert research) involves consent, there are a variety of forms of consent. For example, in negotiating access to an organization, those involved in negotiations will be aware of the research. The rest of the organization will still need to be informed (and then some members may decline to take part in the research). Furthermore, consent can range from signed declarations by ethnographers and organizational members to conversations in the field. Also, some participants may provide clearer consent than others (for example, O'Neill's ethnography of ambulance drivers had drivers' but not patients' consent; O'Neill, 2001).

Anonymity

Access negotiations with organizations often involve declarations that the organization and its members will be made anonymous in any report or publication. Anonymity can prove difficult where there are few organizations which match the description offered (and so its identity is clear for some readers), or where members of the organization or readers might try to figure out the identity of particular members from their description (Ellen, 1984), or where some members want credit for their contribution. What counts as appropriate levels of anonymity should be negotiated with the organization.

Publication

Ethnographers should make it clear to organizations from access negotiations onwards what the purpose is for their research in terms of publication. Where will research be published? Who will be likely to read it? In what form will it be published? Will the organization get to read it prior to publication? Understanding what counts as a viable form of privacy protection for the organization and its members can be important for establishing the basis of the research and for building trust between researchers and the researched (see Hammersley and Atkinson, 1995, for a discussion of making publications too accessible). Including organizational members as co-authors (see sensibility eight) can help.

Sensitivity

On entering an organization, ethnographers might find that there are particular areas of the organization that are treated as sensitive by members (perhaps because of the organization's own ethical concerns or because of a section's market value). These areas need to be assessed: are they particularly important for the ethnography and so worth extra access negotiations? How might they be included in the ethnography? What protection might the organization seek? A colleague recently had to sign an insurance agreement guaranteeing an organization against any loss of market share it might experience as a result of her (anonymous, academic) ethnography

145

(exemplar twelve offers more detail on the moral judgements of ethnographers). Burack (2002) suggests that the ways in which ethnographers deal with sensitive issues through the ethnographic text is an important constituent feature of the types of relations readers build with texts.

Impact

The AAA guidelines suggest that ethnographers should leave ethnographic fields open for further ethnographers to study by acting in appropriate ways (also see Hammersley and Atkinson, 1995). Addressing the questions set out in this section will help ethnographers begin an assessment of what counts as appropriate research activities. However, as the next section will demonstrate, ethnographic ethics and appropriate action have been a historic focus for concern.

Overt and covert ethnography

Covert research has formed one aspect of the ongoing history of ethnographic research. Studies of groups otherwise difficult to access have been completed by ethnographers who have immersed themselves in the field without informing those they have studied. For example, Humphreys (1975) studied male homosexuals' sexual activity in public toilets by acting as a watchman. Such covert research has been criticized for the ways in which it exploits participants (see Burgess, 1984, for a discussion). However, covert research has also been completed by organizational ethnographers (see exemplar seven, although this was tempered somewhat by talking to research participants after the completion of fieldwork). The majority of organizational ethnographies operate in an overt manner and thus sidestep this particular ethical concern. Indeed, through overt research strategies, organizational ethnographers have had the opportunity to explore field relations in more depth and use such relations to gain feedback from organizational members (see sensibility four). However, 'overt' ethnographers still need to give consideration to the extent of their openness. Through access negotiations the ethnographer may come into contact with a select number of organizational members. How other organizational members are informed of the research (by managers, by the ethnographers, prior to the research, during the research), what their reactions are to the research and how the openness of ongoing relationships in the field is managed are all important considerations for the ethnographer. The next section will suggest that managing these questions can have utility for organizational ethnography.

Ethics, representation and writing

Reporting ethical negotiations and standards in an ethnography can be an important way of communicating the reliability and professional standards of the researcher. However, ethics need not be restricted to such concerns. Ethical negotiations with an organization can reveal useful insights into the organization. Sensitive organizational areas, members' (un)willingness to talk about certain issues, concerns over publication, participants wanting credit for their contribution, among many other issues, can all contribute to the ethnographic study of an organization. It should go without saying that these issues require sensitive handling. Analysing ethical negotiations can help to emphasize their importance; ethics are not just a set of rules to adhere to or something to think about when every other aspect of the ethnography is decided. Ethics and ethical negotiations can provide further ethnographic data. Although I have argued in this discussion that ethics should not be left to the end of an ethnographic study, in the next sensibility I will suggest that exits also require much planning.

Recommended reading

American Anthropological Association (1998) *Code of Ethics of the American Anthropological Association*, available from: www.aaanet.org

Ellen, R. (ed.) (1984) *Ethnographic Research: A Guide to General Conduct* (Academic Press, London)

Ong, A. and Collier, S. (eds) (2005) *Global Assemblages: Technology, Politics, and Ethics as Anthropological Problems* (Blackwell, Oxford)

10

Exits ▷▷▷▷▷Sensibility Ten

Introduction

In the last sensibility I argued that ethics can be thought through as an ongoing series of principles which guide research conduct and in this discussion I want to suggest that ethnographic exits can be understood in similar ways. The inevitability of leaving the field at some point to write something about the field can be used to focus several sets of questions. First, do I have enough information about what is going on in the ethnographic field-site? What would count as enough? Second, what responsibilities (to my own institution, members of the research setting and those funding the research) have I built during the research and have I fulfilled these? Third, is there anything going on either inside or outside the field setting which recommend an end to my ethnographic study? These questions will be addressed by first looking at ways in which ethnographers might come to understand whether or not they have sufficient information to produce an ethnographic text. Second, we will discuss the negotiated responsibilities established between researchers and researched, highlighting the ways in which such negotiations can establish a time frame or temporal focus for research. Third, we will look at constraints imposed by the ethnographer on research. Finally, the discussion will analyse those moments where ethnographers might have to make an emergency exit from the field.

Informational sufficiency

Snow (1980) and Shaffir and Stebbins (1991b) suggest that 'informational sufficiency' (Snow, 1980: 101) is complex in ethnographic research. Snow highlights several ways in which ethnographers can come to understand that their data are sufficient for an ethnographic write-up and hence make an exit. Researchers can begin to take for granted features of the field, losing any sense of distance or scepticism regarding the activities taking place. This may be a sign that the ethnographer has to work harder to maintain distance or that every aspect of the field has become familiar, in which case it may be time to leave and revisit field notes from times when the setting seemed strange. Instead, researchers might find that they are not producing any new examples of activities to populate the themes they have produced to understand the organization. This might mean that they have sufficient information to offer a detailed rendition of each of these themes. Alternatively, researchers may have reached a reasonable level of confidence that they can now talk like an organizational member and offer a detailed picture of the actions of members. Snow (1980) also suggests that ethnographers might reach a point where they continue to feel less than confident about their observations, but find nothing new to report. I still think this can be an opportune moment for ethnographers to leave the field and such uncertainties can be reported as part of a modest ethnographic write-up (see exemplar ten). Snow (1980) and Shaffir and Stebbins (1991b) argue that these criteria are necessarily vague and ethnographers need to make their own sense of these criteria in deciding when to leave the field. This might appear to make ethnographic exits sound more or less straight-forward, and indeed Jorgensen (1989: 117) calls field exits 'routine', and Hammersley and Atkinson (1995: 122) suggest that exits are 'generally … a matter of saying goodbye'. However, in organizational ethnography, exiting is not always so easy.

Negotiating with an organization

Exits should not be left to the end of an organizational ethnography. They can be included as part of an ethnographic strategy (see sensibility one) through which the ethnographer can try to figure out approximately how long the research will take. This can be useful for access negotiations with the organization (see sensibility three) where the strategy can be used to establish the basis for the research (what the ethnographer wants to study, why, for whom this will be interesting, and so on). This can help shape the organization's willingness to allow a period of access to the organization. Although ethnographies generally operate on a longer time scale and require more lengthy access than other research methods, being clear about this time at the start of research can encourage organizations to allow access (for more on these temporal issues, see sensibility five). There are two principal means I have found useful for establishing exit strategies for organizational ethnographies. The first of these involves studying a specific phenomenon and the second involves studying a particular time frame. It may be useful for ethnographers to develop field relations in such a way that ethnographic revisits (Gallmeier, 1991; Burawoy, 2003) provide a means to expand the scope (or fill in the blanks) of ethnographic research.

Exemplar Thirteen

C. Morrill (1995) *The Executive Way: Conflict Management in Corporations* (University of Chicago Press, London)

Morrill's research attempts to ethnographically engage with the area of conflict among senior executives in corporate settings. The ethnographic aspect of this research is justified through four points. First, Morrill argues that there is a need to investigate the detail of what can sometimes be hidden aspects of corporate activity. Conflict may not be readily apparent to survey researchers, who may supply surveys to executives and receive the kinds of replies executives are keen to give at that particular moment. Second, Morrill suggests that it was important to study senior executives, as a great deal of ethnographic research focuses on lower levels of organizational activity. The suggestion is that we know little about senior executives' handling of conflicts. Third, much of the current research on executives is dominated by 'great man' accounts, which are often written by or through the executives who form the subject for the text. Such texts often portray executives as the singular driving momentum behind an organization. Alternatively, management texts are caught up with prescriptive arguments on how conflicts should be handled without much attention paid to the detail of particular instances of conflict. Fourth, Morrill suggests that ethnography is particularly suited to the study of executive conflict as executives can form social groupings of their own, located in separate sections of buildings, socializing with each other, without necessarily contacting the rest of an organization. For Morrill, they display similar characteristics to the tribes living in far-flung, exotic and isolated contexts studied by early anthropologists.

These justifications provide those interested in organizational ethnography with an opportunity to enter into an assessment of the ethnography presented by Morrill. Readers are asked to recognize the relevance and paucity of alternative texts presented on conflict, to align with suggestions that conflict can be difficult to find, and to agree that ethnography is an appropriate way to study conflict and overcome some of the apparent problems with recent management research. For Morrill:

> ....organizational conflict management often occurs in the crevices of organizational structures, hidden behind the scenes and inaccessible to macroanalyses of organizational politics or conventional survey and experimental methods. (1995: 8)

This brief summary will investigate the ways in which Morrill's study engages in a particular stylistic approach, attempts particular forms of supplementation and has an interesting approach to access and to exits.

Stylistic ethnographic approach
Morrill suggests that the style of his ethnography is realist. This may appear confusing in the sense that realism has been talked of in this book as not just a style, but also

invoking particular epistemological concerns. However, for Morrill, realism is a form of reportage, a way of presenting the results. In the methodological appendix what we find is a variety of less realist, and what Morrill terms more confessional, asides on the ethnographic study. The results are presented in a straightforward, realist way in the main body of the text as if the events reported straightforwardly occurred as reported. In the appendix readers are presented with more detail on issues of access and exits (see below), researcher influence and ethnographic writing.

Morrill chose to address the problem of researcher influence (that what was included in the text might be a concoction of the researcher, unrecognizable to subjects) by presenting research to colleagues, other academic audiences, the subjects studied and by entering into long discussions with particular subjects where the ethnographer could try out particular suppositions on the subjects. This provides a neat and coherent means to engage with the potential problem of researcher influence. It does differ, however, from alternative ethnographic strategies which might focus on incorporating more of the moves made by the researcher into the main text and argument of the book, rather than being marginalized in an appendix (see exemplar four).

In his methodological appendix, Morrill provides some detail on the writing selections made in putting together the book.

> Like every ethnographer before me, my systematic data collection and coding efforts yielded a Mount Everest of information which even before I left the field I anxiously began to scale. (1995: 253)

Morrill organized his ethnographic observations and interviews (see 'Supplementing' below) by producing an initial coding. This involved producing eight categories ranging from 'gender relations', through to 'life styles of executives' and was followed by more sub-categories. Morrill also produced a narrative architecture for each case of conflict, that set out which of the principal participants were involved in the incident, the history, roles/relationships, formal grievance schemas, threat posed to the organization by the conflict, and so on. These cases of conflict and forms of ethnographic coding provided an initial means to order ethnographic data which could then be used in writing a detailed analysis of the area (for more on writing, see sensibility eight).

Access

Morrill analyses ethnographic access as a complex series of events, relationships, times and places, rather than focusing on a single access story (as demonstrated in exemplar five). The ethnographer is initially dependent upon a close contact for establishing rapport with secretaries who control access to senior executives. However, gaining an appointment was one (difficult) thing, convincing executives to take part in the research was quite another. Morrill draws on a range of resources, from his background at Harvard, his sporting prowess (which some executives were keen to hear about), his tastes in music (which other executives deemed important), his potential role as a listener for those 'lonely' executives with no one to talk to, through to his choice of pastries when meeting executives for breakfast meetings. Morrill's portrayal of these access problems provides organizational ethnographers with a rich array of the possible ways in which access can be negotiated, deferred, managed or refused.

Supplementing

Morrill's study of conflict among executives included extensive observation and inter-viewing. When reading the study it is difficult to assess which provided more data. To term the interviews a 'supplement' to the observational material might appear somewhat misleading. However, I will use this term in order to maintain a consistency in terminology with sensibility seven. Two hundred and twenty eight interviews were conducted as part of this study, apparently ranging from 30 minutes to nearly six hours. Morrill chose not to tape record and transcribe interviews, but instead to take notes during interviews (this is perhaps slightly unusual, see sensibility seven). The interviews became something akin to ethnographic field conversations in that they featured note-taking, were often completed in the field and were (at best) semi-structured. Morrill describes his interviewing technique as adopting the position of the detective: drawing together people, things and events into suppositions which can be offered to research participants in order to generate a response. The technical term Morrill uses for this approach is 'interview by comment'.

Exits

Morrill usefully devotes some consideration to his exit from the field. He suggests that his exit involved three 'traditional' ethnographic concerns. First, he had spent a full cycle with his research subjects, as anthropologists might watch a tribe through a full season from harvest, through planting to harvest again. Second, Morrill's money ran out. This kind of practical consideration is an important feature of ethnographic research, which cannot go on forever. As sensibility ten emphasizes, practical constraints must be taken into account when planning research and possible exits. Third, Morrill suggests he reached the point where he 'had absorbed as much information as I could handle and needed to get beyond the collection and initial coding phases of the study to the write-up' (1995: 241).

Studying a phenomenon

An organizational phenomenon can provide a focus for loosely establishing the boundaries for when an ethnographer will exit the field. Ethnographers can aim to study the development of a new technology (exemplar eight), the implementation of a strategy (exemplar fourteen), a merger or other form of reorganization, or the introduction of a new system (for an example, see Neyland and Woolgar, 2002). At these points of change, organizations might be particularly sensitive to the idea of allowing an ethnographer access. However, these organizational changes also provide moments where more information on what is going on, what is working, what is creating problems in the organization might be particularly welcome. Ethnographers can use such moments of organizational change in negotiating access and a time frame for research, emphasizing how useful ethnography might be in understanding change and its associated problems. Organizational change does not set the limits for studying a phenomenon. For example, Hine's (2000; exemplar ten) work involves the study of a particular media storm around the death of a child, Harper's (1998; exemplar one) ethnography focuses on the organizational life of a document and Leidner (1993; exemplar nine) completes McDonald's staff training. Each of these focal points to some extent prefigures an appropriate exit for the whole study or an aspect of the study.

Studying a time frame

Another means for establishing the exit point for ethnography is to clearly focus the research on a specific time frame. Time frames can range from studying a set time in the lives of factory-floor workers (exemplar seven) to spending a month with recycling collectors (Neyland, Wong and Woolgar, 2006). Although these time frames are arbitrarily imposed, few ethnographers find organizations that start and stop in line with their research (for a notable exception, see Gallmeier's (1991) research on hockey players who disband and disappear from the city where they play at the end of the season). Every ethnographer needs to engage with the ways in which an organization precedes and continues beyond the ethnography. Such imposed time frames and pre-planned exit points go against some of the traditions of ethnographic research, in which ethnographers would spend large parts of their life in the field (see exemplars two, three and five). However, even these studies involved particular time constraints, as the next section will analyse.

Ethnographer constraints

The ethnographer's own constraints can provide another impetus for ethnographic exit. Even long-term, traditional ethnographic studies (such as Whyte's (1955) ethnography of street corner society) require funding. Exits have to be managed in line with such practical constraints as research funding, sabbatical research leave, or for students the constraints of the course they are studying or their supervisor's demands. Ethnographers need to take heed of these impending exits and devise their ethnographic strategies accordingly. This does not mean that one moment of exit then results in the ethnographer leaving that field permanently. Ethnographic revisits are often possible (for example, Whyte revisited street corner society multiple times as funding and time constraints enabled; see Whyte, 1993).

Exemplar Fourteen

D. Neyland and C. Surridge (2003) 'Information strategy stories: ideas for evolving a dynamic strategy process', *Perspectives*, 7(1): 9–13

I decided to include one of my own ethnographic exemplars in this book as I wanted to look in some detail at the constitution of a piece of ethnographic writing and how the process of writing can form a reflexive basis for assessing an appropriate time to exit the field. It seemed clear to me that I could have no greater insight into the process of ethnographic writing than to analyse one of my own ethnographic articles. However, this got me thinking: to what extent could I be considered the author of the text? First, it should be noted that this journal article was co-authored; interaction between co-authors was an important constituent feature of the writing. Second, the text was written for a particular kind of audience; it was written for practitioners and, more precisely, those involved in the practice of higher education. Third, taking into account the reflexive tradition in ethnography (see sensibility two and exemplar four), to what extent should the reader be accredited with making sense of the text? These three areas will be given consideration in turn after a brief introduction to the subject matter of this ethnography.

An ethnography of strategy

This article was developed as part of a three-year ethnographic study of changes in UK universities, particularly in relation to the introduction of new technological systems. A purpose of the research was to assess the extent to which an ethnographic approach to change could provide new and illuminating insights into how change occurred, responses to change, and problematic aspects of change. In this book's Conclusion I will take on the task of assessing whether or not this ethnographic approach proved useful (due to the number of different regimes of assessment in which any UK university is engaged, an assessment of the ethnographic component of this project required something like an ethnography itself). The ethnographic study involved three different IT change projects occurring at three different UK universities.

I began the ethnography by becoming a participant in several of the many committees in operation at the three universities under study. It quickly became apparent that 'IT change' did not happen in one place, at one time, that decisions were made everywhere and nowhere, and that what initially appeared to be three IT change projects could be conceived in innumerable ways. These projects appeared to present something of an organizational mess, characterized by uncertainty, unusual behaviour, odd forms of communication, bitter contests for status, determination to resist change, alongside complete disinterest or lack of knowledge about the projects from some university members apparently involved in the projects. This could be simply rephrased as an ethnographic opportunity. Very little work was required to make interactions between university members strange – all members were happy to provide their own versions of why 'IT change wouldn't work here' (each contradicting the previous version) – and my ethnographic project was welcomed with a mixture of sarcasm and laughter (many of the committees I joined welcomed me with a variation on the phrase 'we have x, y and z issues to discuss today, and we have an ethnographer joining us'. The implication seemed to be either that an ethnographer was yet another issue to take into account, or an ethnographer was hardly likely to reduce the number of issues the committee needed to consider).

After an initial run-through of meetings (each university term was characterized by regular slots for meetings, and so after one term, I had attended one meeting of each committee I had joined), my notes were dominated by mention of Information Strategy and Information Strategy Committees. These seemed to be the location where IT changes were most frequently discussed and perhaps, intriguingly I thought, most likely to happen. I joined the Information Strategy Committee's (ISC) of two universities (termed University 1 and University 2 for the sake of anonymity here).

> University 1 had an Information Strategy Committee and a five-year-old Information Strategy document. The perception amongst members of University 1 was that this document had never been acted on (although it had been useful to wave at funding bodies ... to say yes, we have got a strategy). The strategy had formed a piece of shelf ware. It had set out a future it wanted to achieve, but five years on, that future was out of date. (2003: 10)

This differed from the situation at University 2:

> Although University 2 had established an ISC five years prior to the ethnography, they had never produced an information strategy. Instead ISC meetings were filled out with reports which could be rubber stamped on aspects of university activity under a broad definition of information (most of which was IT-related). (2003: 10)

To reiterate, the aim of this project was to provide a detailed ethnographic analysis of IT change projects at three UK universities and to use that ethnography to try to figure out the problematic aspects of change. Ethnographic writing in this project needed to both demonstrate ethnographic evidence of the way the study had been done (showing that the ethnographer had got close to the action and could provide a detailed account of the problems) and provide a way out of, in this example, an apparent strategic impasse (other change-related issues arose throughout the project and form the basis of, for example, an assessment of audit; Neyland and Woolgar, 2002). The following sections will look at the ways in which ethnographic writing could manage these two aspects of the project.

Co-authoring ethnography

The co-author for this ethnographic article was one of the participants in the research, an IT manager with many years experience of IT change projects in university settings. However, her initial academic interests were in social science, where she received her PhD. In this sense, she proved the perfect co-author; open, interested and willing to listen to social scientists, while also aware of what, for example, university IT managers might expect from a project report, might be willing to listen to and might take on board (taking on board here is intended to signify that the readers of this report might actively make their own interpretation of the report; see below).

Co-authoring ethnography is a complex process (see sensibility eight). For this article, incorporating a participant as co-author proved useful. Other participants also incorporated into project outputs, such as the final project report, included members of the government agency which funded the research. The principle behind including the funders as (limited) co-authors was that the communicative utility of the project's final report would be enhanced by working closely and gaining a contribution from those who would assess the report.

Writing for a practitioner audience

It should not be assumed that having a practitioner as co-author of this article swept away all problems with the production of practical ethnographic findings. In the case of this article, three questions were posed. First, what can we use the ethnography of strategy to say to strategists? Second, how can we get to talk to university strategists? Third, how could we know whether or not or how our ideas were being taken up? These three questions were not step-by-step considerations, but were three principles we used to navigate our way through the process of writing.

To address the first question, the ethnography of strategy was used to suggest that universities taking part in the study were characterized by three strategic 'distances'. There was a distance of time (a strategy document would be produced now to have an impact over the next three to five years, by which time the strategy could be out of date), a distance of space (between the committee and locations where the strategy might be enacted, with the latter identifying the former as a sometimes irrelevant, centralized bureaucracy), and a distance of action (with departments and faculties producing multiple (or no) interpretations of the strategy, completely detached from the committee). The article recommended setting up local groups for each faculty which could each produce an interpretation of the strategy and nominate a representative to report that interpretation back to the committee (the representative could then respond, and so on). This might have a chance, it was argued, of making strategy an ongoing process (diminishing time issues), locally appropriate (overcoming the distance of space) and inclusive (reducing problems with distanced actions).

To address the second question, although these ideas appeared to us, as authors of a strategic ethnography paper, to be a possible way forward, they were meaningless without some connection to university strategists. We were hoping our article would not be another item of strategic shelfware. The paper was presented at conferences and published in a journal for university managers. The strategic committees at each university were then invited to comment on the presentations and the article. This led to a lively debate in University 1 and University 2. This draws in the third question: ethnographic writing for a practitioner audience was as much about providing a (hopefully) useful discussion document to initiate a conversation as it was about providing a definitive and single solution to a neatly circumscribed problem. The length of my ethnographic study meant that I could follow how University 1 and University 2 picked up on and made something of this article (with the latter developing a version of the strategy process that was relevant to them).

Reflexive exit considerations

It is worth noting here that although the reflexive turn in ethnography is frequently associated with ideas of postmodernism and relativism (see sensibility two), in communicating with practitioners, reflexivity has practical value. Investigating the ways in which the ethnographer makes sense of the world, members make sense of the ethnography, and the ethnographer responds to the sense-making practices of the members under study can be a useful means to address the value of ethnography. Finding out what is made of ethnography, the moments where ethnography appears useful and the debates that an ethnographic study can spark in this study formed the basis for assessing the appropriate time for exiting the field. Having engaged with each of these areas of members' sense-making, usefulness and value, I could exit the field having used this engagement to reflexively assess the completeness of the study.

A further set of constraints can derive from an ethnographer's personal life. Ethnography can involve long-term and deep immersion in the field setting. This needs to be managed in such a way as to fit with whatever might be happening in an ethnographer's life outside the field. For example, personal issues, family issues or illness can each form part of the 'foreseen and unforeseen contingencies' (Shaffir and Stebbins, 1991b: 208) of ethnographic research. These issues are likely to be more pronounced in traditional ethnographic settings where distance from 'home' might be more acute. However, organizational ethnography can involve lengthy trips over some distance away from one's personal relationships. The possibility of exits imposed by external problems, needs to be managed by the ethnographer.

One final issue for ethnographers in exiting the field is adjusting back from research life and their ethnographic identity. Several ethnographers have reported difficulties in readjusting to ordinary ways of living after ethnographic study and switching from treating members of their field-site as friends, colleagues and associates to subjects of ethnographic writing (Taylor, 1991). These features of ethnographic exits can form a focus for reflexive ethnography (see sensibility two) and provide ways of considering the extent to which one successfully became a member and could act as a member of the organization studied.

Emergency exits

In most cases organizational ethnographers will be unlikely to require the kind of emergency exit forced upon ethnographers working in areas of deviance. For example, Scott's (1983) covert research on a satanic group was uncovered by members of the group and Scott was told to leave in no uncertain terms (also discussed in Hammersley and Atkinson, 1995). Although this might be an unlikely scenario for organizational ethnographers, what it highlights is the role of field relationships in posing a threat to the continuation of ethnography. An ethnographer creating problems in an organization, a breakdown in field relations with members of the organization, managers beginning to distrust an ethnographer or sudden changes in organizational priority can all lead to a rapid ethnographic exit. These kinds of problems are not limited to exits from the field-site. Ethnographers can also run into problems in the publication of work. A notable example again from studies of deviance involves Wolf's (1991) research on motorcycle gangs. Although he gained permission for the research from the section of the gang he studied, an alternative chapter of the same gang visited Wolf to make it clear that they looked less favourably on the publication (particularly as Wolf's study had been used in a court case against a member of the gang). Once again, such a scenario might seem unlikely in organizational ethnography, but it does highlight the extent to which ethnographers can be held to account for their publication of studies of the field.

The true exit point for an ethnographer from the field can thus seem diffuse and can involve a gradual drift away from spending time in the field setting to spending more time writing to finally publishing an account of the field. However, ethnographers do not exit from their responsibilities when they leave the field. Utilizing field relationships to gain a greater understanding of how organizational members understand, rate or wish to contribute to an ethnographic text can be a useful way of managing this ongoing exit and provide a means to ease publication problems. In the Conclusion to this book I will look at the ways in which these field relationships can be used to establish the utility of organizational ethnography.

Recommended reading

Jorgensen, D. (1989) *Participant Observation: A Methodology for Human Studies* (Sage, London)

Shaffir, W. and Stebbins, R. (eds) (1991a) *Experiencing Fieldwork: An Inside View of Qualitative Research* (Sage, London)

Snow, D. (1980) 'The disengagement process: a neglected problem in participant observation research', *Qualitative Sociology* 3(2): 100–22

The Utility of Organizational Ethnography

Introduction

The preceding sensibilities have highlighted a variety of ways in which ethnography has been engaged in multiple modes of scholarly and practical activity. From the initial development of ethnography in anthropological studies *of* colonial settings, we can also find the early development of ethnography *for* colonial management (for a discussion, see Baba, 2005). From early sociological forays into ethnographic research we find studies *of*, for example, the Boston ghetto (Whyte, 1955; exemplar three). What we also find is that these studies were conducted *for* the express political purpose of providing a detailed rendition of the organizational routines which made up ghetto life and stood in some contrast to the then contemporary political and media accounts of 'what was going on'.

Despite the apparent split in ethnographic theory and practice (Baba, 2005) that followed these earlier studies, ethnography now appears once more engaged in numerous forms of combined scholarly and practical pursuit. These have included forms of design (Hughes, Randall and Shapiro, 1992), technology development (INCITE, 2005), marketing (de Waal Malefyt and Moeran, 2003; including the branding of the methodology itself, Suchman, 2000), and organizational review (for an overview, see Schwartzman, 1993). Further to this recent reinvigoration of the scholarly, practical and pragmatic aspects of ethnography, it increasingly finds a place in business and management schools, even as a 'tool' taught in MBA courses (see Sherry Jr, 2003). While this ethnographic activity might, as Moeran suggests, mostly adhere to its origins in practising 'long-term involvement with and study of the everyday lives, thoughts and practices of a particular collectivity of people' (2005: 3), it has also on occasions become 'a buzzword that covers virtually every kind of data collection available to market researchers, from telephone surveys to focus groups … [and] interviews' (2005: 11).

These activities and broadened scope have raised a range of questions regarding the utility of ethnography, often couched in terms of its value, usefulness and practicality. That is, what might justify a slow, expensive, subjective methodology like ethnography? Such questions have also raised issues regarding ethnography's accountability, finding focus in discussions of the most appropriate ways to assess, measure or even regulate the methodology (at least in attempts at regularizing the 'right' way to do ethnography; see Moeran, 2005). Utility and accountability have become closely intertwined with claims to practical usefulness oriented towards mechanisms of accountability which produce an often numerical sense of ethnography's value (for a critique, see Strathern, 2002). In turn, the multiple activities of differing organizational ethnographies render a singular definition for the methodology elusive.

The objective of this conclusion is to address these recent forms of ethnographic activity and questions of utility and accountability. Although social science provides for a history of ethnographic studies of organizational forms (Wasson, 2000), what makes these questions particularly pressing is the simultaneous recently renewed interest regarding: ethnography *for* (and not just *of*) organizations; using ethnography to understand rapid technological developments (by, for example, Intel, IBM and Kodak; Wakeford, 2003; Pang, 2005); and the use of ethnography in business schools and management research. These are combined with a backdrop of rising demands for academic social science demonstrations of usefulness and value.

This objective will be achieved by synthesizing the conclusions of the preceding sensibilities and establishing the variety of forms organizational ethnography can take. This succinct summary will then provide a basis for analysing the moments during which organizational ethnography comes under scrutiny in assessments of its utility. This analysis will draw on a recent organizational ethnography which engages with the ways in which (and the terms on which) ethnographic utility can be assessed.

Organizational ethnography

Ethnography is increasingly called upon to demonstrate its utility, value and impact, particularly in line with its growing presence in business schools, in practical research methods courses, in organizational activities, in marketing and technology development. Increasing numbers of research centres (such as INCITE, 2005; NERDI, 2005) and conferences (such as DSTSMB, 2004, 2005; EPIC, 2005) are focusing on questions raised by the methodology. In turn, ethnography has been used to inform a broad array of actions from the augmentation of strategy processes to the design of mobile phones.

As suggested in the Introduction to this book, the convention for claims to ethnographic utility has been that: a detailed, in-depth picture of a group, organization and its members can be developed; the social, cultural and political issues which other methods find intangible are at the centre of analysis; ethnography is strongly participative, allowing for members of groups to comment on the data and data gathering as it occurs. With more practical ethnography (see, for example, Neyland and Woolgar, 2002; Neyland and Surridge, 2003), these claims to utility are augmented by a translation of this in-depth data into practical recommendations. It has been suggested (see, for example, Ethnovention, 2001) that these recommendations are particularly robust as they are developed in tandem with local members (and so are inclusive), pay attention to the detail of members' interests (and so are informed) and allow for change to be an iterative and participative process (rather than an enforced set of top-down management decisions). However, what are the particular challenges posed by organizational ethnography? How does ethnography demonstrate and manage its claims to utility? Do the traditions of ethnography come under threat as a result of demands for utility?

Ethnographic sensibilities

Organizational ethnography is not a singular research method, involving the deployment of a straightforward set of instructions. Instead, it has been argued (see preceding sensibilities) that researchers need to address a range of ethnographic sensibilities involving, among other things, issues of strategy, knowledge, entry/access, interaction and field relations, observation and writing, and departures from organizations. The following section will provide a brief summary of these sensibilities.

Ethnographic strategy

It was suggested in sensibility one that ethnographers could think about strategy as a means to orient their research. In place of a fixed, step-by-step approach to planning and executing research, a more fluid ethnographic strategy could be used to manage the myriad of unpredictable events which may occur during any ethnographic research. Often these events can be welcome contributions to the research effort, such as developing an understanding of the appropriateness of a particular research question after some time spent in the organization. Other times these events can be less welcome, such as the cessation of access to a particular part of the organization. A good ethnographic strategy is one that can be constantly worked on and used by the ethnographer in figuring out the most appropriate next moves. What at first may appear to be a research problem (such as the cessation of access) may come to be understood as an informative part of the research (the cessation of access revealing something of what the organization regards as important) or as the next necessary step in which the ethnographer needs to engage (such as new access negotiations, or finding an alternative means – such as interviews – to access information). Discussions in sensibility one suggested ethnographers need to develop a keen sense of when to stubbornly stick to the strategy in its present form and when to adapt the strategy to circumstances.

Questions of knowledge

In sensibility two the basis for perhaps the most complex of ethnographic sensibilities – questions of knowledge – was set out. The epistemological grounds on which an ethnographer researches an organization can be characterized as a variety of forms of realist, narrative or reflexive ethnography. A realist ethnographer might seek to engage with organizational data on the basis that the data are available independently of the ethnography, and the test of a good ethnography (for realists) is the extent to which it can accurately collect and represent this data. A narrative approach may be more focused on utilizing key informants (or even the ethnographer themselves) in order to tell a particular story of the organization. In a variety of ways, this narrative might be presented as one of several possible accounts of an organization. A reflexive ethnographer would provide a more thoroughly sceptical account of the ways in which the ethnographer and other members of the organization are engaged in the production or construction of the ethnography. In this sense, the 'data' would not be presented as existing entirely independently of the study in any straightforward sense, but rather what was included in the study would be the result of a complex process of reflexive engagement between ethnographer, organizational members, the material artefacts of the organization, its documents, and so on. To add further complexity to this picture, it was suggested that the lines between narrative and reflexive ethnography and between some forms of narrative and realist ethnography are blurred.

Locations and access

Discussions in sensibility three established the bases on which ethnographers might make important decisions about locations (where to study, how many locations to study, how to link locations) and access (how to get into, become a member of, spend time in and negotiate further access to areas of the organization). The discussion came with the caveat that multi-site ethnography, although often thought of as more 'complete', was not essential and that rich engagement in one location can often prove more revelatory than brief immersion in multiple locations. It was also suggested that one location (and the stories told there) can offer the ethnographer a great deal of information about other locations. The discussion recommended thinking about access as an active process and a focal point for the ethnography. Gaining entry into an organization was not simply about making phone calls, writing letters or e-mails to the organization, but about first encounters with the ways the organization attempts to express itself to external audiences, and the procedures in place to manage access and the organization's identity.

Field relations

Field relations provide one means for an ethnographer to navigate the field being studied. Ethnographers ideally switch in and out of an organization's membership, being immersed in and reflecting on the organization, its members, how the organization works, how it holds together, how it changes and how the very idea of an organization (its identity, credibility, brand, and so on) is established and maintained. However, field relations are not easily navigated. Although a close relation with participants is important, a principal aim of ethnography is to provide some analytical scrutiny of 'what is going on' in the organization. Thus, close relations in the field are both essential and difficult. The discussion provided a range of examples of field relations which proved valuable to particular pieces of research and other examples which (perhaps) suggested closer forms of involvement than might conventionally be expected between researchers and researched.

Ethnographic time

In sensibility five a case was made for the defence of ethnographic time, for taking time in research and the advantages of doing things slowly. While much research in management and for management appears to be characterized by ever-increasing pace in turn-around (from initiation to completion of research) and expectations regarding research deliverables (practical outcomes which can be identifiably accounted for as contributing to process), ethnography operates on its own time scales. Access often takes a long time and the ethnographer should expect to be immersed in the field over long periods, and organizing and writing up research requires further consideration. It may also be important to move back into the field to report on findings, to analyse any outcomes produced through the ethnography or to see what the natives make of the research. Although this apparent lack of pace can run counter to organizational and management research expectations, part of the negotiating skills of the ethnographer in gaining access is to emphasize the strengths and necessities of ethnographic time.

Observing and participating

Although observing (and forms of participant observation) might at first appear to be the primary sensibility for ethnographers to engage in, observation cannot sensibly be thought through without regard for the other sensibilities. Of particular note for organizational ethnographers are questions of: what to observe (how to choose and how to elicit further information), the practicality of observations (how to record observations, when, where, and using what means) and what to do with these observations (how to organize them in such a way as to make them amenable to the process of writing-up). These questions often also involve considerations of field relations (sensibility four), time (sensibility five) and writing-up (sensibility eight). How participation is managed (as a full member or as an independent observer) can have implications for observation and the ways in which the observer is treated by those researched.   163

Supplementing

The discussion in sensibility seven outlined the grounds on which ethnographers might decide to supplement their ethnographic observations with further forms of ethnography (such as virtual ethnography), further forms of data (through, for example, interviews) and forms of collection and analysis (such as the collection and use of organizational documents). As the discussion in sensibility three had cautioned against assumptions that multi-site ethnography was necessarily or inevitably better than single-site ethnography, in sensibility seven it was suggested that supplementing the research was not always necessary or advisable. The management, organization and writing of the ethnography does not get any easier through supplementing what might be termed more straightforward ethnographic observation and the ethnographer may run into problems attempting to accumulate multiple forms of information (which are not necessarily compatible) into a single write-up. The discussion in sensibility seven suggested that supplementation was a question which ethnographers should incorporate into the research as a possibility, not a necessity.

Writing

Writing ethnographies, as suggested in sensibility eight, involves the ethnographer in constant movement between the observations made (and other information collected, such as organizational documents) and various means of theming, categorizing, indexing and organizing the observations. This process also involves trying out various characterizations of the data, using observations to make particular arguments, referring these arguments back to members of the organization for feedback and the pursuit of further observational material to fill any notable gaps. This 'writing' process should start early. Figuring out how observations could be organized and how putative arguments could be put together can provide the ethnographer with guidance in the continuation of ethnographic research. A little like the ethnographic strategy, the inevitability of a final research write-up can be used as an orienting sensibility in developing understanding of what the ethnographer has seen and what the ethnographer needs to do next.

Ethics

The discussion in sensibility nine established a variety of ethical considerations that have traditionally been drawn into ethnographic research. Questions of informed consent, of anonymity, of publication and use of observational material, of covert or overt participation and of the areas of the organization to be engaged by the ethnographer were analysed. Examples were drawn in to illustrate the ways in which ethics shift between types of study, types of location being studied, types of question being asked, and so on. It was suggested that ethics can be thought of in terms of rules (any breakage of which deems the research unethical), guidelines (which require interpretation for the completion of particular research projects), and as situated accomplishments (where the ethnographer will need to provide evidence to, for example, an ethics committee that they have produced an ethical statement which adequately accomplishes ethical standards for their particular research situation).

Exits

Considering an appropriate exit from an organizational setting should not be left to the end of the study. However, as the discussion in sensibility ten highlighted, there are a variety of forms of exit the ethnographer can consider. Often exits can be tied into access negotiations where an appropriate length of time to spend in the field is decided between the ethnographer and the organization. Partial exits can be a useful way to leave open the possibility of future re-entry into the field to report back on findings, carry out further observations or even ask new research questions in follow-up studies. Alternatively, there are unexpected exits where the ethnographer or the organization initiates the researcher's departure from the field. Although less than ideal, such exits can often form some part of ethnographic analysis and may reveal something of the nature of the organization under study.

Ethnographic exemplars

Alongside the preceding ethnographic sensibilities, a variety of exemplars were used for illustrative purposes. A brief consideration of the status of these exemplars will be useful in foregrounding subsequent discussion of ethnographic utility and accountability. The exemplars incorporated into this text involved a variety of forms of organizational ethnography. These were derived from several distinct theoretical and epistemological traditions. In terms of disciplinary traditions, the work of Malinowski (1929) acted as a demonstration of initial interests expressed by early anthropological ethnographers. The work of Whyte (1955) was used to illuminate early sociological interest in ethnographic research. Leidner's (1993) work was used as indicative of management research attempts to address some traditional (management research) concerns in different ways. As suggested above, these forms of ethnography had both practical and scholarly intent. However, it should not be assumed that this tripartite of anthropology, sociology and management research ethnography exhausts the alternative forms of ethnography. Neither should this mode of description be taken as reflective of a neatly delineated methodology. Other exemplars, such as the work of Hine (2000), drew upon different aspects of these traditions and used their work to pose interesting questions of the field. Ethnographers thus have the opportunity to blur and utilize these distinctions in carrying out and writing up research.

The exemplars also presented opportunities for entering into epistemological considerations. Malinowski's (1929) work might broadly be construed as providing an example of realist ethnographic research, suggesting the field existed to be studied independently of the ethnographer. The work of the ethnographer here was to capture as accurately as possible a detailed representation of the field. In considering the work of Whyte (1955), however, there is a greater focus on the account offered by a key informant (Doc), who provides much of the narrative of the research. This account is still treated as a realist version of the field. Other exemplars, such as the work of Latour and Woolgar (1979), provided an alternative epistemological approach, through radical reflexive-constructivist ethnography. This approach incorporated the ethnographer into the study more explicitly, analysing the ways in which the ethnographer was involved in the constitution of the field. Once again, this tripartite schema of realist, narrative and reflexive ethnography need not be considered as absolute. Several of the exemplars incorporated narrative and reflexive aspects of ethnography into the same study (see exemplars six and thirteen).

In what ways, and with what outcomes, are these ethnographic sensibilities, exemplars, traditions of ethnography and questions of epistemology involved in assessments of ethnographic utility?

Considerations of utility

An important feature of organizational ethnographic research (as highlighted in the exemplars) is the progressive identification and accumulation, in the process of the research, of connections with participants and other potential 'users'. However, in line with recent explorations of 'interactive social science' (Caswill and Shove, 2000; Woolgar, 2000) and engagement in research programmes incorporating novel forms of outreach (Woolgar, 2002a, 2002c), user relations should not be taken for granted. The exemplars explored a variety of ways of enhancing interaction with a range of audiences. These relations ranged from shifts between apparent invisibility and visibility (Geertz, 1973) through to constructing strategic processes (Neyland and Surridge, 2003). The reflexive sensibilities which often form a feature of the production of ethnography (Atkinson, 1990, 1992) can be extended here to considerations such as how and to what extent the researchers were themselves accountable for the value and utility of their research (for discussion of these issues, see Woolgar, 1998, 2002b; Neyland 2006b). However, careful consideration is required of the precise implications of utility in relation to organizational ethnography.

Assessments of utility form one feature of recent moves made to inaugurate a shift towards the marketability or customer orientation of research. As Du Gay and Salaman argue, there is hardly a public service organization in Britain 'that has not in some way become permeated by the language of enterprise' (1992: 622). This language of enterprise, however, is not a 'vague, incalculable "spirit", the culture of enterprise is inscribed into a variety of mechanisms, such as application forms, recruitment "auditions", and communication groups' (1992: 626). For Rappert (1997), one such mechanism can be found in university funding bodies' establishment of particular themes. These themes call for the 'incorporation of users' needs' and suggest that 'customer–contractor relations' are an important basis for research funding (Rappert, 1997: 1,2). These moves are positioned under broader motifs such as the 'need to meet the challenges of international competitiveness and improve the quality of life' (1997: 1). Gibbons (2000) ties this shift in research funding to the shift he identifies from Mode One to Mode Two research activity. Rather than setting research problems and solving them (Mode One), science and social science research is now more closely incorporated into the context of application for research and is produced via teams of mixed-skill researchers in close collaboration with users (Mode Two). In this sense, organizational ethnography could be understood as shifting from the study *of* the organization to combinations of study *of* and *for* the organization.

However, several social scientists (for example, Shove and Rip, 2000; Woolgar, 2000) warn against assumptions regarding the ease or comfort of interacting with practitioner audiences. Shove and Rip (2000: 175) suggest that 'the over-reliance on an embodied notion of use and uncritical acceptance of associated pathways of influence is understandable but unnecessary. ... In short, the challenge is to understand better the process of use even if that means abandoning the comforting fairy-tale of the research user'. This aligns with Woolgar's (2000: 169) suggestion that 'we should accept that users' needs rarely pre-exist the efforts and activities of producers to engage with them'. These arguments contribute to a social science history of the difficulties of user interaction. For example, caution is advocated as to the 'circumstances under which social science research enters the decision-making domain' (Weiss and Bucuvalas, 1980: 248), with suggestions made that social science findings are prone to be misinterpreted, misunderstood or misused. Furthermore, it is argued that social science is often 'underutilized' (Wagner et al., 1991: 5), with findings on policy principles not used to their full extent. Warnings are also given against any assumptions that good social science will automatically be utilized. Thus Heller (1986: 1) suggests that 'while only a few people would argue specifically against making use of existing social science knowledge, it should not be assumed too readily that a broad-based advocacy of more utilization is either logical or practical'.

The challenges posed to organizational ethnography in attempting to demonstrate its utility cut to the centre of the methodology employed. Concerns with, for example, ethnographic time scale and its mismatch with claims regarding the necessity of organizational speed (see, for example, Jeffrey and Troman, 2004) and organizational sensitivities regarding the provision of access for long periods to particular areas of organizational activity (see, for example, Harrington, 2003) are frequently cited as problematic features of ethnography's attempts at addressing practitioner audiences. However, preceding discussions have suggested that more active participation in exploring notions of use and relations with users can inform our understanding and development of ethnographic utility. Engaging in detail in ethnography's multiple forms of accountability can help us understand the conditions under which ethnography's utility is assessed.

In the next section I will present findings from a recent organizational ethnography in which I was engaged. I will argue that the research involved three distinct modes of ethnographic research: ethnography *of* the organization, ethnography *for* the organization and (eventually) ethnography *with* the organization. As we shall see, each of these ethnographic modes carried with it distinct approaches to questions of utility and accountability, distinct forms of epistemological claim and were predicated upon very different conceptions of the nature of ethnographic field relations (particularly relating to questions of which type of field relation might be most suited to demonstrating ethnography's utility).

Demonstrating ethnographic utility

The following discussion is based on a recent ethnographic study I carried out of IT change in universities (exemplar fourteen also provides some information on one aspect of this study). The specific ethnographic details of this study (presented below) can tell us a great deal about the complexities of demonstrating the utility of organizational ethnography.

Ethnography of the organization

The ethnography of universities began in a conventional manner with a great deal of work to build a collaborative research team which spanned four universities and could make claims to operate in a practically oriented, Mode Two (Gibbons, 2000) fashion. However, the collaborative team were bidding for money from the Higher Education Funding Council for England's (HEFCE) Good Management Practice fund. This fund came with specific expectations that projects should: identify 'stakeholder needs', likely 'management process improvements', 'top-level support' from within participating universities, a clear 'dissemination plan' and evidence of 'performance measures'. The latter seemed particularly difficult for organizational ethnography: what would an ethnographic performance measure include? Measures can involve benchmarking (establishing a figure against which to measure change or a target to aim towards; QAA, 2002; PSBS, 2006) or establishing performance indicators (particular areas of activity which will be measured according to a standard metric at specific time intervals; Audit Commission, 2006; Reh, 2006). It has been argued that such measures risk reducing the exploratory scope of ethnography, raising questions regarding the ways in which detailed description can be translated into a prescribed range of numbers (Strathern, 2002). Performance measures would appear to stand in opposition to the principal, exploratory strengths of ethnography outlined in the preceding sensibilities.

Partly in response to these foreshadowed problems, the research began by operating in a conventional academic ethnographic mode. The initial publications and conference presentations were designed for academic audiences (see, for example, Neyland and Woolgar, 2002). These project outputs were very much based on ethnography *of* the organizations. The research was carried out by academics, studying university administrators and managers and was published for academics. The basis for epistemological claims in this mode of research was that the findings of these outputs were an original and incisive contribution to academic knowledge. This aspect of the research was important: increasingly academics are coming under scrutiny to demonstrate their value, usefulness and relevance. Many of these demonstrations occur through peer review by other academics. Therefore, successfully demonstrating academic utility was a vital aspect of this organizational ethnography for the academics involved. However, such demonstrations of academic value through ethnography *of* the organization contributed little to the research funding body's expectations regarding value and usefulness. In order to address these concerns, the project team began to engage in ethnography *for* the organization.

Ethnography for the organization

It still remained unclear how the organizational ethnography could engage with the funding body's demands for numerical ethnographic measures. However, as the project progressed, the collaborative team succeeded in producing evidence that matched the funders' other assessment criteria by demonstrating that the research had top-level support, would provide management process improvements, had a dissemination plan and would address stakeholder needs. These demonstrations took place in meetings between the research team and representatives from the funding body. Each meeting involved reports on the latest dissemination activity and progress being made in introducing new processes in the universities. Presenting the ways in which the ethnography was contributing to local changes and was receiving a favourable response from presentations to the university community (for example, at conferences of university managers) began to shift the emphasis of the ethnography away from ethnography *of* the organizations. These reports were based on a form of ethnography *for* the organizations. The epistemological claim made in these meetings was that the ethnography was providing a detailed analysis of activity in the organizations and evidence was presented that this ethnographic detail was being translated into practical changes. This claim to value was based on presentations of feedback received from, for example, university managers at management conferences and responses from members of the universities present at the meetings who could attest to the ethnography's ongoing contribution to process change.

This might suggest that the meetings were relatively straightforward occasions with people simply turning up and agreeing at the correct moment that the research was useful. The meetings were not so straightforward. The funding body had requested demonstrations of top-level support from within the participating universities. This suggested that evidence of utility had to involve top-level people both turning up to meetings and being the people who recognized the utility of the research. In order to achieve this, first, senior individuals who had agreed to take part in the project in pre-project negotiations had to turn up to the meetings. Turning up demonstrated that they had taken time out from their busy schedules in order to attend a project meeting. However, the project team were worried that, if questioned by the funding body representative about their involvement in the project, senior individuals may have been left with little to say. As a result, second, a member of the project team attempted a series of briefings before each meeting for senior individuals (so that they were able to convincingly demonstrate involvement in the project should they be required). However, top-level figures did not always turn out to be faithful allies to the project. On occasions they were unavailable for the briefings, at times they forgot the content of briefings in the meetings and even missed the meetings with the funding body. As a result, third, 'missing meetings' was then used by the project team to demonstrate to the funding body that these senior people had busy and important schedules. Demonstrating that the ethnography *for* the organizations was actually useful for the organizations was an important and complex ongoing issue during the research. Without such demonstrations, organizational ethnography's utility would have remained as an unanswered question. However, these demonstrations still avoided addressing the funding body's request for performance measures. Engaging with these measures involved the development of a form of ethnography *with* the organizations.

Ethnography with the organization

Ongoing uncertainties regarding the utility of the ethnographic research led to the development of closer relationships with members of the organizations involved in the research. First, these closer relations took the form of joint-authorship of written publications and presentations for university management audiences (more detail on this is provided in exemplar fourteen). Members of the research team from each of the participating universities were asked to read and comment on papers in draft stages and contribute ideas that they had in order that the ethnographer could draw together a range of different inputs for publication. These were then presented to the community of university managers as the result of collaborative work. The epistemological strength of these papers was not that they had been produced by an independent expert whose voice could be relied upon as a guarantor of original thought and likely useful information. Instead, the claim of these papers was that their strength lay in the opportunity members of the research team had been given to think outside the narrow and immediate confines of their day-to-day job and consider instead what might improve their working position. This aspect of ethnography *with* the organizations differed from ethnography *of* the organizations (where claims to knowledge were based on academic prerequisites of theoretical and methodological innovation, designed for academic audiences) and ethnography *for* organizations (where claims to knowledge were provided by the ethnographic research in the hope that the universities which took part in the research would find the claims useful). This feature of ethnography *with* the organizations was deemed a success by research participants.

However, second, the research team noted that the universities were not the only organizations involved in this research; the funding body was also a notable organizational participant in the project. Regular meetings between the funding body representative and the research team had not led to the development of performance measures, neither had they led to any diminishment in enthusiasm for such measures from the funding body. Instead, the establishment of numeric measures had been deferred. The project team suggested that it would be possible to collect numbers through the ethnography and the funding body remained interested in these numbers. However, the project team continued to stress that the kinds of numbers the ethnography could collect might not be particularly illuminative (number of research participants, number of publications, feedback scores from conference audiences, etc.) and certainly were not a principal purpose of the ethnography (the observational material, it was emphasized, would provide greater insights than these somewhat limited metrics). Over time the funding body representative began to increase his interest in outputs from the research, which were both based on ethnography and offered some practical utility. In phone conversations, on e-mail and in face-to-face meetings, the representative asked about the latest 'findings'.

On one such occasion the representative was putting together a package of publicity material for a forthcoming event designed to highlight the outputs from across the Good Management Practice projects they had funded. He wanted a contribution from the research team. I sent the representative the paper on information strategy (Neyland and Surridge, 2003; described in exemplar fourteen). Remembering the previous instruction that ethnographic material formed an important part of the research, the

171

representative took the ethnographic section of the paper (which high-lighted the messy, inconclusive and confused state of information strategy in two English universities) and promoted this as Good Management Practice. A member of the project team suggested the representative had read the paper 'about as carefully as everything else'. In response to this apparent misreading of the ethnography, I suggested an alternative focus for the promotional material. This involved further e-mail negotiations between the research team and the funding body representative which acted as a form of ethnography *with* the (funding body) organization. First, the project team had to establish that the representative's initial attempts to promote the messiness of strategy as Good Management Practice were misguided. Second, to ease any burden this might create in terms of extra workload, the project team made it clear that they would be happy to pro-vide an alternative focus for the promotional material. Third, the project team came up with the suggestion of writing such a promotional focus. Fourth, the representative suggested that he was happy to read any alter-native and would offer helpful recommendations on how to change it if nec-essary. Fifth, I submitted an alternative promotional text. Sixth, the representative e-mailed some minor changes to the text. Seventh, it was agreed that this text was now a suitable promotional text to be incorpo-rated into the publicity material.

This back-and-forth process highlighted the complexity of funding body–project team relations. Even the relatively straightforward matter of a promotional paragraph about the project involved several attempts at straightforward communication and several further realizations that 'things were not going to be as easy as that'. However, this experience also suggests that forms of ethnography *with* organizations can be a useful way for redistributing the ways in which ethnography might be held to account (for more on accountability, see Neyland, 2006b). Although it would have been possible to provide the funding body with numeric measures as a basis for holding the utility of the ethnography to account, the project team were clear that this risked undermining the value of the research. Instead, estab-lishing close relations with the funding body resulted in opportunities to hold the funding body representative to account in order to pay attention to the ways in which ethnographic outputs might be used. This shifted assessment of the utility of our ethnography from solely handing over data to be assessed, to inviting the would-be assessors to take part in the production of material. This appeared to offer a greater likelihood of maximizing value from the ethnographic research.

Further evidence of the utility of this ethnographic research is somewhat speculative. A variety of different claims could be made that the research demonstrated its utility, based on a variety of distinct occasions where the research appeared to succeed in achieving something useful. First, the project could be assessed by academic peers through its publications. This was a form of ethnography *of* organization. Papers were well received by reviewers and subsequently published. It was not the case, however, that publications were universally noted as demonstrative of ethnographic utility. The publications were of marginal interest to the funding body, which suggested that academic publications were of little more status than a 'side product' of a Good Management Practice project. The funding body emphasized on several occasions that they wanted to see 'results'.

Second, the project played a role in organizational change. This was agreed by the organizations which took part in the ethnography (this agreement was fostered through time spent in the field and the development of close field relations). For example, as a result of the project, the organizations (to some extent) changed the way they approached strategy. Third, the project was instrumental in changing (possibly improving) the material artefacts of the organization through providing recommendations on IT purchases, which took into account ethnographic observations of employee activities in the organizations. These two areas shifted back and forth between ethnography *for* and ethnography *with* the organization.

Fourth, the project team were successful in negotiating a way around conventional performance indicators and benchmarks which may have stifled the exploratory aspects of ethnography. The alternative 'indicators' of senior support, collaboration and dissemination were achieved in communications between the project team and the funding body. Communicating these to the funding body required a form of ethnography *with* the (funding body) organization. This led to the promotion of the research through the funding body's Good Management Practice text (as negotiated above) and their day-long event which promoted the Good Management Practice projects they had funded. During this day-long event the project team delivered a well-attended presentation. This led to several conversations about the utility of ethnography over lunch, attended by the key-note speaker for the day (Dr David Ward, President, American Council on Education and Chancellor Emeritus of the University of Wisconsin, Madison). A concluding remark of his key-note speech was that, in order to understand the way universities operate, everyone needs an ethnographer. This assertion formed the fifth claim to utility that the research could mobilize. Recognition for the value of this statement would depend upon the recognizability of David Ward (or the kind of person he represents), agreement that this is the kind of thing he (or someone like him) could have said, and recognition that this comment is demonstrative of utility. In this sense, the utility of organizational ethnography retains its status as a research question.

Summary

This Conclusion has suggested that organizational ethnography can draw on its ten principal sensibilities in making claims to utility. Engaging with detailed analysis of questions of knowledge, getting close to the action of what goes on in particular organizations, having the flexibility to incorporate further methodological forms (such as interviewing and document analysis), and having a reasonably clear research strategy can all feature in claims to utility. However, these claims to utility can be predicated upon different research orientations. First, I suggested ethnography *of* organizations is an important research orientation for making claims about the focus of study for academic audiences. Presenting research as the outcome of an engaged and intensive exploration of the organization under study can provide a means for methodological and theoretical innovation.

Second, ethnography *for* organizations was presented as a summary term for those ethnographic projects which seek to provide something, or are commissioned by the organization to provide something, useful for the organization. This usefulness can take many forms and often requires elaborate communication strategies to present initial findings to the organization, gain feedback on what the organization might find useful and further incorporating this feedback into ongoing research. Providing something useful through ethnography for organizations requires ongoing work.

Third, I introduced ethnography *with* organizations as an alternative means to work through the complexity of ongoing research. Rather than carry out research which can then be presented to an organization or an academic audience, research with the organization entails a more extensive collaborative relationship between researchers and researched such that the boundary between these two positions becomes less clear. Members of the organization are invited to take an active part in the research process and the production of research outputs. At the same time the researcher shifts in focus from being the principal source of research outputs to being the co-ordinator of research and one of several collaborating authors for outputs. Although in the research I presented in this Conclusion, ethnography with the organization proved useful, it should be noted that this utility is tied into traditional concerns with ethnography. For example, ethnography *with* the organization takes perhaps even more time than conventional ethnography and it involves an even closer relationship between the ethnographer and research participants. In my own research I have always found these principles to be advantageous rather than problematic features of research.

Having read this far, would-be ethnographers should have a clear idea of the challenges posed by doing ethnography and have read through some of the ways ethnographers have engaged with these issues. The remaining challenge is now to go and take on these challenges, sensibilities and exemplars by entering the field and doing organizational ethnography.

Recommended reading

Caswill, P. and Shove, E. (eds) (2000) 'Interactive Social Science', special issue, *Science and Public Policy* 27(3)

Rappert, B. (1997) 'Users and social science research: policy, problems and possibilities', *Sociological Research Online* 2(3): http://www.socresonline.org.uk/socresonline/2/3/10.html

Weiss, C. and Bucuvalas, M. (1980) *Social Science Research and Decision Making* (Columbia University Press, New York)

References

AAA (1998) Code of Ethics of the American Anthropological Association, available from: www.aaanet.org

AAA (2004) American Anthropological Association Statement on Ethnography and Institutional Review Boards, available from: www.aaanet.org

Ackoff, R. (1981) *Creating the Corporate Future – Plan or Be Planned For* (John Wiley and Sons, Chichester)

Arfield, J. (1995) *Information Strategies in UK University Libraries* (http:educate2. lib.chalmers.se/IATUL/proceedcontents/abs196/Arfield.html)

Armstrong, G. (1998) *Football Hooligans Knowing the Score* (Berg, London)

Arnould, E. and Wallendorf, M. (1994) 'Market-oriented ethnography: interpretation building and market strategy formulation', *Journal of Marketing Research* 31(4): 484–504

Ashmore, M. (1989) *The Reflexive Thesis* (University of Chicago Press, Chicago)

Atkinson, P. (1990) *The Ethnographic Imagination: Textual Constructions of Reality* (Routledge, London)

Atkinson, P. (1992) *Understanding Ethnographic Texts* (Sage, London)

Audit Commission (2006) Performance Indicators, available from: http://www.audit-commission.gov.uk/performance/index.asp?page=index.asp&area=hpbvpi

Baba, M. (1986) 'Business and Industrial Anthropology: An overview', National Association for the Practice of Anthropology bulletin, American Anthropological Association

Baba, M. (2005) 'To the end of theory-practice "apartheid": encountering the world', Ethnographic Praxis in Industry Conference, *Conference Proceedings of EPIC 2005* (American Anthropological Association, Arlington, VA) pp. 205–17

Ball, M. and Smith, G. (2001) 'Technologies of realism? Ethnographic uses of photography and film', in Atkinson, P., Coffey, A., Delamont, S., Lofland, J. and Lofland, J. (eds), *Handbook of Ethnography* (Sage, London), pp. 302–19

Banks, M. and Murphy, H. (eds) (1997) *Rethinking Visual Anthropology* (Yale University Press, New Haven, CT)

Barber, B. (1983) *The Logic and Limits of Trust* (Rutgers University Press, New Brunswick, NJ)

Bate, S. (1997) 'Whatever happened to organizational anthropology? A review of the field of organizational ethnography and anthropological studies', *Human Relations* 50(9): 1147–76

Beaulieu, A. (2004) 'Mediating ethnography: objectivity and the making of ethnographies of the internet', *Social Epistemology* 18(2–3): 139–63

Becker, H. (1973) *Outsiders: Studies in the Sociology of Deviance* (Free Press, New York)

Becker, H. (1998) *Tricks of the Trade* (University of Chicago Press, Chicago)

Bell, G. (2003) *'Other homes: alternate visions of culturally situated technologies for the home'*, Computer–Human Interaction conference 2003, 5–10 April, (Fort Lauderdale, FL)

Bergman, M. (2003) 'The broad and narrow in ethnography on organizations', *Forum Qualitative Social Research* 4(1): http://www.qualitative-research.net/fqs-texte/1-03/1-03tagung-bergman-e.pdf

Bestor, T. (2004) *Tsukiji: The Fish Market at the Center of the World* (University of California Press, Berkley, CA)

Blaikie, N. (1993) *Approaches to Social Enquiry* (Polity Press, Cambridge)

Blythin, S., Rouncefield, M. and Hughes, J. (1997) 'Never mind the ethno stuff: what does all this mean and what do we now? Ethnography in the commercial World', *Interactions* May: 38–47

Boelen, W. (1992) 'Street corner society: cornerville revisited', *Journal of Contemporary Ethnography* 21(1): 11–51.

Brewer, J. (2000) *Ethnography* (Open University Press, Buckingham)

Burack, T. (2002) 'Book Review of *Turning Words, Spinning Worlds* by M. Rosen', *Journal of Business and Technical Communication*, April: 220–22

Burawoy, M. (2003) 'Revisits: an outline of a theory of reflexive ethnography', *American Sociological Review* 68(5): 645–79

Burgess, R. (1984) *In the Field: An Introduction to Field Research* (Routledge, London)

Caswill, P. and Shove, E. (eds) (2000) 'Interactive social science', special issue, *Science and Public Policy* 27(3)

Clifford, J. (1986) 'Introduction: partial truths', in Clifford, J. and Marcus, G. (eds), *Writing Culture: The Poetics and Politics of Ethnography* (University of California Press, Berkley CA), pp. 1–26

Clifford, J. and Marcus, G. (eds) (1986) *Writing Culture: The Poetics and Politics of Ethnography* (University of California Press, Berkley, CA)

Coffey, A. (1999) *The Ethnographic Self: Fieldwork and the Representation of Identity* (Sage, London)

Cohen, S. (1972) *Folk Devils and Moral Panics* (MacGibbon & Kee, London)

Collier, S. and Lackoff, A. (2005) 'On regimes of living', in Ong, A. and Collier, S. (eds), *Global Assemblages: Technology, Politics, and Ethics as Anthropological Problems* (Blackwell, Oxford), pp. 22–39

Cooper, G. (2001) 'Conceptualising social life', in N. Gilbert (ed.) *Researching Social Life* (Sage, London), pp. 1–13

Cooper, G., Green, N., Murtagh, G. and Harper, R. (2002) 'Mobile society? Technology, distance and presence', in Woolgar, S. (ed.), *Virtual Society? Technology, Cyberbole, Reality* (Oxford University Press, Oxford), pp. 286–301

Coopman, C., Neyland, D. and Wedgar, S. (2004) 'Does STS Mean Business? Some Issues and Questions', June 2004, Said Business School, University of Oxford available from: http://www.sbs.ox.ac.uk/NR/rdonlyres/DFSAS36C-F691-4056-BDTC-ADB610F9B2C3/893/stsworkshop.

Corrall, S. (1994) *Strategic Planning for Library and Information Services* (Aslib, London)

CUREC (2006) Central University Research Ethics Committee guidelines, available from: http://www.admin.ox.ac.uk/curec/oxonly/ethicalapp/checklistJan06.doc

Czarniawska-Joerges, B. (1992) *Exploring Complex Organizations: A Cultural Perspective* (Sage, London)

Darrah, C. (1996) *Learning and Work: An Exploration in Industrial Ethnography* (Garland Science, Newyork)

de Waal Malefyt, T. and Moeran, B. (eds) (2003) *Advertising Cultures* (Berg, Oxford)

Dellbridge, R. (1998) *Life on the Line in Contemporary Manufacturing* (Oxford University Press, Oxford)

Denzin, N. (1992) 'Whose Cornerville is it anyway?', *Journal of Contemporary Ethnography* 21: 120–32

Dey, C.R. (2002) 'Methodological issues: the use of critical ethnography as an active research methodology', *Accounting, Auditing and Accountability Journal* 15(1): 106–21

DSTSMB? (2004) 'Does STS mean business?', June, Said Business School, University of Oxford, see: http://www.sbs.ox.ac.uk/news/archives/Main/Does+STS+Mean+Business.htm

DSTSMB? (2005) 'Does STS mean business too?', June, Said Business School, University of Oxford, see: http://www.sbs.ox.ac.uk/sts2

Ducheneaut, N. and Moore, R. (2005) 'More than just XP: learning social skills in massively multiplayer online games', *Interactive Technology and Smart Education* 2: 89–100

Du Gay, P. and Salaman, G. (1992) 'The cult(ure) of the customer', *Journal of Management Studies* 29(5): 615–33.

Earl, M. (1999) 'Strategy making in the information age' in Currie, W. and Galliers, B. (eds), *Rethinking Management Information Systems: An Interdisciplinary Perspective* (Oxford University Press, Oxford)

Ellen, R. (ed.) (1984) *Ethnographic Research: A Guide to General Conduct* (Academic Press, London)

Ellis, C. (2004) *The Ethnographic I: A Methodological Novel* (Altamira Press, London)

Ellis, C. and Bochner, A. (eds) (1996) *Composing Ethnography* (Altamira Press, London)

Ellis, C. and Bochner, A. (2000) 'Autoethnography, Personal Narrative, Reflexivity', in Denzin, N. and Lincoln, Y. (eds), *Handbook of Qualitative Research* (2nd edn, Sage, London), pp. 733–68

Emerson, R., Fretz, R. and Shaw, L. (1995) *Writing Ethnographic Fieldnotes* (University of Chicago Press, Chicago)

EPIC (2005) 'Ethnographic Praxis in Industry Conference', Microsoft, Redmond, USA, see: http://www.epic2005.com/

Ethnovention (2001) http://www.co-i-l.com/coil/knowledge-garden/kd/ethnovention.shtml

Evans Pritchard, E. (1940) *The Nuer: A Description of the Modes of Livelihood and Political Institutions of a Nilotic People* (Clarendon Press, Oxford)

Festinger, L., Riecken, H. and Schachter, S. (1956) *When Prophecy Fails* (University of Minnesota Press, Minneapolis)

Fetterman, D. (1989) *Ethnography Step by Step* (Sage, London)

Fielding, N. (2001) 'Ethnography', in Gilbert, N. (ed.), *Researching Social Life* (2nd edn, Sage, London), pp. 147–63

Fielding, N. and Thomas, H. (2001) 'Qualitative Interviewing', in Gilbert, N. (ed.), *Researching Social Life* (2nd edn, Sage, London), pp. 123–44

Fjelstad, O. and Haanaes, K. (2001) 'Strategy tradeoffs in the knowledge and network economy', *Business Strategy Review* 12(1): 1–10

Freeman, D. (1983) *Margaret Mead and Samoa: The Making and Unmaking of an Anthropological Myth* (Harvard University Press, Cambridge, MA)

Freidberg, S. (2001) 'On the trail of the global green bean: methodological considerations in multi-site ethnography', *Global Networks* 1(4): 353–68

Gallmeier, C. (1991) 'Leaving, revisiting and staying in touch,' in Shaffir, W. and Stebbins, R. (eds), *Experiencing Fieldwork: An Inside View of Qualitative Research* (Sage, London), pp. 224–31

Garfinkel, H. (1963) 'A conception of and experiments with "trust" as a condition of stable concerted actions', in Harvey, O. (ed.), *Motivation and Social Interaction* (Ronald Press, New York), pp.197–238

Garfinkel, H. (1967) *Studies in Ethnomethodology* (Prentice-Hall, Englewood Cliffs, NJ)

Geertz, C. (1973) *The Interpretation of Cultures* (Basic Books, New York)

Gibbons, M. (2000) 'Mode 2 society and the emergence of context-sensitive science', *Science and Public Policy, Journal of the International Science Policy Foundation*, special issue on Interactive Social Science 27(3): 159–63

Gilbert, N. and Mulkay, M. (1984) *Opening Pandora's Box: A Sociologists' Analysis of Scientific Discourse* (Cambridge University Press, Cambridge)

Golden-Biddle, K. and Locke, K. (1993) 'Appealing work: an investigation of how ethnographic texts convince', *Organization Science* 4(4): 595–616

Goodman, R. and Lawless, M. (1994) *Technology and Strategy: Conceptual Models and Diagnostics* (Oxford University Press, Oxford)

Graham, L. (1995) *On the Line at Subaru-Isuzu: The Japanese Model and the American Worker* (Cornell University Press, New York)

Grimshaw, A. (1997) 'The eye in the door: anthropology, film and the exploration of interior space', in Banks, M. and Murphy, H. (eds), *Rethinking Visual Anthropology* (Yale University Press, New Haven, CT), pp. 36–53

Grimshaw, A. (2001) *The Ethnographer's Eye: Ways of Seeing in Modern Anthropology* (Cambridge University Press, Cambridge)

Hammersley, M. (1992) *What's Wrong with Ethnography* (Routledge, London)

Hammersley, M. and Atkinson, P. (1995) *Ethnography: Principles in Practice* (2nd edn, Routledge, London)

Harper, R. (1998) *Inside the IMF: An Ethnography of Documents, Technology and Action* (Academic Press, London)

Harrington, B. (2003) 'The Social Psychology of Access in Ethnographic Research', *Journal of Contemporary Ethnography* 32(5): 592–625

Headland, T., Pike, K. and Harris, M. (1990) *Emics and Etics: The Insider/Outsider Debate* (Sage, London)

Heller, F. (1986) 'Introduction', in Heller, F. (ed.), *The Use and Abuse of Social Science* (Sage, London), pp. 1–18

Hess, D. (1989) 'Teaching ethnographic writing: a review essay', *Anthropology and Education Quarterly* 20(3): 164–76

Hine, C. (2000) *Virtual Ethnography* (Sage, London)

Hine, C. (2001) 'Ethnography in the laboratory', in Gellner, D. and Hirsch, E. (eds), *Inside Organizations: Anthropologists at Work* (Berg, Oxford), pp. 61–76

Hirsch, E. (1992) 'The long-term and the short-term of domestic consumption: an ethnographic case study', in Silverstone, R. and Hirsch, E. (eds), *Consuming Technologies* (Routledge, London), pp. 208–26

Hovland, I. (2005) '"What do you call heathen these days?" The policy field and other matters of the heart in the Norwegian Mission Society', Paper presented at: Problems and Possibilities in Multi-Sited Ethnography Workshop, University of Sussex, 27–28 June, available from: http://www.ncrm.ac.uk/research/documents /WhatdoyoucalltheheathenthesedaysIngieHovland.pdf

Hughes, J., Randall, D. and Shapiro, D. (1992) 'Faltering from ethnography to design', Proceedings of the 1992 ACM conference on Computer Supported Co-operative Work (ACM Press, New York, New York), pp. 115–22

Humphreys, L. (1975) *Tearoom Trade: Impersonal Sex in Public Places* (Duckworth, London)

Humphreys, M., Brown, A. and Hatch, M. (2003) 'Is ethnography jazz?', *Organization* 10(1): 5–31

INCITE (2005) 'Critical Inquiry into Technology and Ethnography', University of Surrey, see: http://incite.surrey.ac.uk/

Jeffrey, B. and Troman, J. (2004) 'Time for ethnography', *British Educational Research Journal* 30(4): 535–48

Jermier, J. (1991) 'Critical epistemology and the study of organizational culture: reflections on street corner society', in Frost, P., Moore, L., Reis Louis, M., Lundberg, C., Martin, J (eds), *Reframing Organizational Culture* (Sage, Thousnd Oaks, CA), pp. 223–32

Jordan, S. and Yeomans, D. (1995) 'Critical ethnography: problems in contemporary theory and practice', *British Journal of Sociology of Education* 16(3): 389–408

Jorgensen, D. (1989) *Participant Observation: A Methodology for Human Studies* (Sage, London)

Junker, B. (1960) *Field Work: An Introduction to the Social Sciences* (University of Chicago Press, Chicago)

Kuper, A. (1983) *Anthropology and Anthropologists: The Modern British School* (Routledge and Kegan Paul, London)

Latour, B. and Woolgar, S. (1979) *Laboratory Life: The Construction of Scientific Facts* (Princeton University Press, Princeton, NJ) (2nd edn, 1986)

Law, J. (1994) *Organizing Modernity* (Blackwells, Oxford)

Law, J. (2004) *After Method: Mess in Social Science Research* (Routledge, London)

Lee, A. (1999) 'Researching MIS', in Currie, W. and Galliers, B. (eds), *Rethinking Management Information Systems: An Interdisciplinary Perspective* (Oxford University Press, Oxford), pp. 7–27

Lee, J. (1984) 'Innocent victims and evil-doers', *Women's Studies* 7(1): 69–73

Lee, N. (1999) 'The challenge of childhood: distributions of childhood's ambiguity in adult institutions', *Childhood* 6(4): 455–74

Leidner, R. (1993) *Fast Food, Fast Talk: Service Work and the Routinization of Everyday Life* (University of California Press, Berkeley)

Liebow, E. (1967) *Tally's Corner* (Routledge and Kegan Paul, London)

Livingston, E. (1987) *Making Sense of Ethnomethodology* (Routledge and Kegan Paul, London)

Lofland, J. (1971) *Analyzing Social Settings: A Guide to Qualitative Observation and Analysis* (Wadsworth Belmont, CA)

Luhman, N. (2000) 'Familiarity, confidence, trust: problems and alternatives', in Gambetta, D. (ed.), *Trust: Making and Breaking Cooperative Relations* (Blackwell, Oxford)

Lynch, M. (2004) 'Science as a vacation: deficits, surfeits, PUSS and doing your job', Does STS Mean Business? workshop, Said Business School, University of Oxford, 30 June, available from: http://www.sbs.ox.ac.uk/NR/rdonlyres/DF5A536C-F691-4056-BD7C-ADB610F9B2C3/896/stsbuslynch.pdf

Macdonald, K. (2001) 'Using documents', Gilbert, N. (ed.), *Researching Social Life* (2nd edn, Sage, London), pp. 194–210

Mainwaring, S. and Woodruff, A. (2005) 'Investigating mobility, technology, and space in homes, starting with "great rooms"', Ethnographic Praxis in Industry Conference, conference proceedings of EPIC 2005 (American Anthropological Association, Arlington, VA), pp. 188–95

Malinowski, B. (1922/2002) *Argonauts of the Western Pacific* (Routledge, London)

Malinowski, B. (1929) *The Sexual Life of Savages in Western Melanesia* (Harcourt Brace and World, New York)

March, W. and Fleuriot, C. (2005) 'The worst technology for girls?' Ethnographic Praxis in Industry Conference, conference proceedings of EPIC 2005 (American Anthropological Association, Arlington, VA), pp 165–72

Marcus, G. (1994) 'On ideologies of reflexivity in contemporary efforts to remake the human sciences', *Poetics Today* 15(3): 383–404

Marcus, G. (1995) 'Ethnography in/of the world system: the emergence of multi-sited ethnography', *Annual Review of Anthropology* 24: 95–117

Martinez, W. (1992) 'Who constructs anthropological knowledge? Towards a theory of ethnographic film spectatorship', in Crawford, P. and Turton, D. (eds), *Film as Ethnography* (Manchester University Press, Manchester), pp. 131–64

Mead, M. (1928) *Coming of Age in Samoa* (William Morrow, New York)

Millen, D. (2000) 'Rapid Ethnography: Time Deepening Strategies for HCI Field Research', available from: http://delivery.acm.org/10.1145/350000/347763/p280-millen.pdf?key1=347763&key2=5298738411&coll=GUIDE&dl=GUIDE&CFID=76517993&CFTOKEN=44873025

Miller, D. and Slater, D. (2000) *The Internet: An Ethnographic Approach* (Berg, Oxford)

Misztal, B. (1996) *Trust in Modern Societies* (Polity Press, Cambridge)

Moeran, B. (2005) *The Business of Ethnography: Strategic Exchanges, People and Organizations* (Berg, Oxford)

Mondada, L. (2003) 'Working with video: how surgeons produce video records of their actions', *Visual Studies* 18(1): 58–73

Morrill, C. (1995) *The Executive Way: Conflict Management in Corporations* (University of Chicago Press, Chicago)

Morton, M. (1988) 'Strategy formulation methodologies and IT', in Earl, M. (ed.), *Information Management: The Strategic Dimension* (Clarendon Press, Oxford), pp. 54–69

NERDI (2005) 'Networked Research and Digital Information', Royal Netherlands Academy of Arts and Sciences, Amsterdam, see http://www.niwi.knaw.nl/en/ nerdi2/

Neyland, D. (2004) 'Closed-circuits of interaction? The mobilisation of images and accountability through high street CCTV', *Information, Communication and Society* 7(2): 252–71

Neyland, D. (2006a) 'Dismissed content and discontent: an analysis of the strategic aspects of actor–network theory', *Science, Technology and Human Values* 31(1): 29–51

Neyland, D. (2006b) *Privacy, Surveillance and Public Trust* (Palgrave-Macmillan, Basingstoke)

Neyland, D. and Surridge, C. (2003) 'Information strategy stories: evolving a dynamic strategy process', *Perspectives*, 7(1): 9–14

Neyland, D. and Woolgar, S. (2002) 'Accountability in action? The case of a database purchasing decision', *British Journal of Sociology* 53(2): 259–74

Neyland, D. and Woolgar, S. (2005) 'Governing the sole: the mundane socio-technical accountability of walking', 4S Annual Meeting, Pasadena, USA, 20–22 October

Neyland, D., Wong, J.M. and Woolgar, S. (2006) 'What a load of rubbish: governance, accountability and space in UK recycling', European Association for Studies of Science and Technology Paper presented at conference, Lausanne, Switzerland, 22–26 August

O'Neill, M. (2001) 'Participation or observation? Some practical and ethical dilemmas', in Gellner, D. and Hirsch, E. (eds), *Inside Organizations: Anthropologist at Work* (Berg, Oxford), pp. 223–30

Ong, A. and Collier, S. (eds) (2005) *Global Assemblages: Technology, Politics, and Ethics as Anthropological Problems* (Blackwell, Oxford)

Oreszczyn, S. (2005) 'GM crops in the United Kingdom: precaution as process', *Science and Public Policy* 32(4): 317–24

Orna, E. (1999) *Practical Information Policies* (2nd edn, Gower, Aldershot)

Orr, J. (1996) *Talking about Machines: An Ethnography of a Modern Job* (Cornell University Press, New York)

Pang, A. (2005) 'The Futures of Science and Technology Studies', available from: http://www.sbs.ox.ac.uk/sts2

Pettigrew, A. (1987) 'Context and action in the transformation of the firm', *Journal of Management Studies* 24(6): 649–70

Pink, S. (2001) *Doing Visual Ethnography* (Sage, London)

Pinney, C. (1992) 'The quick and the dead: images, time and truth', in Crawford, P. and Turton, D. (eds), *Film as Ethnography* (Manchester University Press, Manchester), pp. 26–49

Plath, D. (1990) 'Fieldnotes, filed notes, and the conferring of note', in Sanjek, R. (ed.), *Fieldnotes: The Making of Anthropology* (Cornell University Press, New York), pp. 371–84

Public Sector Benchmarking Service (2006) 'What is benchmarking?', available from: http://www.benchmarking.gov.uk/about_bench/whatisit.asp

Quality Assurance Agency (2002) 'Subject benchmark statements Academic standards – Anthropology', available from: http://www.qaa.ac.uk/academicinfra-structure/benchmark/honours/anthropology.asp

Radcliffe-Brown, A. (1922) *The Andaman Islanders: A Study in Social Anthropology* (Cambridge University Press, Cambridge)

Rappert, B. (1997) 'Users and social science research: policy, problems and possibilities', *Sociological Research Online* 2(3): http://www.socresonline.org.uk/socresonline/2/3/10.html

Rayner, S. and Malone, E. (1998) *Human Choice and Climate Change* (Battelle Press, Columbus, OH)

Reed-Dehaney, D. (ed.) (1997) *Auto/Ethnography* (Berg, Oxford)

Reh, J. (2006) 'Key Performance Indicators', available from: http://management.about.com/cs/generalmanagement/a/keyperfindic.htm

Reponen, T. (1993) 'Strategic information systems: a conceptual analysis', *Journal of Strategic Information Systems* 2(2): 100–104

Richardson, L. (2000) 'Writing: a method of inquiry', in Denzin, N. and Lincoln, Y. (eds), *Handbook of Qualitative Research* (2nd edn, Sage, London), pp. 923–48

Rory, F. (1996) *The Third Eye: Race, Cinema and Ethnographic Spectacle* (Duke University Press, Durham, NC)

Rosen, M. (1991) 'Coming to terms with the field: understanding and doing organizational ethnography', *Journal of Management Studies* 28(1): 1–24

Rosen, M. (2000) *Turning Words, Spinning Worlds: Chapters in Organizational Ethnography* (Routledge, London)

Rubin, H. and Rubin, I. (2004) *Qualitative Interviewing: The Art of Hearing Data* (2nd edn, Sage, London)

Ruby, J. (2000) *Picturing Culture* (University of Chicago Press, Chicago)

Sanjek, R. (ed.) (1990a) *Fieldnotes: The Making of Anthropology* (Cornell University Press, New York)

Sanjek, R. (1990b) 'On ethnographic validity', in Sanjek, R. (ed.), *Fieldnotes: The Making of Anthropology* (Cornell University Press, New York), pp. 385–415

Schwartzman, H. (1993) *Ethnography in Organizations* (Sage, London)

Scott, G. (1983) *The Magicians: A Study of the Use of Power in a Black Magic Group* (Irvington Publishers, New York)

Sellen, A. and Harper, R. (2001) *The Myth of the Paperless Office* (MIT Press, Cambridge, MA)

Shaffir, W. and Stebbins, R. (eds) (1991a) *Experiencing Fieldwork: An Inside View of Qualitative Research* (Sage, London)

Shaffir, W. and Stebbins, R. (1991b) 'Leaving and keeping in touch', in Shaffir, W. and Stebbins, R. (eds), *Experiencing Fieldwork: An Inside View of Qualitative Research* (Sage, London), pp. 207–10

Shapin, S. (1994) *A Social History of Truth: Civility and Science in Seventeenth Century England* (University of Chicago Press, Chicago)

Sherman Hayl, B. (2001) 'Ethnographic interviewing', in Atkinson, P., Coffey, A., Delamont, S., Lofland, J. and Lofland, J. (eds), *Handbook of Ethnography* (Sage, London), pp. 369–83

Sherry Jr, J. (2003) 'Foreword: A word from our sponsor – anthropology', in de Waal Malefyt, T. and Moeran, B. (eds), *Advertising Cultures* (Berg, Oxford), pp. xi–xiii

Shore, B. (1983) 'Paradox regained: Freeman's Margaret Mead and Samoa', *American Anthropologist* 83: 935–44

Shove, E. and Rip, A. (2000) 'Symbolic users – users and unicorns: a diagnosis of mythical beasts in interactive science', *Science and Public Policy, Journal of the International Science Policy Foundation*, special issue on Interactive Social Science 27(3): 175–82

Smith, D. (1993) *Texts, Facts and Femininity* (Routledge, London)

Smith, M. (1981) *Baba of Karo: A Woman of the Muslim Hausa* (Yale University Press, New Haven, CT)

Smith, V. (2001) 'Ethnographies of work and the work of ethnographers', in Atkinson, P., Coffey, A., Delamont, S., Loftland, J. and Lofland, L. (eds), *Handbook of Ethnography* (Sage, London), pp. 220–233

Smits, M., van der Poel, K. and Ribbers, P. (1997) 'Assessment of information strategies in insurance companies in The Netherlands', *Journal of Strategic Information Systems*, 6: 129–48

Snow, D. (1980) 'The disengagement process: a neglected problem in participant observation research', *Qualitative Sociology* 3(2): 100–22

Spradley, J. (1979) *The Ethnographic Interview* (Harcourt, Brace, Jovanovich Publishers, New York)

Spradley, J. (1980) *Participant Observation* (Holt, Rinehart and Winston, New York)

Strathern, M. (2002) 'Abstraction and decontextualisation – an anthropological comment', in Woolgar, S. (ed.), *Virtual Society?* (Oxford University Press, Oxford), pp. 302–13

Suchman, L. (1987) *Plans and Situated Actions* (Cambridge University Press, Cambridge)

Suchman, L. (2000) 'Anthropology as 'brand': reflections on corporate anthropology', American Anthropological Association annual meeting, San Francisco, 15 November)

Sunday Times (2003) 'Somebody's watching you', *Sunday Times Magazine*, 11 May: 44–50

Taylor, S. (1991) 'Leaving the field', in Shaffir, W. and Stebbins, R. (eds), *Experiencing Fieldwork: An Inside View of Qualitative Research* (Sage, London), pp. 238–47

Thompson, H. (1967) *Hell's Angels* (Penguin, London)

Thompson, J. (1995) *Strategy in Action* (Chapman and Hall, London)

Urry, J. (1984) 'A history of field methods', in Ellen, R. (ed.), *Ethnographic Research: A Guide to General Conduct* (Academic Press, London)

Vallas, S. (2003) 'The adventures of managerial hegemony: teamwork, ideology, and worker resistance', *Social Problems* 50(2): 204–25

Van Maanen, J. (1988) Tales of the Field: On Writing Ethnography (University of Chicago Press, Chicago)

Van Maanen, J. (1979) 'The fact of fiction in organizational ethnography', *Administrative Science Quarterly* 24(4): 539–50

Van Maanen, J. (2001) 'Natives R Us: some notes on the ethnography of organizations', in Gellner, D. and Hirsch, E. (eds), *Inside Organizations: Anthropologist at Work* (Berg, Oxford), pp. 233–61

Visual Anthropology (2005) http://www.visualanthropology.net/

Wagner, P. Weiss, C. Wittrock, B. and Wollman, H. (1991) 'The policy orientation: legitimacy and promise', in Wagner, P., Weiss, C., Wittrock, B. and Wollman, H.

183

(eds), *Social Sciences and Modern States National Experiences and Theoretical Crossroads* (Cambridge University Press, Cambridge), pp. 2–27

Wakeford, N. (2003) 'Research note: working with new media's cultural intermediaries', *Information, Communication and Society* 6(2): 229–45

Wasson, C. (2000) 'Ethnography in the field of design', *Human Organisation* 59(4): 377–88

Watson, T. (1994) 'Managing, crafting and researching: words, skill and imagination in shaping management research', *British Journal of Management* 5: 77–87

Watson, T. (2001) *In Search of Management* (Thomson Learning, London)

Weeks, J. (2004) *Unpopular Culture: The Ritual of Complaint in a British Bank* (University of Chicago Press, Chicago)

Weiss, C. and Bucuvalas, M. (1980) *Social Science Research and Decision Making* (Columbia University Press, New York)

Whittington, R. (2004) 'Strategy after modernism: recovering practice', *European Management Review* 1(1): 62–68

Whittle, A. (2001) '"Work anywhere" or "go somewhere"? The career dynamics of mobile workers', Mobilize! Conference, Digital World Research Centre, University of Surrey, May

Whittle, A. (2005) 'Preaching and practicing flexibility: implications for theories of subjectivity at work', *Human Relations* 58(10): 1301–22

Whyte, W. (1955) *Street Corner Society* (2nd edn, University of Chicago Press, Chicago)

Whyte, W. (1993) 'Revisiting *Street Corner Society*', *Sociological Forum* 8(2): 285–98

Willis, P. (1977) *Learning to Labour* (Arena, London)

Willis, P. (2000) *The Ethnographic Imagination* (Polity Press, Cambridge)

Wittel, A. (2000) 'Ethnography on the move: from field to net to internet', *Forum: Qualitative Social Research* 1(1), available from: http://www.qualitative-research.net/fqs-texte/1-00/1-00wittel-e.htm

Wolf, D. (1991) 'High-risk methodology: reflections on leaving outlaw society', in Shaffir, W. and Stebbins, R. (eds), *Experiencing Fieldwork: An Inside View of Qualitative Research* (Sage, London), pp. 211–23

Woolgar, S. (1998) 'De toekomst van privacy ('The futures of privacy'), in Schoenmaker, M., van den Starre, G. and Baten, I. (eds), *Privacy Geregistreerd: visies op de maatschappelijke betekenis van privacy* (Rathenau, The Hague)

Woolgar, S. (2000) 'Social basis of interactive social science', *Science and Public Policy, Journal of the International Science Policy Foundation*, special issue on Interactive Social Science, 27(3): 165–73

Woolgar, S. (2002a) *Virtual Society? The Social Science of Electronic Technologies*, ESRC End of Programme Report, University of Oxford

Woolgar, S. (2002b) 'The boundaries of accountability: a technographic approach', Paper presented to European Association for Studies of Science and Technology Conference, University of York, 2nd August

Woolgar, S. (ed.) (2002c) *Virtual Society? Technology, Cyberbole, Reality* (Oxford University Press, Oxford)

Wynne, B. (1996) 'May the sheep safely graze? A reflexive view of the expert-lay knowledge divide', in Lash, S., Szerszynski, B. and Wynne, B. (eds), *Risk, Environment and Modernity: Towards a New Ecology* (Sage, London), pp. 44–83

Index

▷▷▷▷▷

Note: Page numbers in **bold** refer to the sensibilities which guide organizational ethnography